A Guide to the Vegetation of the Lopé Reserve

Lee WHITE & Kate ABERNETHY

This guide is a revised, English version of a book previously published in French:

Guide de la Végétation de la Réserve de la Lopé
Lee White & Kate Abernethy
Published by ECOFAC Gabon

Available from:
ECOFAC Gabon, BP 9352, Libreville, Gabon.
Fax. (+ 241) 775534

WILDLIFE CONSERVATION SOCIETY
185th St. & Southern Blvd., Bronx, New York 10460-1099, U.S.A.
Second edition 1997
ISBN 0-9632064-2-7
Printed by: Multipress-Gabon, Libreville
D.L.B.N. 1246/11/97

Forward

For non Gabonese, this book offers a trip to a new world. For a tropical forest expert, even one familiar with the exotic nature of the Guide's subjects, the sensitivity and beauty with which they have been illustrated and the interconnected and habitat-based way in which they are discussed is a stimulating treat. Consider one of the first illustrations: «Gorilla dung with seedlings»! The Guide is a treasure trove and model of ecological interrelationships which do not stop with Lopé vegetation.

A prerequisite in the process of conserving natural environments is an understanding of what they contain and how they work, most especially of their plants and animals within the context of local climate, geology and history. Unfortunately, few West African nations have handy, available references. Few tropical nations anywhere have such technically competent ones. The author's and artist's overview of the fragile and fascinating 5,000 square kilometre Lopé Reserve, potentially one of the most important protected wild lands in Africa, make this guide particularly useful.

Dr. Lee White, a staff scientist with the Wildlife Conservation Society, has conducted research in the Lopé Reserve since 1989. He has focussed upon the impact of big mammals, such as elephants and gorillas, on vegetation and upon the history and effects of human colonization of Lopé savannas. Kate Abernethy is both a scientist and an artist who studies primate ecology from the Station for the Study of Gorillas and Chimpanzees of the International Center for Medical Research in Franceville. Dr. Abernethy began her work in Lopé in 1993. Both have had the important advantage of insights gained through the long-term work of Caroline Tutin and Michel Fernandez and their associates at the Station, which they founded in Lopé in 1983.

The current work is a translation and up-dating of White and Abernethy's *Guide de la Végétation de la Réserve de la Lopé, Gabon,* published in 1996 which has a related volume by Patrice Christy and William Clarke, the *Guide des Oiseaux de la Réserve de la Lopé,* published in 1994. Both guides were published by Ecofac-Gabon, a far-sighted project financed by the Development Program of the European Union. This is sound science in the service of education, solid conservation and rational national development.

William Conway
President
Wildlife Conservation Society
New York

Moabi

Brachycorythis pleistophylla **(Orchidaceae) - a savanna orchid which blooms after the dry season fires.**

Forward to the French edition

Le Gabon est un pays de forêts et d'eau.

Pendant des siècles, la vie de ses habitants a prospéré en harmonie autour de ces deux éléments. La culture traditionnelle s'est toujours fondée sur une profonde connaissance des arbres et de la forêt toute entière et cette maîtrise a permis de maintenir un équilibre entre l'homme et l'environnement.

L'urbanisation de ces dernières décennies a entraîné un relâchement de la liaison fonctionnelle avec le milieu naturel: en même temps que la technologie moderne permet d'exploiter ses richesses en bois et en gibier à un rythme sans commune mesure avec les équilibres d'antan, sa connaissance par une population de plus en plus citadine s'effiloche: les Gabonais n'ont jamais autant pénétré la forêt, mais ils n'en ont jamais été aussi éloignés culturellement.

Ce livre nous ouvre une porte sur ce monde fascinant et peu connu.

Nous nous trouvons à la réserve de la Lopé, dans un parc de grand intérêt pour la conservation de la forêt tropicale humide, situé au coeur du Gabon, en Afrique équatoriale.

C'est sur ce lieu magnifique qu'un projet de conservation de la nature, fruit de la coopération entre l'Union Européenne et la République Gabonaise, a concentré des efforts considérables pour préserver un écosystème unique et le rendre accessible aux yeux du monde.

Ce livre, deuxième après le "Guide des oiseaux de la Lopé" d'une série de publications issues de ce projet, est une sorte de vade-mecum pour les passionnés de la forêt ou simplement pour les curieux qui voudront se lancer à la découverte de ce milieu si particulier.

Avec un peu de fantaisie, ce livre rappellera aux touristes, de retour dans leurs contrées, l'expérience vécue sous l'équateur. Dans ces planches ils reverront, dans un crescendo de couleurs et de formes, le foisonnement de plantes qui les avait frappés et qui fait la richesse de la forêt gabonaise.

Les dessins nous accompagnent dans une promenade unique sur les traces d'espèces végétales souvent rares, parfois propres uniquement au Gabon; une immersion au fond d'une forêt dont beaucoup de secrets sont dévoilés par des descriptions détaillées.

Mais le véritable enjeu de ce livre est la sauvegarde, au profit des Gabonais, d'une mémoire orale de l'utilisation de plusieurs plantes dans la vie de tous les jours et dans la pharmacopée traditionnelle, mémoire qui risquait de se perdre.

La conservation de ce savoir passe forcément par le maintien de la capacité de reconnaître une plante de l'autre, ainsi que ses propriétés.

Le "Guide de la végétation de la Lopé" accomplit cette tâche et donne aux jeunes étudiants des villes gabonaises une idée sommaire de l'immense patrimoine que leur a confié en héritage une nature si généreuse.

Je suis convaincu que, grâce à la multiplication des ouvrages de ce genre, sur l'ensemble du pays, des passions mûriront pour une meilleure connaissance de la forêt dans laquelle il faut chercher, non seulement le passé, mais aussi l'avenir du Gabon.

Marco MAZZOCCHI-ALEMANNI
Délégué de la Commission Européenne
en République Gabonaise

This book was made possible by financial support from:

The Wildlife Conservation Society (WCS), in collaboration with the CARPE project of the U.S. Agency for International Development.

ECOFAC-Gabon, financed by the European Fund for Development

The Centre International de Recherches Médicales de Franceville (CIRMF)

ACKNOWLEDGEMENTS

In many respects this guide represents a collective effort on the part of all researchers who have lived and worked at the Station d'Etudes des Gorilles et Chimpanzés (SEGC), which was founded in 1983 in the Lopé Reserve by Caroline Tutin and Michel Fernandez. Keys to identification are available elsewhere, but in this guide we try to introduce you to the natural history of the plant species featured. In this respect we have made extensive use of records and observations made at SEGC and elsewhere in the Lopé Reserve over the years. We thank Jean-Phillipe Bitou, Allard Blom, Henri Bourobou-Bourobou, Catherine Bouchain, Patrice Christy, Jean-Yves Collet, Alick Cruikshank, Anna Feistner, Benoit Fontaine, Stephanie Hall, Rebecca Ham, David Harris, Mike Harrison, Jennifer Hedin, Ard Louis, Karen MacDonald, Alphonse Mackanga-Missandzou, Boo Maisels, Gordon McPherson, Richard Oslisly, Richard Parnell, Patricia Peignot, Jan Reitsma, Liz Rogers, Ann Pierce, Liz Williamson, Ben Voysey, Frank White, Chris Wilks, Dorothea Wrogemann and especially Michel Fernandez and Caroline Tutin. More recently various members of the ECOFAC forest team have helped us to increase our botanical knowledge. Thanks in particular to Vincent Bossissie, Joachim Dibakou, Edmond Dimoto, Jean-Toussaint Dikangadissi, Gilbert Kella-Isalla, John Koumouzokou, Theodore Makonde, Daniel Mala, Pierre Mayouma, Alain-Roger Mboni, Francis Nzinga, Claud Passilende and Andre Siniboure.

Jean-Hubert Eyi-Mbeng, Directeur de la Faune et de la Chasse, Ministère des Eaux et Forêts, has given enthusiastic support throughout our years of study in Gabon, as have Alphonse Mackanga-Missandzou and Joseph Maroga-Mbina, who have served as 'chefs de brigade' at Lopé during our stay in the Reserve.

We have had a great deal of help with identifications over the years from a number of colleagues. In particular, without the continued efforts of Gordon McPherson at Missouri Botanical Garden, our knowledge would still be in its infancy. Caroline Tutin, Chris Wilks and Liz Williamson also deserve special thanks for introducing one of us (LW) to the vegetation of the Lopé.

The first (French) edition of this guide was funded by the ECOFAC programme, funded by the European Union and managed by AGRECO-GEIE, in collaboration with The Wildlife Conservation Society. This edition is funded by The Wildlife Conservation Society with funds from the CARPE initiative of US-AID. Throughout our time in Lopé we have been resident at the Station d'Etudes des Gorilles et Chimpanzés of the Centre International de Recherches Médicales de Franceville and received additional logistical and financial support from this institution.

Michel Fernandez, Benoit Fontaine, Gordon McPherson, Robert Nasi, Caroline Tutin and Chris Wilks read earlier versions of the text. Their comments and suggestions were extremely useful. Serge Akagah helped design the layout of the French version, on which this edition is based.

Finally, special thanks to Michel Fernandez-Puente, without whose help and encouragement this book would never have germinated.

TABLE OF CONTENTS

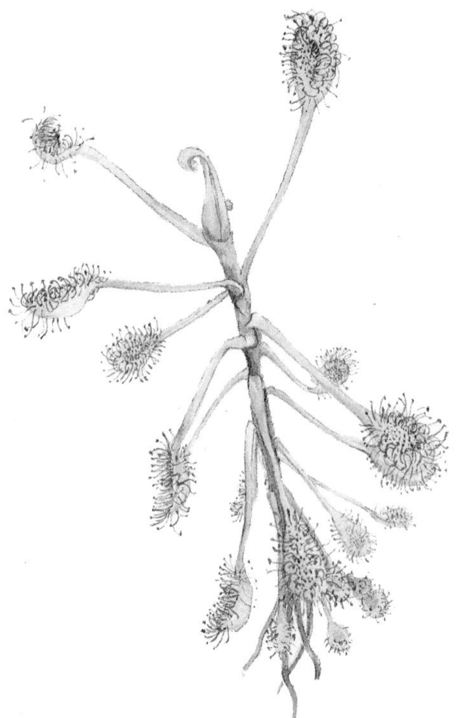

Drosera madagascariensis **(Droseraceae) - a sundew which grows in savanna marshes**

PLANT LIFE CYCLE

Each year innumerable seeds germinate on the forest floor and gradually unfold their first tender new leaves. The odds against any individual surviving to flower and fruit are enormous. Countless numbers of them will die through lack of light in the shaded conditions of the forest understorey, or because they are scorched by the sun out in the savanna. Others will be eaten or trampled by animals, or will gradually sicken, because the conditions where their seed happened to fall are not quite right. However, a small proportion of seeds will fall in optimal conditions and, if they escape the attentions of hungry herbivores or unfortunate accidents, they will gradually grow and mature. Small herbs may live for only a year, withering after they have fruited, whilst some trees live to be over 1000 years old and produce many crops of fruit during their life-time.

If a plant is to reproduce its flowers must be fertilised, its fruits must ripen, and its mature seeds must find a suitable place to grow. Since they are rooted in the ground they are unable to move in search of a mate, or to care for offspring, as animals do. The first stage in plant reproduction is pollination. Pollen grains need to be transferred from the flower's male anthers, where they develop, to the female stigma, which gives access to the tiny eggs, or ovules, within the ovary. In some plant species pollen from the anthers can fertilise ovules in the same flower, or in other flowers on the same tree. In other species pollen has to be transported to flowers on a second plant if fertilisation is to take place. Some species have separate male and female flowers. These are sometimes on the same individual, but some species have separate male and female plants.

In temperate regions many plant species release large quantities of pollen into the air to be transported by the wind. This wind-borne pollen is the cause of allergies such as hay fever. Other species are visited by insects, such as bees or butterflies, which collect pollen on their bodies as they sip nectar from the flower and transport it to other flowers of the same species. The majority of plants in the tropical rain forest are pollinated by animals such as insects, birds or bats. These animal-pollinated plants tend to have colourful flowers, which are often scented, whilst those pollinated by the wind are drab and odourless.

After pollination, the ovules develop into seeds, within a fruit. Plants have developed many mechanisms to achieve this. Some produce light seeds with wings, or feathery attachments which allow them to drift long distances on the wind. Others have fruits which gradually dry out and then suddenly explode, physically throwing seeds away from the parent - a process known as dehiscence. Some drop their seeds into water, to be carried away by the current. In tropical forests about three-quarters of species have seeds which are dispersed by animals.

A few of these animal-dispersed species have seeds which hook onto fur or feathers and are carried away, finally falling off some distance from the parent plant. The majority, however, have succulent fruits which are eaten by animals. The animals either carry the fruits away from the parent plant and drop the seeds as they feed, or swallow the seeds and pass them in their dung. Some seeds actually need to pass through the digestive system of an animal before they can germinate. The seeds of some plants are dispersed by many different animals, whilst others are specially adapted for dispersal by particular species. The seeds in fruits which are not eaten and which fall to the ground under their parent tree tend to rot, or to be eaten by seed predators, such as rodents or pigs. Hence, dispersal is a vital part of plant reproduction and is often the key to understanding the distribution of a given species.

In addition, the means of dispersal has a great bearing on the relationship of a plant species with animals. Animal dispersed species tend to have sugary or oily fruits, to attract and reward their dispersers, whilst those dispersed by explosive mechanisms or by the wind often have seeds which are physically or chemically protected, to prevent animals from eating them. Understanding the means of pollination, or seed dispersal, often gives clues to the reason for their flowers or fruits having a particular form. Unless we have an understanding of a plant's natural history its name has little relevance. To understand why a particular plant is common in small forest patches isolated within the savanna one has to understand how its seeds are dispersed; or if we are to be able to explain and predict movements of frugivorous mammals and birds we must know which fruits they eat. A knowledge of the distribution and behaviour of plants is the key to understanding how the forest works.

d
c
b
a
e
h
d
f
g
b
c
a
e
KA'95

In this guide we hope to enable you to identify many of the plant species you notice during your visit to the Lopé. We place particular emphasis on the natural history of the plants which are illustrated, rather than simply giving descriptions of their forms, because we feel that it will be much more satisfying and useful if you understand why any plant is interesting. So, for each species we will try to provide tips to aid identification and then give any additional information we think will be useful or interesting. Where we provide little more than a description it is more likely to reflect our lack of knowledge than to suggest that that plant is of little interest. Our understanding of the biology of tropical plants is poor, so any observations you are able to make during your stay in Lopé may contribute new information.

Left:

1) Gorilla dung with seedlings (above) :

- *a) Cola lizae*
- *b) Dialium lopense*
- *c) Ganophyllum giganteum*
- *d) Santiria trimera*
- *e) Uapaca guineensis*

2) Elephant dung with seedlings (below) :

- *a) Diospyros mannii*
- *b) Duboscia macrocarpa*
- *c) Irvingia gabonensis*
- *d) Myrianthus arboreus*
- *e) Omphalocarpum procerum*
- *f) Swartzia fistuloides*
- *g) Tetrapleura tetraptera*
- *h) Trichoscypha acuminata*

Paristolochia flos-avis, **(Arictolochiaceae) a species of liane found in Marantaceae Forest which attracts insect pollinators with an odour which resembles rotting meat.**

KA 96

INTRODUCTION TO THE LOPÉ RESERVE

No matter how you arrive at the Lopé, you will see a marked change in the landscape as you near your destination. Lopé is known for its attractive mosaic of forest and savanna. However, unlike the other changes you may have noted along the route, such as lush gallery forests along rivers, cultivation around villages, and secondary vegetation along the road, railway, or in logging chantiers, the reason for the sudden appearance of grasslands in the middle of the equatorial forest is not immediately apparent. To understand this change, and its wider implications, one has to go back in time about 18,000 years, to a period when much of Europe was hidden under a layer of ice.

During this period, as the last ice sheet advanced across northern Europe, there were widespread implications for global climate. In equatorial Africa the climate became cool and dry. In these conditions large expanses of the African rain forest, which depends upon a warm, moist climate for its survival, were gradually replaced by grasslands. The forests of central Africa retreated into a few small patches, or refugia, located in areas which are now swamps, or in montane regions close to the coast, where rainfall remained relatively high. These refuges acted as sanctuaries for rain forest plants and animals. As the ice sheets retreated, about 12,000 years ago, the global climate warmed and rainfall in equatorial Africa increased, allowing forest to spread out again into the grasslands.

It is thought that there were three forest refuges in Gabon during this period, one close to Libreville, in the Monts de Cristal, and two to the southwest of the Lopé, in the Massif du Chaillu and the Monts Doudou. As a result, Gabon has a very rich flora. There are about 6,000 species of plant in Gabon, more than for the whole of West Africa combined.

The Lopé savannas are, therefore, a reflection of how much of equatorial Africa looked during the arid phase between 18,000 and 12,000 years ago. As you step out of your plane, train or vehicle, you are effectively stepping back in time, to a period when the world's climate was in flux. Of course, it requires a good deal of imagination to see Lopé today as a small settlement of hunter gatherers in the Late Stone Age, but we hope that as we guide you through the vegetation of the Reserve and introduce some of the plants that grow here, you will be able to make this leap into the past.

Left:
Engraved rocks in gallery forest along the banks of the Ogooué.

The forest -savanna mosaic at the Lopé.

Cameroun
Equatorial Guinea
Sao Tomé
Equator
Gabon
Congo
Zaire
0
500 km
1
2
3
Libreville
Ndjolé
Booué
Lastoursville
Franceville
Makokou
Port Gentil
Lopé Reserve
Forest refuges:
1 Monts de Cristal
2 Massif du Chaillu
3 Monts Doudou

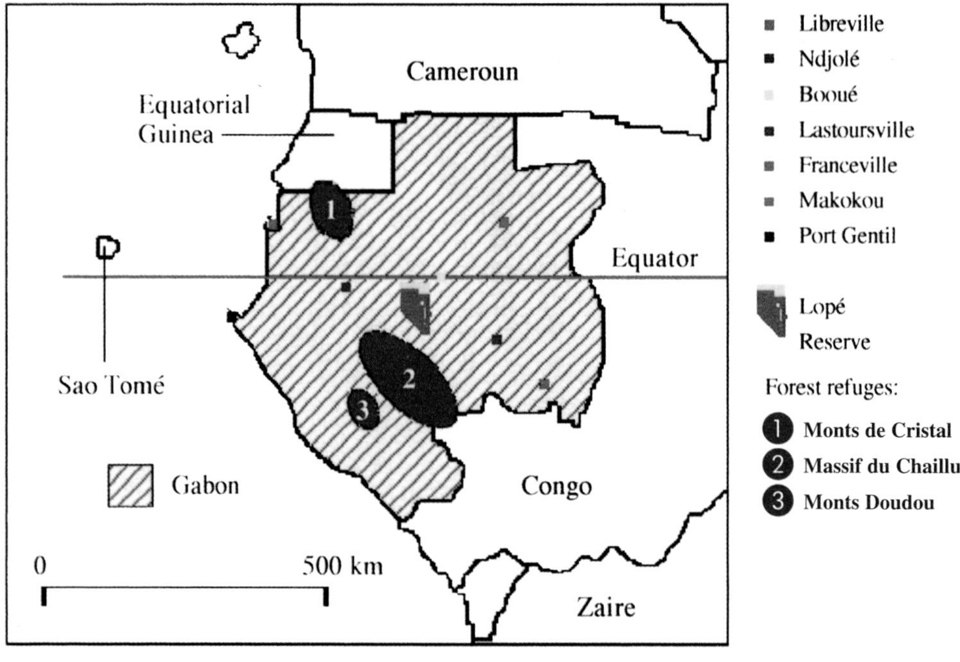

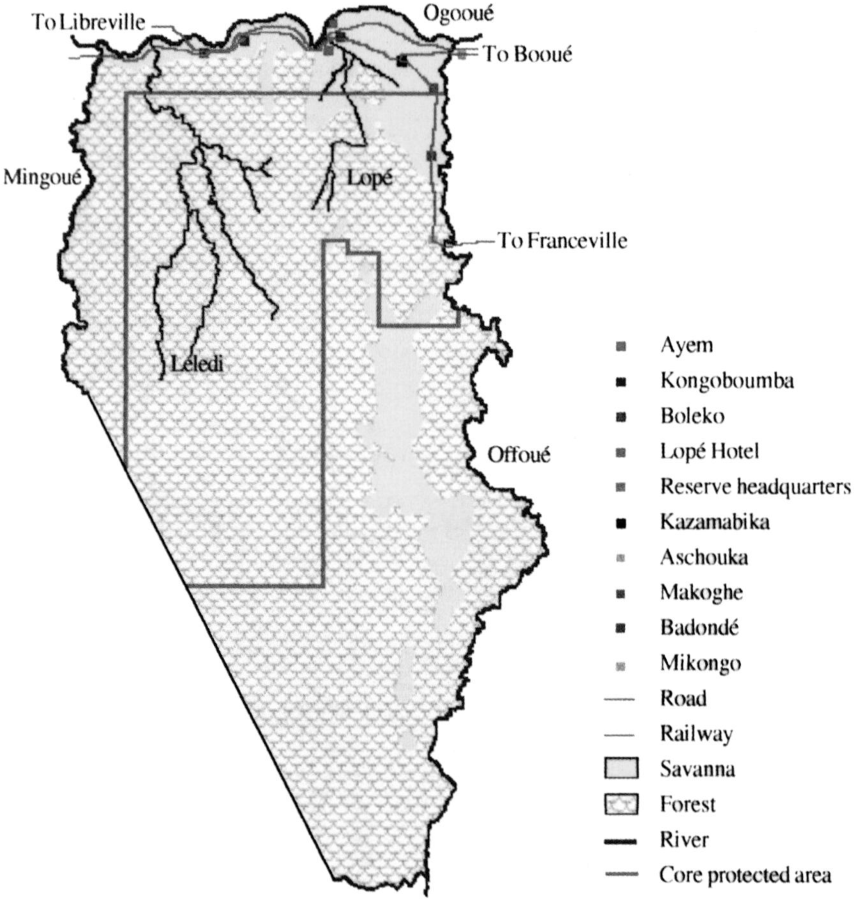

To Libreville
Ogooué
To Booué
Mingoué
Lopé
To Franceville
Lélédi
Offoué
Ayem
Kongoboumba
Boleko
Lopé Hotel
Reserve headquarters
Kazamabika
Aschouka
Makoghe
Badondé
Mikongo
Road
Railway
Savanna
Forest
River
Core protected area

To understand why Lopé survives as a living record of the past, you need a grasp of the geology and climate of the region and of the history of the peoples who have inhabited the area for many thousands of years. The map shows that Lopé is the geometric centre of Gabon. The Reserve covers 5000 km², bordered in the north by the River Ogooué, to the east and west by the Offoué and Mingoué rivers respectively, and tapering to its southern limit, about 120 km to the south (lower map). The savannas form bands along the northern and eastern limits of the Reserve.

Annual rainfall in northern parts of the Lopé averages about 1500 mm. This is low compared to much of Gabon. For example, annual rainfall in Libreville is about 3000 mm. The low rainfall in the Lopé region is due to a rain shadow effect: air currents are cooled as they rise over the Massif du Chaillu, to the southwest, and rain falls on the western side of these mountains, depriving the region to the east of rainfall. Because of this, Lopé has the driest climate in Gabon, and it is therefore the area where the forest is naturally most fragile. It is generally thought that tropical rain forest needs an annual rainfall of about 2000 mm in order to survive. The forests of Gabon survive because cold sea currents during the dry season result in the formation of a dense cloud layer, which reflects the heat of the sun and prevents vegetation from drying out excessively. However, given its low rainfall the Lopé region is the area of Gabon which is most susceptible to any changes in climate. Therefore, during periods when the earth's climate became drier, Lopé was one of the first places to lose its forests, and equally, is one of the last places to be reclaimed by the forest.

A *Syzygium cf. guineense* tree growing on a 700 year old iron furnace.

As you will discover during a stay in Lopé, the region posesses the richest archaeological remains in central Africa. Humans are thought to have lived in the middle valley of the Ogooué river for about the last 400,000 years. The only known settlements dating back to this time are at Otoumbi, just outside the Lopé Reserve to the west. However, there is ample evidence of humans living within the reserve during the last 60,000 years. A succession of Stone Age (up to about 4000 years ago), Neolithic (4000 to 2500 years ago) and Iron Age peoples (2500 to the present) have occupied the area. As you will see on your journey up to Lopé, humans can have a severe impact on the rain forest. Where today we can cut through the forest, sitting comfortably in a bulldozer, the primitive peoples who lived in the Lopé region probably used fire to modify their environment.

Burning of savanna has long been practised as an aid to hunting. The tender regrowth, that soon sprouts up after a fire, attracts animals like buffalo and bushbuck out into the savanna, where they are an easier target for hunters. There is no reason to think that the Stone Age peoples resident in the Lopé region did not burn savannas regularly. In doing so they would have prevented the forest from recolonising areas of savanna that had been formed during dry periods in Africa's climatic history, hence maintaining the mosaic of forest and savanna that we see today.

Fire is used today as a management tool. If representatives of the Ministry of Water & Forests did not burn the savannas in the Lopé each dry season, the forest would gradually expand and replace the grasslands. These annual fires are responsible for maintaining sharp boundaries between forest and savanna.

Iron age pottery found in the Lopé Reserve.

Many people, particularly those who have not lived in the tropics, have the impression that the rain forests of the world are lush 'Gardens of Eden' where warmth and moisture combine to give life a stability that does not exist at higher latitudes. This is true to some extent, but once you are in tune with the forest you soon realise that there are quite extreme seasonal changes, despite the relatively constant, green exterior. As elsewhere, these changes are closely related to seasons, although wet and dry are the most obvious variables, not hot and cold. Lopé's 1500 mm of rain is not evenly distributed. Four seasons can be defined by rainfall patterns: the 'long-dry season' which runs from mid-June to mid-September; the 'short-dry season' which tends to last for anything from a few days to about four weeks, anytime between mid-December and mid-February; and two 'rainy seasons'. There is less variation in annual temperatures. The average temperature for the hottest part of the day (recorded in the shade of the forest) vary between 27 and 31 °C whilst night-time lows average between 20 and 22°C. The dry season is the coolest part of the year since the sun rarely breaks through the low cloud cover.

These four seasons are reflected in the forest. In effect, the long dry season is Lopé's winte; the temperature falls and conditions are gloomy. It is a time of hardship, when little fruit is available and forest animals go hungry. Monkeys and birds move around quietly, spending all their time searching for food, gorillas appear thin of face and the elephants' hips are prominent on their gaunt frames.

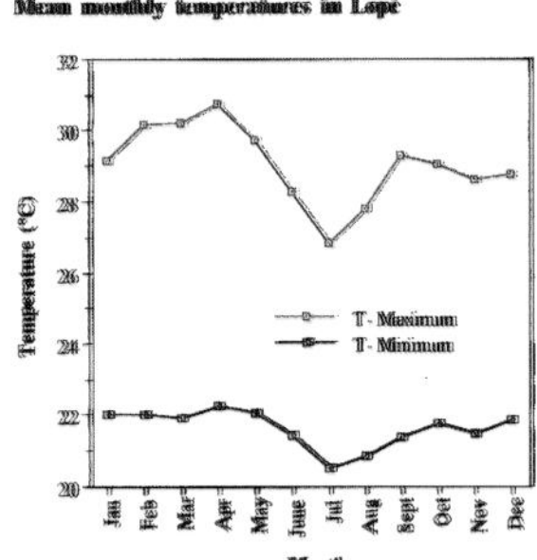

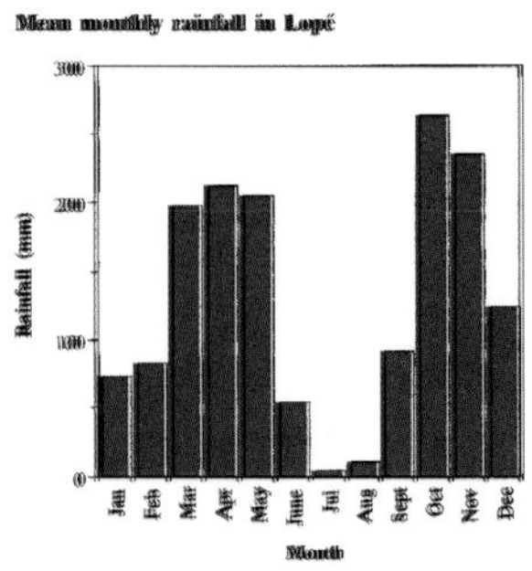

The months immediately after the long dry season are our spring, the peak time for flowering, when the forest hums to the buzz of bees busily working their way around the sweet smelling canopies of forest trees. More importantly for many of the animals, fruit crops increase. Christmas and the New Year are a time of plenty, when young gorillas are spoilt for choice of succulent fruits and take on a chubby appearance.

There is great variability between years, perhaps reflecting variations in weather patterns. In some years fruit is available right through the long dry season, but in others little fruit is to be found between April and October. Since many of the animals in the forest rely upon plants, especially fruits, for their food, the plants determine the rhythm of the forest. To understand the animals you have first to understand the plants. However, plants also rely on animals. The majority of rain forest plants are pollinated by insects and in Gabon, 70% of plants depend upon animals to disperse their seeds. Hence, there are many complex interactions between plants and animals, most of which remain poorly understood. In this guide we try to provide as much information as possible about the relationships between the plants we describe and the animals with which they interact. In order to understand the distribution patterns of plant species we have to know how their seeds are dispersed, so we try to provide this information whenever possible. For plants whose seeds are dispersed by animals we must also understand how their fruiting patterns affect animal movements, since this will determine where the seeds are deposited. Consequently, this guide also provides relevant information about certain animals, although other more detailed guides are, or will soon be available for the birds and mammals of the Lopé Reserve.

When you first enter the forest you are surrounded by hundreds of plants and animals which may be unfamiliar. In such circumstances the first question that springs to mind is 'what'. "What is that plant with a bright red fruit?" . . . "What is that beautiful flower?" In this guide we hope not only to give you a tool to enable you to identify plants which might catch your eye, but also to introduce you to the ecology of the forest. We hope to anticipate the next question, which will almost invariably be 'why' or 'how'. We cannot possibly cover all the plants in the Reserve - we currently know of about 1500 species which occur within its limits. Nor do we intend this book to stand alone. It should be seen as an addition to the tour guide who will take you out into the forest. It is they who will help to bring the forest to life around you. The book may help to clarify some of the things they show you and remain as a souvenir of the things that you see.

Variation in ripe fruit production through the year in the Lopé Reserve.

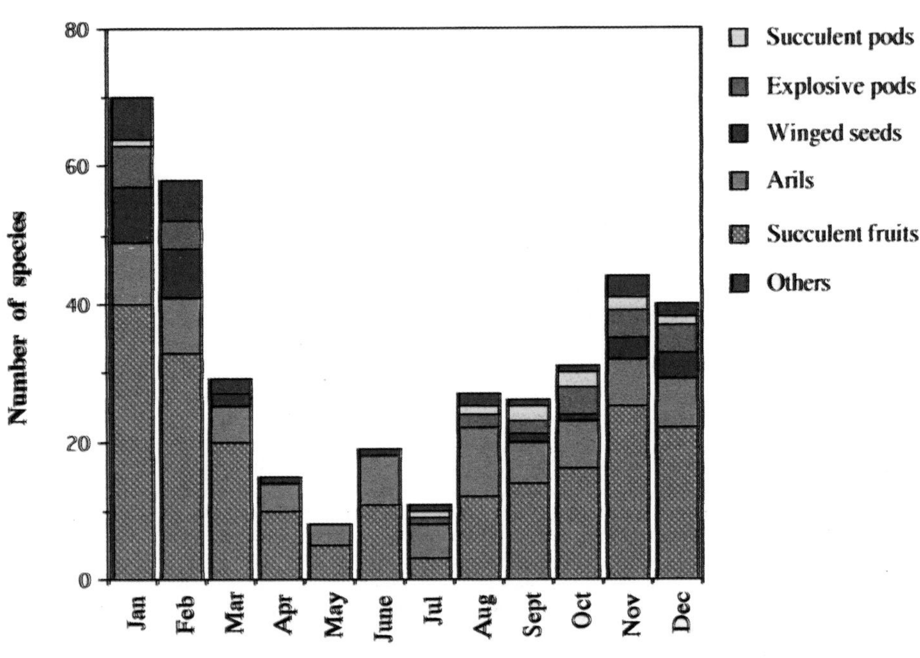

HOW TO USE THIS GUIDE

For most people the diversity of the rain forest is formidable. When we first arrived in Lopé we knew only those species that are grown as house plants in Europe. Our principal aim in this guide is to make the forest less daunting for people who share our desire to get to know some of the many attractive and fascinating plant species growing in Lopé. Most plant guides include a key to species, but this one does not. Keys are rather dry and unless you are lucky enough to find a specimen with flowers, rarely result in a firm identification. In this guide we divide plants by their growth form (tree, shrub, liane etc.) and group them within the habitat type in which you are most likely to find them. As far as these criteria allow, species in the same taxonomic families are grouped together. Hence, if you notice a tree with attractive flowers growing in the gallery along the Ogooué, below the Lopé Hotel, by turning to the relevant section of the guide the possibilities should be narrowed down to the extent that you can quickly pick it out from the illustrations and then learn about it from the facing text. In doing so there is every chance that you will spot other species from the same habitat that you have already noticed, or which you would like to see. In order to enable you to do this we will now describe the various habitats you will encounter in Lopé.

You will encounter several habitat types in the Lopé :

1) The gallery forests of the Ogooué are particularly varied, being rocky in certain places, sandy in others, and sometimes seasonally flooded (see p.15).

2) The savannas are dominated by grasses, but also contain a variety of small perennial herbs, as well as several species of fire resistant shrubs (see p.29).

3) Two types of forest occur as more or less isolated patches in the savanna: gallery forests snake out of the main forest block, and small isolated patches or 'bosquets' tend to occur on hill tops (see p.45).

4) Young forest types develop after savanna colonisation by (see p.45).

5) Marantaceae forest, one of two dominant vegetation formations in Lopé, is characterised by a dense understory of herbaceous vegetation composed principally of wild gingers and plants in the Marantaceae family (see p.94).

6) Mature forest is a classic rain forest, with many large and medium sized trees which result in a complex structure. The upper canopy is more or less continuous, producing cool shady conditions at ground level. The understory vegetation consists mostly of shrubs and lianes (see p.163).

7) Rocky areas are colonised by scrambling shrubs and lianes, which scramble over outcrops in the forest. Close to rock outcrops small shrubs scratch a living in thin soils. A little further away there are dense stands of small trees, rarely exceeding 15m tall (see p.188).

8) The banks of forest rivers are often fringed with lush vegetation, with many species of ferns, wild gingers and occasionally small, yellow flowered *Begonia*. Certain small trees grow at the waterside (see p.197).

9) Two types of disturbance which alter natural vegetation occur in Lopé: agriculture and logging (see p.206).

10) Mountains (see p. 212)

11) Introduced species are often found at sites of past or present human habitation (see p.213)

Few plants are restricted to just one habitat, although most tend to be more common in one or two vegetation types. Therefore, if you do not find the species you are looking at in the corresponding habitat do not give up hope; there is a fair degree of overlap between several of the habitats described here. Once you have checked the habitat in which you find yourself try elsewhere in the book. The following guidelines will enable you to search through the guide efficiently:

If you are in the Ogooué gallery and fail to find a plant of interest in this section, try looking in "galleries, bosquets and young forest types" or in "forest rivers".

If you find a shrub or small tree which is not illustrated in the "savanna", section look in "galeries, bosquets and young forest types" or "disturbed areas".

If the unidentified plant is in a gallery, bosquet or young forest type, check in "savanna", "rocky areas", "forest rivers" or "Marantaceae forest".

After Marantaceae forest try "galleries, bosquets and young forest types" or "forest rivers".

After mature forest, try under "Marantaceae forest".

After rocky areas try "Marantaceae forest" or "galleries, bosquets and young forest types".

After gallery forests try in "mature forest", "rocky areas", "Marantaceae forest" or "young forest types".

After disturbed areas try in "savanna" or "galleries, bosquets and young forest types".

If you have already looked through a botanical text you will realise that this science has a technical language all of its own. We have tried to minimise the use of technical terms. We have replaced strict botanical terminologies with words or phrases which are more familiar, if less precise. Scientists may find this unsatisfactory, but we hope that it will make this guide more accessible for the majority of our readers. However, if you are unfamiliar with certain terms employed check the illustrated glossary at the end of the book.

NOMENCLATURE

The plant kingdom is divided into Families of related species. All plants in any given family share a set of common features which facilitate classification and identification. The structure of the flower is the most important feature for most plants (except for plants without flowers - see p. 216) and this sometimes results in small savanna herbs and large forest trees confusingly being classified in the same Family or even in the same genus. Most plants have common names in local languages. These vary between different languages, so one plant may have tens or hundreds of different names, depending on where in the world it is living. Every species of animal and plant that has been documented by science has been assigned a Latin name unique to that species. In fact, each species receives two names, the first, or generic name, which refers to a group of closely related species, and the second, the specific name, which is only applied to one species in any genus. Some species vary from place to place and where separate races can be recognised these are described by a third, or sub-specific name. The Latin name is often chosen to describe a striking feature of the plant so it is usually interesting to understand the origins of the scientific name.

In this guide all species are described by their scientific name. For some of the commoner or more striking species and particularly for those with economic importance, there is a widely used common name which we also give, but for many species no such name exists.

You will note for some species we give only the generic name and use the abbreviation sp. (meaning species) in place of the specific name. This is because we have so far been unable to fully identify the species in question. Often this is because no comprehensive scientific study has been undertaken on that genus or family and it is therefore extremely difficult to identify them, but in other cases it is because the species in question may be new to science. It may seem strange to visitors from Europe or America, but the fact is that our knowledge of tropical forests is still in its infancy. Only 10 years ago a new species of monkey, the sun-tailed guenon, *Cercopithecus solatus*, was discovered just outside the Lopé Reserve to the east of the river Offoué. In this guide you will read about several newly described plant species and when you go out into the forest you will soon realise how common and easily recognised some of these are. Imagine how many more there are out there waiting to be discovered.

THE TOURIST ZONE

During a typical guided visit to the Reserve you will see a wide variety of habitats. The canoe ride to see pre-historic rock engravings provides an ideal introduction to the vegetation of the Ogooué River gallery, although we recommend you take a short walk along the river bank from the hotel for a close up view of some of the trees and flowers. If lucky you will see orchids in bloom, but remember that you cannot pick flowers in the Reserve. This walk is to be recommended to anybody interested in birds, as many of Lopé's 350 or so species are only to be found in this habitat. If you are lucky you may catch a glimpse of the large cape clawless otter out in the current. It is also an ideal place to search for animal tracks.

During the savanna tour you will be driven through a mosaic of grassland and gallery forests. When not watching buffalo or elephant take time to look for attractive savanna flowers or for fruiting trees in the narrow belts of forest. These are often given away by the crash and chatter of monkeys or by noisy flights of African grey parrots.

The forest into which guided tours are taken has been specially selected for its diversity of vegetation types. With the exception of the highest mountains, which are only found in remote parts in the centre of the Reserve, all forest types are represented. So you will have an opportunity to walk through savanna and to see it evolving into younger forest types; to follow elephant paths through dense Marantaceae fields; and to peer up into the high canopy of the Mature Forest. The map on the following page will enable you to follow your route and help you to recognise the forest type you are moving through.

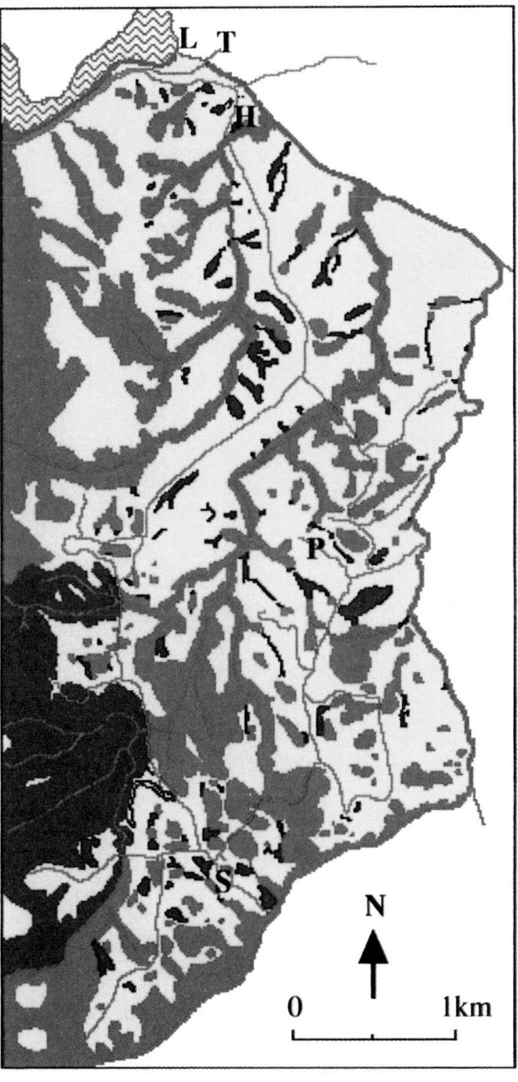

L	Lopé Hotel
T	Train station
H	Reserve headquarters
S	Research station (SEGC)
P	Prehistoric village
——	Railway
——	Road
——	River
	Ogooué
	Marshes
	Forest
	Tourist zone
	Savanna

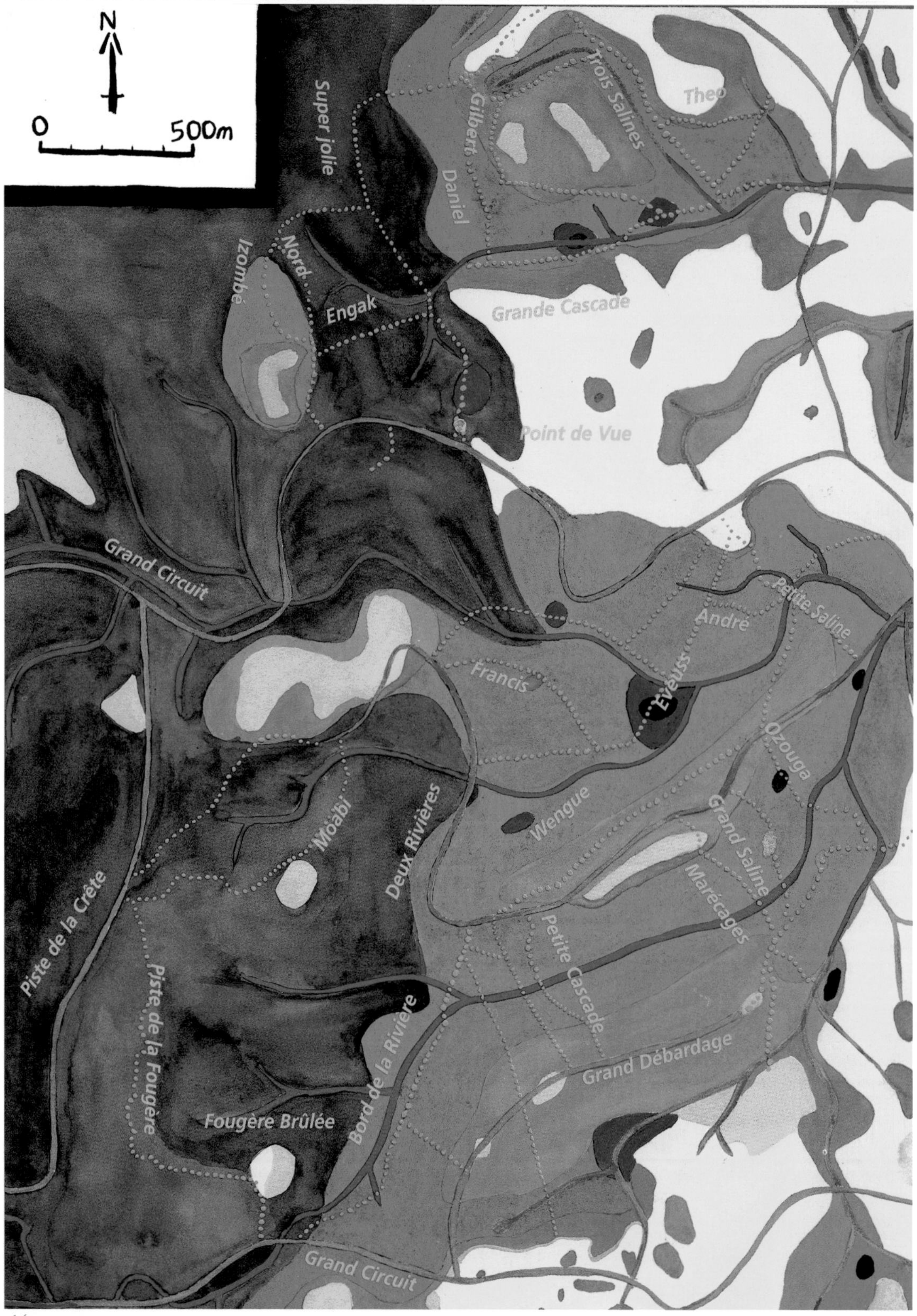
N
0
500m
Super jolie
Gilbert
Trois Salines
Theo
Daniel
Izombé
Nord
Engak
Grande Cascade
Point de Vue
Grand Circuit
André
Petite Saline
Francis
Eveuss
Ozouga
Wengue
Grand Saline
Moabi
Deux Rivières
Marécages
Piste de la Crête
Petite Cascade
Piste de la Fougère
Bord de la Rivière
Grand Débardage
Fougère Brûlée
Grand Circuit

1/ GALLERY FORESTS ALONG THE RIVER OGOOUÉ

Gallery Forests are forests which grow along rivers and streams. They usually contain some plant species which only grow close to water. Because of their proximity to water and because light penetrates to the ground from the opening in the canopy above the river or stream, vegetation tends to be particularly lush. In Lopé, the majority of gallery forests are enclosed within the forest, but in the north and east of the Reserve galleries snake out into the savanna along water courses.

The Ogooué is one of Africa's largest rivers, draining almost the whole of Gabon. The gallery forests along its banks vary greatly in width, but rarely disappear. These form a varied habitat; in places vegetation seems to grow out of the rocks which form the bed of the river, whilst elsewhere there are extensive areas which are seasonally flooded. Seasonal changes in the height of the river have an important influence on the vegetation along its banks, so bear in mind when you look at the gallery that what you see is not necessarily representative year-round.

If you take time to walk along the river in the shade of the gallery you will see a rich diversity of plants that do not occur elsewhere in the Reserve. It is the best habitat in which to see orchids, with several species covering the trunks of some of the larger trees.

If you visit in the dry season you will see extensive grassy banks revealed by the low waters. These were once grazed by herds of hippo, animals which were hunted close to extinction before the Reserve was established. Beautiful lilies grow in other areas revealed by the low waters. When the waters rise, at the end of the dry season, the gallery becomes as spectacular a flower show as you can hope to find. Trees covered with white or pink blossoms line the river, some giving out pungent perfumes which drift out over the water.

There are many fruit trees growing in the gallery, so many animals are attracted to the waterside after the long dry season. However, it is not just the forest mammals and birds which enjoy this bounty. Many of the river fishes, such as the Yara, *Eutropus grenfelli*, eat large quantities of fruit. In this way the forest sustains fresh-water fisheries, which are vital for the local economy in much of rural Gabon, as well as being a favourite source of protein.

Left:

Vegetation map of the tourist zone.

Savanna

Young forests

Stands of *Aucoumea*, *Lophira* and *Sacoglottis*.

Marantaceae forets

Mature forest

Exposed rocks

Rocky forest

Rivers with old galleries

Rivers with young galleries

Old logging roads

Paths.

Herbaceous plants

AMARYLLIDACEAE

This family includes familiar genera such as *Narcissus*, the daffodils that signify the arrival of spring in Europe, and many species of ornamental lily, found in florists around the world.

Crinum purpurescens is a white flowered lily which springs up and flowers on mud flats revealed by the low dry season waters on the Ogooué. Like a daffodil it is only visible for 2-3 months but survives as an underground (and in this case underwater) bulb. Its close relative, *Crinum natans*, is an aquatic plant which has long wavy submerged leaves, which drift in the current of a few of the smaller channels of the Ogooué. Its white flowers are held above the water on thick, fleshy stalks.

Scadoxus cinnabarinus is a spectacular, red flowered lily, which grows up to about 60 cm tall, found on the forest edge, particularly close to rock outcrops, as well as in the forest itself.

ARACEAE

This family contains many ornamental plants, such as *Monstera deliciosa*, from South America, commonly known as the Swiss cheese plant. Others are cultivated for their edible tubers, such as 'taro', *Colocasia esculenta*.

Anchomanes difformis is found in all forest types in Lopé. It is a distinctive plant with a prickly, fleshy stem up to 3 m high and an intricate leaf. Both the stem and leaf are eaten by gorillas, but dry the back of the throat causing a choking sensation, so are not to be recommended! The inflorescence consists of a phallic "spadix', with tightly clustered male flowers on the upper portion, and numerous female flowers below. This is enclosed within a purplish hood, the spathe, a modified rolled leaf. Numerous white berries develop on the spadix, turning pink when ripe. These are sweet to taste, but dry the back of the throat in the same way as the leaves. The underground tubers are eaten by humans in times of famine.

Pseuderanthemum tunicatum **(Acanthaceae) in the Ogooué gallery -** **see p. 101.**

Below :

Amaryllidaceae
- ***a) Crinum purpurascens***
- ***b) Scadoxus cinnabarinus***

Araceae
- ***c) Cercestes congoensis***
- ***d) Culcasia scandens***

Cercestes congoensis is an epiphytic plant found on the trunks of trees in the Ogooué gallery. It can be recognised by the characteristic shape of its leaves. It has small red fruits in February / March.

Culcasia scandens is common in the gallery of the Ogooué and along some other rivers in the Reserve. It grows over rocks and climbs up the trunks of trees with the aid of special 'brace-roots', subsequently living as an epiphyte. It has a greenish spathe and white spadix, on which a few small red fruits develop.

ORCHIDACEAE

The family Orchidaceae contains over 500 genera with about 20,000 species and may account for up to one tenth of all flowering plants. Only the Compositae contains a greater number of species worldwide. Almost 500 orchid species are found in west and central Africa. They are herbs, which may live on the ground, on trees as epiphytes, or on decomposing plant matter as 'saprophytes'. Most epipytes grow best in humid conditions and on hardwood trees, which gradually accumulate a cover of these 'hitch-hiking' plants during their long lives. Because the climate in Lopé is relatively dry and much of the forest quite young (see p. 7-10) and dominated by resinous trees like *Aucoumea klaineana*, epiphytes are generally rare. One exception is in the gallery of the Ogooué River. Here, ancient trees which arch out over the river are often covered in epiphytic ferns, lilies and orchids. When flowering, the orchids are instantly recognisable by their intricate blooms, which tend to open in September, at the end of the long dry season and in March.

Eulophia gracilis

Several species of epiphytic orchid can be seen in the Ogooué gallery close to the Hotel. ***Ansellia africana***, the leopard orchid, is often found in quite exposed places on living or dead *Vitex doniana* (p. 72) trees. It produces beautiful spotted flowers and large dangling fruits, which release thousands of tiny seeds into the air. ***Cyrtorchis chailluana*** tends to grow on the trunks of large trees of the Caesalpiniaceae family (p. 23), particularly those overhanging the river. It favours more shady conditions than *Ansellia africana*, but does not grow well unless relatively free of other vegetation, such that the afternoon breeze dries out its leaves and roots. ***Plectrelminthus caudatus*** is found in similar habitat to *Cyrtorchis chailluana*, but is uncommon and its spectacular bunches of flowers are rarely seen. The more discrete ***Polystachya***, often found in association with *Cyrtorchis chailluana*, has not yet been identified to species, but is locally abundant in the Ogooué gallery.

Eulophia gracilis, is found growing in leaf litter in the Ogooué gallery and becomes common in a few places. It can grow as a saprophyte amongst leaf litter, or in the ground, and is also found around rock outcrops in galleries and disturbed forest elsewhere in the Reserve.

Cyrtorchis chailluana

b
c
a
KA'
94

Lianes

CUCURBITACEAE

This family includes many cultivated species like cucumbers, melons, gourds and marrows. In Lopé they are all lianes, found in galleries and disturbed areas.

Cogniauxia podolaena is a herbaceous climber which can rise to 6 m, or trail along the ground. It is found in disturbed areas around villages and in open areas along streams and rivers. Its leaf, with five distinct lobes, is typical of many Cucurbitaceae. Twisted tendrils, characteristic of the family, grow from close to the leaf axil. The large, delicate, yellow flowers last only 1-2 days. The fruit is about 15 cm long, pale green in colour, with darker longitudinal lines. When dry, numerous black, flattened seeds, like those of a marrow, fall from an opening at its tip. The dried fruit is used locally as a sponge and, elsewhere in Gabon the dried leaves are powdered and used to treat burns. This plant is frequently eaten by elephants and its seedlings, with leaves similar to the adult plant, are sometimes found germinating in dung.

Physedra longipes, is found in galleries in the savanna and in Marantaceae Forest. It is a liane which climbs up to about 20 m. Its leaves are up to 15 cm long and are like those of *Cogniauxia podolaena*, with five distinct lobes. The flowers have pale orange petals about 1 cm across. It is particularly eye catching when it has large bunches of crimson fruit.

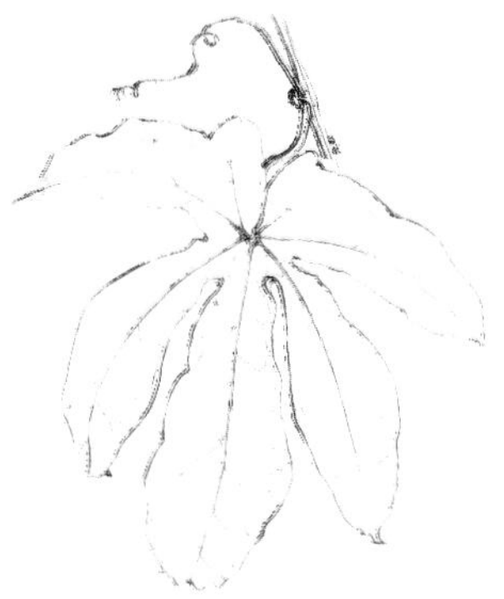

Physedra longipes

Telfairea occidentalis, commonly known as the 'fluted pumpkin' or 'oyster nut', is a liane with herbaceous stems which can be up to 30 m long. It has digitate compound leaves with 3-5 leaflets, which can be up to 15 x 10 cm and are toothed from about a third of the way up their edges. The showy flowers are 4-5 cm across with creamy petals and a red-purple centre. Its spectacular, deeply ridged, gourd-like fruit is pale green, drying yellow-brown. It is up to about 60 cm x 25 cm, with bright yellow flesh within containing up to 155 large, flattened seeds about 3 cm across. It was introduced to Gabon by Bantu peoples migrating southwards from the Nigeria-Cameroon border, perhaps as long as 3,000 years ago In some parts of Africa it is still cultivated and where it occurs in Lopé it may be a sign of past habitation. The leaves and young stems are rich in minerals and are eaten as a vegetable. The seeds are flavoured like almonds and can be cooked whole or ground up and added to soups. They are rich in oil, similar to olive oil, which can be extracted and used for cooking.

Left:

a) Ansellia africana
b) Plectrelminthus caudatus
c) Polystachya sp.

Page 20:

a) Cogniauxia podolaena
b) Physedra longipes
c) Telfairea occidentalis

Page 21:

Compositae
a) Grangea maderaspatana
Euphorbiaceae
b) Antidesma venosum
Loganiaceae
c) Mostuea brunonis
Malphigiaceae
d) Acridocarpus longifolius
Ochnaceae
e) Ouratea cf. arnoldiana
f) Ouratea dusenii
Olacaceae
g) Olax gambecola
Oxalidaceae
h) Biophytum zenkeri
Pedaliaceae
i) Sesamum radiatum
Rubiaceae
j) Morelia senegalensis
k) Psychotria sp.

Shrubs

A number of characteristic small and medium sized shrubs live in the galleries of the Ogooué and its larger tributaries. They are particularly noticeable when growing on rocks in the Ogooué, crowning the great boulders which emerge from its waters in the dry season, or half submerged, thrashing back and forth in the wet season spate. Most species can be identified from their flowers or fruits. Some have traditional uses.

Garcinia cf. ovalifolia (**Clusiaceae**) is a small shrub often seen clinging tenaciously to rocks out in the middle of the river. Its small, edible, yellow fruits are eaten by fishes when they fall into the river.

Mostuea brunonis (**Loganiaceae**) is a small shrub reaching 1 m in height, which is common on the rocky banks of several rivers. A second, rarer species, *Mostuea gabonica,* is very similar but can be distinguished by its hairy leaves. Its roots contain a strong aphrodisiac and stimulant, whose effect is similar to that of the renowned Iboga, *Tabernanthe iboga* (Apocynaceae), and of the Yohimbe tree, *Pausinystalia johimbe* (Rubiaceae, see p.152), but which is dangerous if taken in too large a dose. It is often used to soothe the pain after a circumscision ceremony.

Olax gambecola (**Olacaceae**) is a small shrub with a sweet, edible fruit which is orange when ripe.

Biophytum zenkeri (**Oxalidaceae**) is a small shrub rarely more than 20 cm high, resembling a bonsai tree in a Japanese garden, which grows out of rock crevices along the banks of the Ogooué.

Sesamum radiatum (**Pedaliaceae**) is an attractive wild sesame whose seeds yield an edible oil. Archaeologists excavating caves close to Lastoursville recently found the seeds of this species on the inside of clay pots several thousand years old, suggesting that the seeds of this species were collected and eaten by stone age peoples living in the region.

Donella ogowensis (Oyiop - **Sapotaceae**) has bright yellow fruits which catch one's eye when they are ripe. They are much prized by gorillas and chimpanzees and make an agreeable snack if you take a walk along the river.

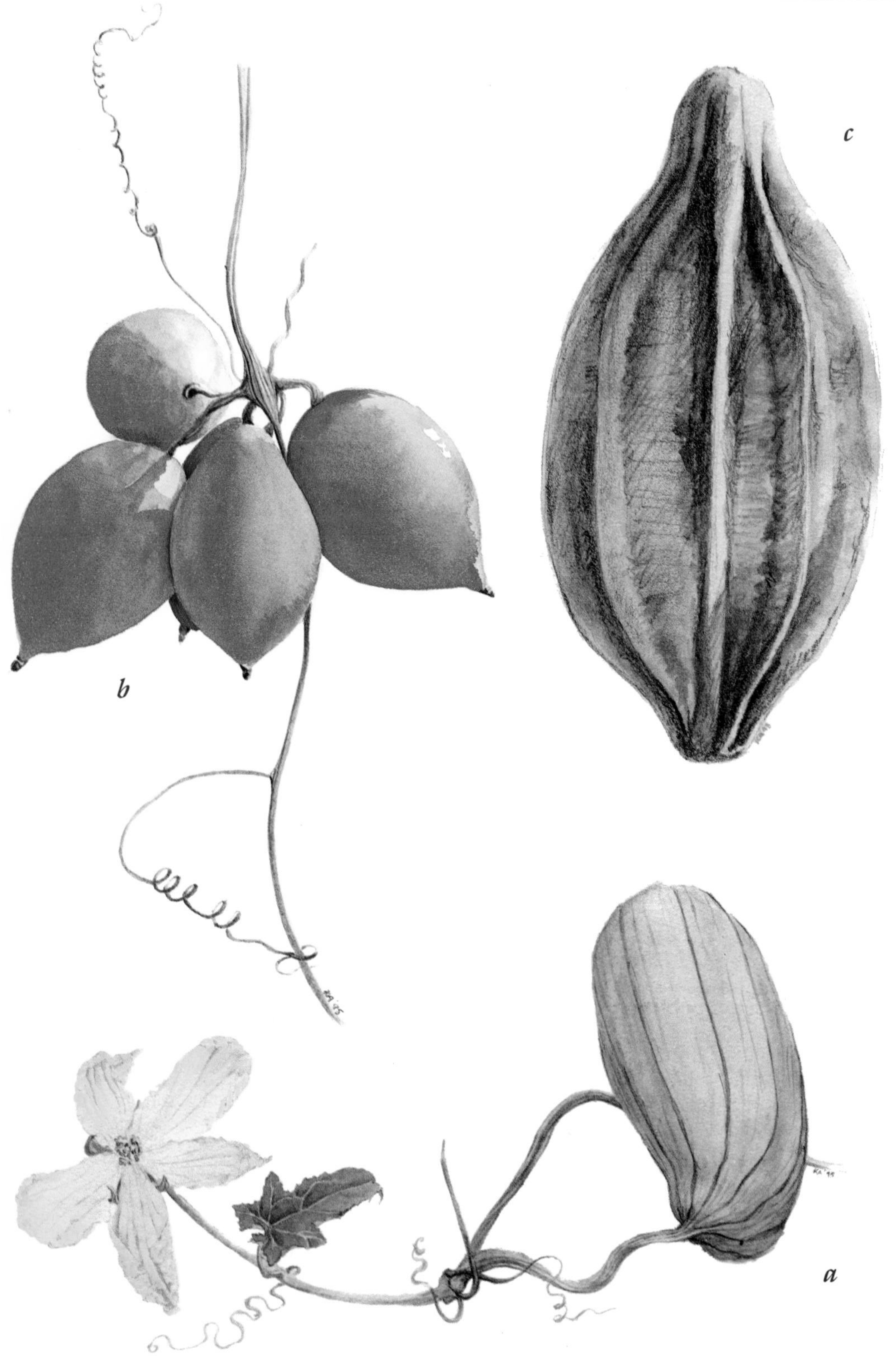
c
b
a

d
k
c
g
b
i
a
e
h
KA'05
f

a
b
c
d
e
f
KA'94

Trees

Trees found along the banks of the Ogooué River and its major tributaries form a distinct botanical community, with characteristic structure and species composition. The gallery vegetation tends to be restricted to a narrow strip about 20 m wide along the banks of the river, although it is more extensive where there are areas of ground which are seasonally flooded. Beyond the gallery the forest, if present, resembles that elsewhere in the Reserve.

EUPHORBIACEAE

There are several species of *Uapaca* in the Reserve, commonly known as the "rikios". They all have stilt roots, which are a special adaptation to enable them to get a firm grip and become common in seasonally flooded areas and along river banks, although they are also found on dry land. They all have leaves arranged in whorls, very similar scented flowers, and succulent fruits like little bobbles along the smaller branches. Like all plants in the Euphorbiaceae family, the flowers of *Uapaca* are unisexual, being either male or female. Individual plants have either male or female flowers, but not both; in technical terms, they are dioecious.

Uapaca heudelotii is abundant in some parts of the Ogooué Gallery, particularly in seasonally flooded areas, where its characteristic stilt roots are reminiscent of mangrove vegetation. The intricate mat of fine roots helps to retain soil when the river is in flood and their shelter provides an important breeding ground for river fishes. The bushy, rounded form and dense foliage are also characteristic.

The flowers of *U. heudelotii* are yellow-green in colour. They develop at the end of the dry season as the waters rise. Their green fruits grow to be about 2 cm long, turning slightly yellow when ripe. They contain three characteristic seeds (see page 214) which are often visible in large numbers on the ground below, having been spat out by monkeys or parrots. The fruits are eaten by a great variety of animals. Gorillas, chimpanzees and monkeys, along with many species of bird, consume the fruits on the tree; elephants, duikers, pigs and civets collect them from the ground; and those which fall into the water are eaten by fishes.

Uapaca heudelotii also occurs in some of the galleries in the savanna, along many of the larger rivers in the forest, in some swamps and occasionally in the forest on dry land. However, the dominant species of *Uapaca* in the savanna galleries and along the edge of the main forest block is ***Uapaca guineensis***. This species can be distinguished from *U. heudelotii* by its thicker and less numerous stilt roots, its more erect form with spreading branches, which curve upwards towards their tips and its large, bunched leaves with prominent veination. In addition, the flowers are yellow and the fruits more rounded. They usually flower in March / April. The fruits (see p. 84) develop rapidly, but then change little during the long dry season, ripening in October / November with the onset of the rains. In years when *U. guineensis* produces large crops the galleries become extremely active as many of the forest animals move out to feed on their bounty. Look for the spectacular giant blue turaco hopping around in its branches or the bright blue face of a moustached guenon, its cheek pouches bulging with fruit.

Deeper in the forest there are several other species of *Uapaca*. The commonest of these is ***Uapaca paludosa***. It is similar to *U. guineensis* but has a more open crown, less curved terminal branches and cream coloured flowers. In addition, the leaf tends to be somewhat larger and is rounded, rather than acute, at its base. This species is often found in well drained valley bottoms in Mature Forest, but also occurs higher up the sides of valleys and occasionally on ridges. Two other species which are rarely encountered are ***Uapaca vanhouttei***, which is easily distinguished by its hairy leaves and ***Uapaca togoensis***, similar in form to *U. paludosa*, but with leaves which are difficult to distinguish from those of *U. heudelotii*.

LEGUMINOSAE; SUBFAMILY: CAESALPINIOIDEAE

Trees in the family Leguminosae; sub-family Caesalpinioideae, dominate the Ogooué Gallery vegetation. This family seems to dominate vegetation along all of the major rivers which flow through the rain forest in tropical Africa. They are specialised to grow on the poor, sandy soils. However, their presence has greater significance, since their fruits are pods and their dry seeds tend to be dispersed by explosive mechanisms which are only able to propel them 20 or 30 m at best. Their presence therefore indicates that some forest vegetation was able so survive along the Ogooué during periods when Africa's climate became arid, when forest was generally replaced by savanna (see p. 7).

Pachystella brevipes **(Sapotaceae) - a large tree with a sugary fruit eaten by many species of animal, which is common overhanging the Ogooué and in some forest galleries.**

A mangrove tree, *Rhizophora racemosa* (Rhizophoraceae) forms extensive stands along coastal lagoons in Gabon.

Left:

Clusiaceae
a) Garcinia cf. ovalifolia
Ixonanthaceae
b) Ochthocosmus congolensis **(see p. 191)**
Rubiaceae
c) Gaertnera cf. paniculata
d) Pouchetia gilletii
Sapotaceae
e) Donella ogowensis
f) Synsepalum cf. dulcificum.

b
a
c

Trees of the sub-family Caesalpinioideae which occur in the Ogooué gallery, as well as several species belonging to other families, share a common, characteristic form. They tend not to be very tall, but spread their long, thick branches out low over the river. They usually branch low, or have several trunks each of which may be 70 cm or more in diameter. Their roots spread far along the bank, searching for a firm hold, to ensure that they have sufficient anchorage to resist the dual forces of gravity and swift flood waters.

Aphanocalyx djumaensis is easily recognised by its compound leaves which have two asymmetric leaflets (5 x 2 cm), with distinctive shape and veination. The soft, limp, young leaves are hot pink. A few young leaves are visible almost year round, but at the end of the long dry season many trees flush, creating a spectacular display along the river. They produce showy bunches of bright white flowers at the same time, enhancing the effect. The pods are 5-6 cm long.

Baikiaea robynsii has very characteristic dark brown, fissured bark. Its leaves have 5-9 alternate, leathery leaflets (10 x 4 cm), with indistinct lateral nerves and rolled margins. It produces spectacular flowers in July / August. These emerge from furry, pale brown, protective sepals. They have one large yellow petal up to 12 cm long and four smaller white petals. From a distance they can be confused with the flowers of *Berlinia bracteosa* (p. 200), which also occurs along the Ogooué. The furry golden brown pods are 8-13 x 6-9 cm. A second species, ***Baikiaea insignis***, is occasionally encountered in galleries along rivers in the forest and in the forest-savanna mosaic and flowers at the same time. *B. insignis* is easily distinguished by its large leaflets, often at least 30 x 15 cm, its huge white petals, which can reach 20 cm long, and its characteristic black-brown, velvety sepals, about 12 cm in length. The black velvety pods are 20-40 x 6-12 cm. Its leaves and seeds are edible. The seeds are particularly appreciated by mangabeys and black colobus, who rip open the unripe pods with their strong jaws.

Cryptosephalum staudtii is common in the Ogooué gallery and along some smaller rivers. It has compound leaves with 10-13 pairs of small leaflets (10 x 3.5 mm) with a characteristic indented apex. In September / October they create a spectacular display of pale pink young leaves and white flowers. The pods are about 6 cm long. They split with a sharp crack and pepper the ground with seeds in January / February. The young leaves are eaten by all of the primates, and by elephants, which often break off quite large branches.

Cymometra schlechteri is easily identified from its compound leaves, with 3 pairs of leaflets, which gradually increase in size from the base of the leaf. The terminal pair of leaflets are about 5 x 2 cm, with a characteristic indented tip. It has peculiar, fleshy, warty pods which do not split open and are perhaps dispersed by water.

Dialium guineensis has leathery leaves which otherwise are similar to those of *Dialium soyauxii* (p. 138). It has yellow-green flowers. The fruits are velvety black-brown capsules, typical of all *Dialium* species, containing a single seed and a tangy, sugary flesh which is excellent to eat. Dried, dessicated capsules persist on the tree long after fruiting is over.

A species worthy of note, but which to date has only been found along the River Offoué within the reserve, is ***Gilbertiodendron dewevrei*** (Limbali). This species closely resembles *G. grandistipulatum* (p. 202), but is easily distinguished because it only has 3, occasionally 2-5, pairs of leathery leaflets and its petals are red-pink and only about 2.5 cm long. In north eastern Gabon and other parts of central Africa *Gilbertiodendron dewevrei* forms extensive, almost pure, stands, which can cover hundreds of square kilometers. In years when most trees fruit, up to almost 5 tons of nutritious seeds fall to the ground in each square kilometer of Limbali forest, attracting large numbers of elephants, pigs and gorillas. Until recently these seeds were also an important food source of forest dwelling people.

Guibourtia demeusii has pale grey-brown, lightly fissured bark, which becomes scaly in older trees. Its leaves have two asymmetrical leaflets in the form of lobster claws (10 x 4 cm) similar to the other *Guibourtia* species (p. 176). If wounded the bark exudes a clear resin which sets like glass. This is copal. Ancient stands of *Guibourtia demeusii* are thought to be the main source of fossil copal, which is extracted from swampy areas and used in the manufacture of varnish. In October / November the crown is covered in white flowers, about 1 cm across. The pods (3 x 2.5 cm) ripen in February and contain a single seed.

Hymenostegia klainei is relatively rare along the Ogooué gallery, but catches the eye in August when its canopy is covered in pink flowers (see p. 200). There is some confusion of the taxonomy of this species, as the same name has been assigned to two varieties, now thought to be different species. The trees found in Lopé correspond to the second variety which may soon be given a new name.

Left:

a) Uapaca heudelotii
b) Uapaca guineensis
c) Uapaca paludosa.

Pachypodanthium staudtii
(Annonaceae - see p. 76)

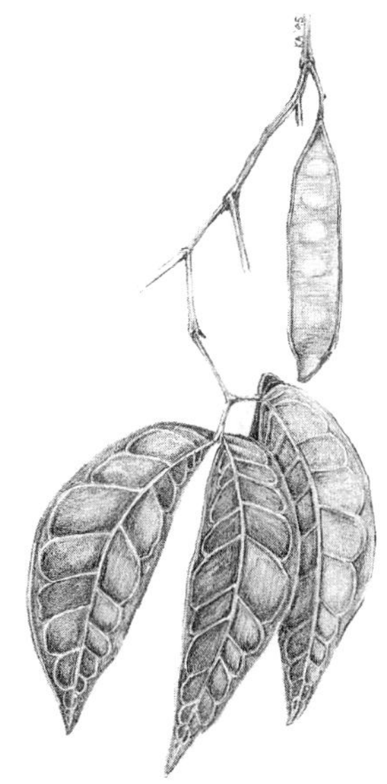

Albizia laurenti
(Leguminosae - Mimosoideae) is common in rocky areas along the banks of the Ogooué. It is easily recognised by its compound leaves with two pairs of leaflets arranged in crab claws, and its papery pods.

d
b
a
c
f
e

This *Baikiaea robynsii* has the characteristic form of trees overhanging the Ogooué.

MORACEAE

Treculia africana (African breadfruit) is one of the trees often seen overhanging the Ogooué. However, the most remarkable individuals are those growing on isolated rocks and small islands, which have the stunted form of large bonsai trees. The spherical flowers are up to 10 cm diameter and develop into fruits the size of footballs. They contain numerous soft seeds which are eaten by many of the forest animals, including gorillas, chimpanzees and elephants. Fruits falling into the river are eaten by fishes. The seeds, if roasted and ground into a flour, can be used to make a kind of bread. *Treculia* seeds were probably an important food for the iron age peoples who carved numerous engravings into boulders along the river. *Treculia africana* is also found along rivers in the forest, where they tend to be taller and straighter.

Left:

a) Aphanocalyx djumaensis
b) Baikiaea robynsii
c) Cryptosepalum staudtii
d) Cymometra schlechteri
e) Dialium guineense
f) Guibourtia demeusii

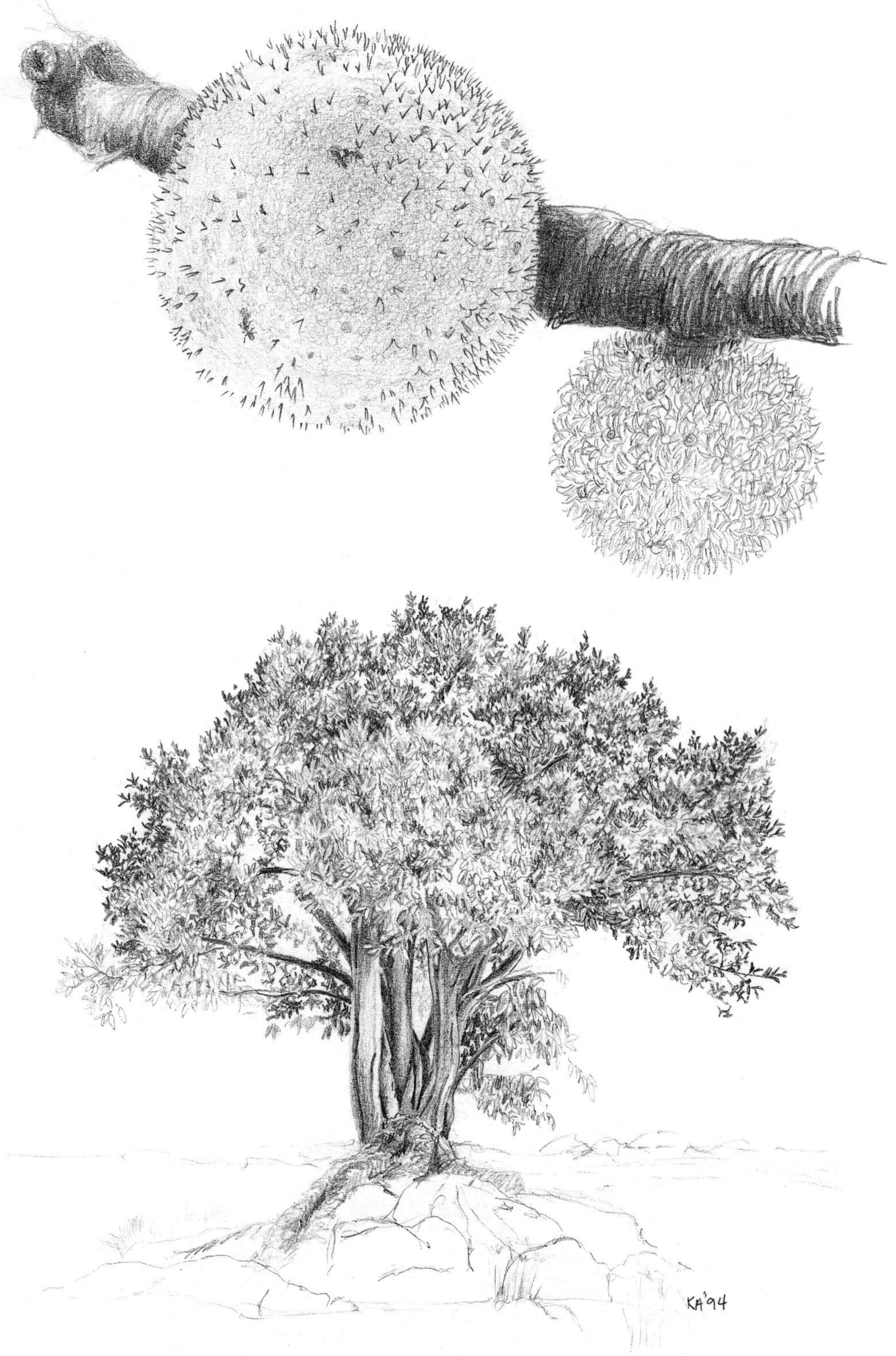
KA'94

2/ SAVANNA

The Lopé savannas are a remnant of a vegetation type that has extended over much of central Africa at various times in the past. They are dominated by a small number of grasses which are found widely in central Africa. Small, perennial herbs grow in amongst the grasses. The savannas support a large number of animals which cannot survive in the forest, adding greatly to the diversity of the Lopé. For example, the bushbuck, a species found in savannas and woodland, but which never lives deep in the forest. In addition the savannas are visited by many species of migratory birds.

There is a similar annual cycle in the savanna to that found in the forest. As the dry season advances the tall grass begins to die and dry out. There is little nutritive value in the dessicated stems and savanna animals hunger for fresh young grass. The buffalo, a prominant feature of the Lopé savannas during most of the year, become brown sacks of bones, and retreat more and more often into the forest, where they subsist on ferns and aquatic plants growing in marshes. Birds, such as the startling yellow-mantled whydah, lose their bright plumage and become a drab brown, more fitting perhaps to the gloomy, oppressive weather.

Then savanna fires crackle through the silence, lighting the night with an orange glow, scorching away a year's growth in smoke and ashes. Flocks of birds follow the fire, devouring insects thrown up by its heat. Within days there are buffalo to be seen, standing motionless, or lying, as if waiting for the grass to grow. It seems strange that something so destructive and violent should bring release to the savanna animals, but as new grass sprouts from burnt tussocks herds of buffalo congregate out in the open. They are joined by elephants, yellow back duikers and red river hogs. This is spring in the savanna, a time of plenty. With the first rains, which cleanse the dry season haze, all memory of the 'winter' fires is gone; the ashes are washed away and the ground becomes a bright green carpet. Small flowering plants add a splash of colour, taking advantage of the open conditions before the grass grows up to smother them. Young buffalo frolic in the early morning dew and the male whydah bobs busily around in his bright mating plumage.

This process of renewal has been underway since savannas first grew in the Lopé area. It is in the savanna that Stone and Iron Age peoples made their villages. Many of their settlements can still be located even today, appearing as patches of erosion on hill tops in the savanna. It is likely that for at least the last 400,000 years, humans living in Lopé area have torched the dry grasslands around their villages. Before the arrival of man, natural fires caused by lightning would also have burnt the savanna, on a less regular basis.

Annual fires kill any seedlings of forest plants which germinate in the savanna. The only woody species that occur in savannas which are regularly burnt are fire resistant shrubs. However, in places which are naturally protected by marshes or gallery forest, dense thickets of shrubs and small trees establish. If the savannas were not burnt they would soon be replaced by forest, but due to the presence of humans and their fires, vegetation in some parts of the north of the Reserve has changed little since the late Stone Age. Then, as now, there were gallery forests along the larger streams, where people would have gone to collect water in their clay pots, to gather firewood or medicinal plants or to hunt.

In view of the biological and historical importance of the savannas, the Ministry of Water and Forests conducts a programme of controlled burns in the dry season, in order to maintain the grassland habitat. Some savannas are burnt each year, to maintain open conditions ideal for the observation of buffalo; others are burnt every two or three years and have greater numbers of shrubs, providing ideal nesting sites for many of the savanna birds; and a few are left to gradually regenerate into forest.

As the September-January rainy season progresses the grass grows higher and birds begin to nest. Down in the marshes orchids abound. This is 'summer' in the Lopé. After the short dry season the grass grows high enough to make it difficult to see buffalo and elephant. As the grass begins to dry out we come full circle.

Low lying areas in the savanna are often poorly drained and become marshes, dominated by sedges or *Pandanus*. These are home to the sitatunga, a large antelope whose toes are splayed to enable it to walk across the soft, moist ground. In the heat of the day buffalo, forest pigs and elephants spend long hours wallowing in the mud in these areas. Their dung adds nutrients to the small streams and still pools in the marshes, stimulating the growth of aquatic plants whose flowers float on the surface. They also feed the large leeches which lurk in these pools.

Left: ***Treculia africana***

Right, some common grasses:

a) Ctenium newtonii
b) Hyparrhenia diplandra
c) Jardinea gabonensis
d) Imperata cylindrica
e) Panicum fulgens
f) Pennisetum polystachyon
g) Peratis indica
h) Anadelphia (Pobeguinea) arrecta

Olyra latifolia **is a forest grass whose hollow stems can be used as drinking straws.**

Grasses

GRAMINEAE (or POACEAE)

There are about 10,000 species of grasses in the world, and at least 500 in tropical Africa, including crops such as millet (species in the genera *Sorghum, Pennisetum* and *Penicillaria*), rice (*Oryza*), corn (*Zea*) and sugar cane (*Saccharum*). The Lopé savannas have at least 70 grass species, although they are often difficult to distinguish from one another for the untrained eye. Species composition in different savanna areas is determined by two main factors: the depth and fertility of the soil, and soil moisture. On the infertile, eroded soils found on hilltops vegetation is sparse and there are only a few grass species. Moving down towards the valley bottom soils become deeper and more fertile and diversity increases. The greatest diversity of grasses, as well as sedges and herbaceous plants, is found in moist savanna marshes.

A few of the commoner and more characteristic grasses are illustrated. ***Anadelphia (Pobeguinea) arrecta*** is the dominant grass on well drained soils in the Lopé savannas, standing about 1m tall when fully grown. On poor soils the grass ***Ctenium newtonii*** and the sedge ***Bulbostylis laniceps*** are most commonly found with *Pobeguinea.* On deeper soils other species such as ***Hyparrhenia diplandra, Andropogon fastigiatus*** and ***Panicum fulgens*** become common. *Hyparrhenia diplandra* is the largest of the grasses commonly seen in Lopé, sometimes exceeding 2m in height. ***Imperata cylindrica***, easily identified by its fluffy, white flowers, which resemble cotton and develop shortly after dry season fires, is common in disturbed areas, as is ***Jardinea gabonensis.***

Sedges

CYPERACEAE

The Cyperaceae, or sedges, are found throughout the world. There are about 200 species in tropical Africa, mostly found in open, humid or swampy areas. They have tufts of leaves like grasses, but can be distinguished by the triangular cross-section of the stem of their inflorescence. The family includes papyrus, *Cyperus papyrus*, the 'bulrush' of the Bible, which grows to 5 m tall and is often found in floating mats, anchored by massive woody rhizomes, in lakes and along waterways. In the Ancient World its main use was for making parchment for writing upon, but it was also used to make boats, sails, cord and cloth and as a food. Today it is plaited into large mats, used as house partitions in Gabon. There are a large number of sedges in Lopé, of which 25 have been identified to date.

Bulbostylis cf. densa and ***Bulbostylis laniceps*** are small sedges with thin leaves, about 10 cm long, like strands of fine wire, arranged in dense tufts. They occur in dry savanna and are generally only noticed when flowering or fruiting, when they are easily distinguished.

Cyperus rotundus is a sedge found along the banks of the Ogooué which becomes particularly common when the waters are low in the dry season. In English it is known as 'nut-grass' because of its small, nut-like, edible tubers. The tuber is slightly fragrant, and contains a volatile essential oil. It has numerous medical applications related to urinary troubles, indigestion and childbirth, amongst others. ***Cyperus sphacelatus*** is a similar species found in the savanna, which has a larger inflorescence.

Eleocharis variegata is a small sedge found in damp and flooded savannas.

Fimbristylis pilosa is a small sedge found in dry savannas in Lopé. It is similar to *Bulbostylis*, but tends to have only 1-3 leaves, and is only noticed when fruiting or flowering. A second species, ***Fimbristylis sp.***, is a small sedge, about 10 cm high, which grows in sandy banks along the Ogooué, exposed by low waters in the dry season.

Kyllinga cf. echinata is a compact sedge, about 20 cm high, found in marshes in the savanna.

Rhynchospora corymbosa, commonly known as knife-grass, is a large sedge which grows to over 1 m tall, which forms dense stands in marshes in the savanna and occasionally also in the forest. It is sometimes used to weave baskets in the Lopé area. Elsewhere it has been effective in tsetse fly control, because the dense cover it produces over water prevents tsetse flies depositing puparia, and hence from breeding.

Scleria boivinii or razor grass (see p. 206), forms dense thickets along old logging roads and in young vegetation types. As its name suggests, its leaves have razor-sharp edges, which cut through human skin with ease. The endemic sun-tailed guenon, *Cercopithecus solatus*, delicately pulls back the abrasive leaves and eats their tender bases.

g
h
c
b
f
d
e
a
KA'96

Right:

a) Ascolepis capensis
b) Bulbostylis cf. densa
c) Bulbostylis laniceps
d) Cyperus rotondus
e) Cyperus sphacelatus
f) Eleocharis variegata
g) Fimbristylis pilosa
h) Fimbristylis sp
i) Kyllinga cf. echinata
j) Rhynchospora corymbosa

Ferns

PTERIDOPHYTES

A number of Pteridophytes, or ferns (see p. 95), are typical of savannas. They are more abundant in moist areas, but some species are particularly resistant to hot, dry conditions. One species, ***Dicranopteris (Gleichenia) linearis*** is typical of roadside vegetation and landslides throughout Gabon, and occasionally forms 'fern savannas' in Lopé, particularly on steep hillsides. These may well be the result of ancient landslides. It is easily identified by its branched fronds.

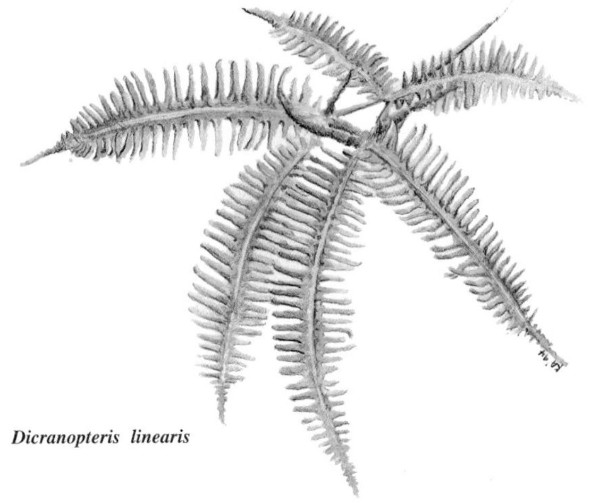

Dicranopteris linearis

Ceratopteris cornuta is found in marshy areas in the savanna, and in large, open marshes within the forest.

Cyclosorus striatus is a large fern found in marshes in the savanna. The leaf can be up to about 130 cm long.

Lycopodium cernuum is common in savanna marshes. Its can be identified by its characteristic form, like a Christmas tree, about 30-40 cm high, with pale brown sporangia on its downturned fronds.

Lygodium microphyllum is a climbing fern found in moist areas in the savanna and along the forest edge. It has small leaves about 4 cm long, which grow numerous tiny 'fingers' on which sporangia develop. ***Lygodium smithianum*** is similar, but has leaves about 8 cm long.

Pteridium aquilinium is the familiar 'bracken', found throughout much of the world. In Lopé it is found in savanna close to the forest edge, although, like *Dicranopteris linearis,* it dominates some savannas on hillsides in southern parts of the reserve.

Selaginella myosurus is a climbing fern found in unburnt parts of the savanna and along the forest edge.

Forest buffalo

j
g
i
b
e
c
KA'95
a
d
f
h

f
e
c
a
b
d
KA '95

Herbaceous plants

Left (see p. 32):

a) Ceratopteris cornuta
b) Cyclosorus striatus
c) Lycopodium cernuum
d) Lygodium microphyllum
e) Lygodium smithianum
f) Selaginella myosurus

ORCHIDACEAE

A number of species of Orchidaceae grow in the savannas of the Lopé. They are all perennial herbs with underground rhizomes, whose leaves sprout up after the dry season fires. In this way they behave rather like bluebells in Europe, which grow in the spring, after the scorching frosts of winter, and whose leaves persist through the summer, after the flowers have fallen. Most of the savanna orchids flower from September to February. In December and January some marshes are filled with hundreds of beautiful blooms swaying in the wind. The flowers which are pollinated successfully (and are not eaten by bushbuck or elephants), develop fleshy fruits which dry and open, releasing thousands of tiny seeds, which drift like puffs of smoke on the breeze. The large, attractive flowers of the different ***Eulophia*** species are easily recognised. ***Platycorne buchaniana*** and ***Liparis rufina*** are more discrete. They are both found in moist areas and grow to be about 30 cm tall.

Platycoryne buchaniana

Liparis rufina

Page 36:

a) Eulophia angolensis
b) Eulophia cucullata

b
KA '94
a

Herbs in recently burnt savannas

The annual savanna fires leave the ground charred and bare. Small herbs, which cannot grow when there is a dense cover of tall savanna grasses, seize this opportunity to reproduce. During the days and weeks after the fire, and particularly once the first rains have moistened the soil, numerous small plants germinate and grow, racing to set seed before they are swamped by tall grasses.

Below:

Compositae
a) Vernonia smithiana
Hypoxidaceae
b) Curculigo pilosa
c) Hypoxis angustifolia
Leguminosae - Caesalpinioideae
d) Cassia mimosoides
Scrophulariaceae
e) Cycnium camporum

Savanna herbs encountered year-round

Other plants are found growing amongst the grasses all year round. Herbs with characteristic flowers belonging to the Leguminosae, subfamily Papilionoideae (see p. 58) are particularly common, although other families also occur. Several species, such as ***Desmodium ramosissimum,*** have seeds which stick to your clothes and have to be removed one by one after a walk through tall grass. This adaptation is an ingenious dispersal mechanism since the seeds stick to the hair and feathers of animals, which carry them away. They are removed later during grooming or fall off naturally as they dry.

Below:
Savanna Papilionoidae

a) Crotalaria ochroleuca
b) Crotalaria pallida
c) Desmodium ramosissimum
d) Eriosema glomeratum
e Indigofera cf. welwitschii
f) Indigofera sp. 1
g) Indigofera sp. 2
h) Uraria picta
***i) Vigna multinervis* (a second species, *Vigna gracilis,* has a blue flower).**
j) Zornia latifolia

Below:

Acanthaceae
a) Asystasia gangetica
Compositae
b) Aspilia africana
Convolvulaceae
c) Ipomoea blepharophylla
Gentianaceae
d) Neurotheca loeselioides
Malvaceae
e) Hibiscus rostellatus
f) Sida linifolia
g) Sida stipulata
Melastomataceae
h) Heterotis decumbens
Scrophulariaceae
i) Lindernia decumbens
Verbenaceae
j) Stachytarpheta cayennensis

Herbs in moist savanna

Many herbs are more common or restricted to humid areas in the thalwegs of the savanna:

Aquatic plants

The fast flowing rivers and streams in the forest in Lopé tend to be crystal clear, except when in flood in the rainy season, when the sediment load increases. Their temperature varies between 24-28°C and the pH is around 7. The water contains very few nitrates or phosphates, which are important indicators of aquatic productivity. In fact, it could be considered as little more that slightly dirty distilled water; an aquatic desert. Almost no genuine water plants occur, although some terrestrial plants, including a number of species of fern, do sometimes trail in the current.

To find water plants you have to search in the slow flowing streams in galleries and marshes in the savanna, or in some of the seasonal channels of the Ogooué. Here green blooms of algae indicate an increased nutrient concentration, perhaps because the water is fertilised by the dung of buffalo and elephants, who often pass the warmest part of the day wallowing in the mud in these areas. In amongst the sedges and herbs, which thrive in permanently moist ground, there are small clear pools in which water plants grow.

HYDROCHARITACEAE

Ottellia ulvifolia is found throughout much of Africa. The leaves are up to 30 x 6 cm and are delicate, soon disintegrating if taken out of the water. They are pale green in colour, sometimes with a purple tinge, and are gathered in a rooted tuft at the base of the plant, drifting free in the current. The yellow flower is held above the surface of the water on an air filled 'spathe', a specially modified leaf. There are three petals each up to 2 cm long. The flower is almost invariably occupied by one or more small black flies, which presumably are the pollinators. The fruit has numerous small seeds and is enclosed within the spathe. The leaves are edible, but in Lopé the large quantities of animal dung in the water tend to discourage potential human herbivores.

NYMPHAEACEAE

Nymphaea maculata (the water lily) is a perennial herb which grows from an underground rhizome. The leaves are reddish when young and float on the surface of the water. The perfumed flower is held above the water on an erect stem and is about 4 cm across when open. The petals are white, often tinged with pink and the anthers are bright yellow. The fruit is fleshy with numerous arillate seeds, suggesting that it depends on animal dispersers.

PONTEDERIACEAE

Heteranthera callaefolia is small aquatic herb which has hollow petioles which hold the leaves above water. The leaves are heart shaped, with numerous parallel veins ascending from the base. The flowers have small, white petals and yellow anthers and are arranged on an erect spike.

The water hyacinth, ***Eichhornia crassipes***, is another Pontederiaceae. It is distributed throughout the world and has invaded many of the larger African rivers. It holds its leaves and purple-blue flowers erect above the water, by means of swollen, air filled petioles. It is an attractive plant when seen bobbing down an otherwise featureless river, but can form compact patches which hinder navigation. In some places it has become a major pest. It does not seem to occur in the Lopé region, but is to be seen downstream on the Ogooué.

Shrubs

The savannas in Lopé are characterised by a small number of fire resistant shrubs. These species are able to grow in the middle of the savanna, where other species would be killed by annual fires. Their density and form vary with soil depth and quality, as well as the intensity of fires. Some steep slopes, which have poor, thin soils and where intense fires race uphill, have very few shrubs; whilst in flatter, low lying areas, they can become relatively big and numerous.

EUPHORBIACEAE

Bridelia ferruginea is a common shrub, or small tree, in savannas close to the Ogooué. It grows to be about 5 m tall, with a diameter up to about 20 cm. The smaller branches often have numerous small protective spines. The alternate leaves are variable in size, between 4-11 by 3-6 cm and have secondary veins which extend right to their margin. The underside is generally furry to the touch and dull in colour, but may be smooth, and occasionally has a coppery hue.

Left:

Commelinaceae
a) Murdannia simplex
Ochnaceae
b) Sauvegesia erecta
Oxalidaceae
c) Biophytum petersianum
Polygalaceae
d) Polygala sp.
Rubiaceae
e) Otomeria elatior
Violaceae
f) Hybanthus enneaspermus

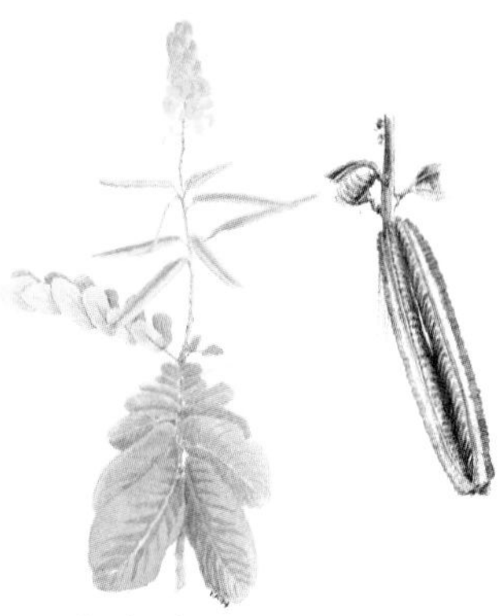

Cassia alata **(Leguminosae-Caesalpinioideae) An attractive shrub found in savanna and along the forest edge, whose leaves are used to treat gonorrhoea**

Euphorbia cf. venenifica **(Euphorbiaceae) is an erect shrub usually found close to rock outcrops in the savanna. The stem and leaves contain opaque white sap which causes severe irritation if rubbed into eyes or cuts on the skin.The sap is mixed with the seeds of *Strophanthus* (Apocynaceae) to produce an arrow poison.**

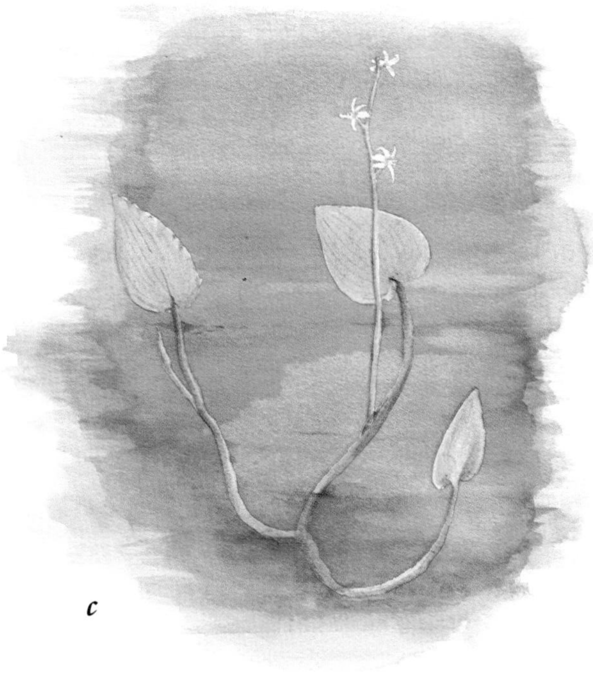

c

b

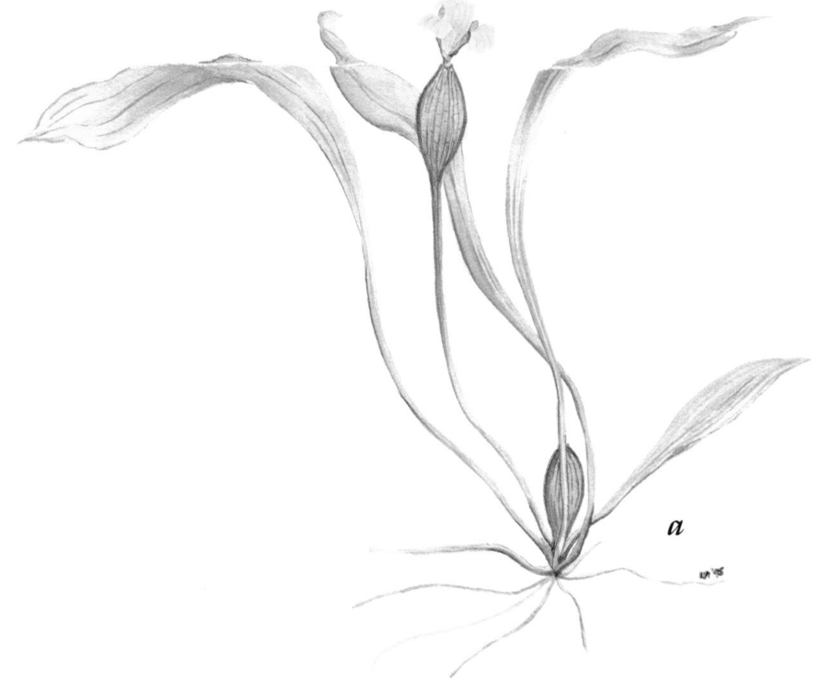

a

Its flowers develop in a small bunch in the leaf axils. They have small green sepals and tiny white petals. It has small, dark, berry-like fruit which have a thin, sugary flesh eaten by birds. If not plucked by a potential seed disperser these tend to dry in situ and can remain on the tree in this dessicated state for several months.

LEGUMINOSAE; SUBFAMILY: PAPILIONOIDEAE

Erythrina vogellii is a rare tree found in savannas close to the Ogooué. It is easily recognised by its spectacular red flowers and twisted pods. It has pale silvery bark with many horizontal ridges and some spines. The spiny branches resemble those of *Bridelia*, as do the leaves at first glance - but do not be fooled, they are in fact leaflets on a compound leaf. There are obvious swollen glands on the leaf stalk where the leaflets are attached.

RUBIACEAE

Crossopteryx febrifuga is the commonest shrub in the Lopé savannas. When protected from fire it can become a small tree of up to 30 cm diameter and about 7 m in height, but individuals regularly burnt tend to remain as small shrubs. When large, it has pale grey, flakey bark and a twisted form. It is easily distinguished from *Bridelia ferruginea* because its branchlets and petioles are reddish-orange and the leaves (7 x 4 cm), like those of all Rubiaceae, are opposite, with distinct stipules between each pair. Their underside is velvety to the touch. It has creamy-white flowers which are sometimes pinkish, in quite showy bunches. The fruits (7 mm long) are green when unripe. They darken to black as they ripen, drying out to form capsules. These open, releasing small seeds (2 mm long) surrounded by a toothed wing, for dispersal by the wind.

Nauclea latifolia is more patchily distributed than the other two species of common savanna shrub. It is easily recognised because of its large, opposite, leathery leaves (18 x 14 cm), with red petioles. These are arranged on long curving branches. There are usually several branches spreading out from a common base, which give younger shrubs a scrambling appearance. The bark is silvery, with deep longitudinal fissures on larger individuals. *Nauclea* produces large, white, spherical inflorescences with a strong perfume, which seems to drive bees to frenzied distraction in the early morning. These flowers develop into large red-brown, succulent fruits with thousands of tiny seeds in a carmine pink flesh. They are a favourite elephant food but are also eaten by many other species, including man.

A young *Lophira alata* (Ochnaceae) growing in savanna (see p. 88).

Left:

Hydrocharitaceae
a) Ottellia ulvifolia
Nymphaeaceae
b) Nymphaea maculata
Pontederiaceae
c) Heteranthera callaefolia

Nauclea latifolia
(Rubiaceae)

a
c
d
b
KA'95

3/ GALLERY FORESTS AND BOSQUETS IN THE SAVANNA
4/ YOUNG FORESTS RESULTING FROM SAVANNA COLONISATION.

Left:

Euphorbiaceae
a) Bridelia ferruginea
Leguminosae; Papilionoideae
b) Erythrina vogellii
Rubiaceae
c) Crossopteryx febrifuga
d) Nauclea latifolia

The gallery forests which snake out into the savanna from the main forest block and associated small, isolated forest patches, or bosquets, represent a habitat more typical of the extreme limits of the rain forest zone in Africa. During the long droughts that have affected Africa in its past these galleries have played an important role, allowing some plants and animals to survive outside the major forest refuges.

The Lopé galleries are a mixture of old forest dating back to the Iron Age and beyond and younger vegetation which is gradually colonising along water courses. Trees in the galleries in the savanna tend not to grow very tall, rarely exceeding 25 m. They often have rounded canopies and the larger branches of trees growing on the edge of the gallery arch out over the savanna. Vegetation along the savanna edge tends to be dense, with a tangle of small or medium sized shrubs and lianes, which makes it difficult to enter galleries from the savanna, except on elephant paths. Once inside, the ground vegetation tends to be quite sparse, consisting mostly of small shrubs and lianes. This is particularly so in areas where rocks emerge above the surface of the soil (see p. 188).

Whilst it is easy to see why galleries exist along water courses in the savanna, where they are protected from fires by soil moisture, the origins of bosquets is often less apparent. If savannas are regularly burnt how could a small patch of forest get established ? The answer lies with people. Beside every bosquet there are the remains of an Iron Age village, often still visible as patches of erosion. When people lived in these villages they probably maintained small plantations nearby, or perhaps even small patches of forest which, as in other parts of Africa, were reserved for the worship of primitive gods. When the people left these areas remained as a living testimony to their presence.

These galleries and bosquets are home to some species which can survive neither deep in the forest nor out in the savanna, such as birds like the double-toothed barbet. They also provide shelter for many animals during the heat of the day, as well as enabling some of the forest species to move out to the savanna edge. For forest species there is a risk associated with foraging trips out into the galleries, and particularly to bosquets, which are surrounded by savanna. Smaller animals are easily detected by vigilant birds of prey when they venture out of the cover of the forest, whilst larger animals often fall prey to leopards, which are common in this habitat. Some of the forest animals never venture out into the galleries, whilst others, such as the spot-nosed or moustached guenons do occasionally take the risk but are forever vigilant and move stealthily in gallery habitats, rarely calling and generally making much less noise than they do in the forest. They will often spend long periods perched high in trees on the savanna edge, searching for sources of danger before crossing, just as a young child might wait to cross a large, busy road.

Just as some animals are unable, or unwilling, to cross the savanna, plants have to overcome the same obstacle if they are to grow in galleries and bosquets. Some species have feathery or winged seeds which can travel long distances on the wind. For other plant species, animal seed dispersers which move out into the forest-savanna mosaic, to visit galleries and bosquets, provide a vital link with the main forest block. It is the movement patterns of these animals which determine the distribution of many of the plants in galleries and bosquets. Many of the plant species which become common in these habitats have small, succulent fruits eaten by bats and birds, which are able to move easily between different forest patches. Elephants and apes are also vital dispersers for many plant species, particularly some of the larger trees.

At certain times of the year the galleries become particularly important for some forest mammals. During the long dry season several species of lianes and a few trees, including the characteristic oil palms which fringe many of the galleries, provide a valuable source of fruit. At this time of year large groups of mandrills and red river hogs are seen crossing between galleries. Mandrill troops can number over 1,000, whilst red river hogs form noisy groups of a hundred or more, which root through the leaf litter, eating up fruit, roots and insects, like living vacuum cleaners, leaving the forest with a swept appearance.

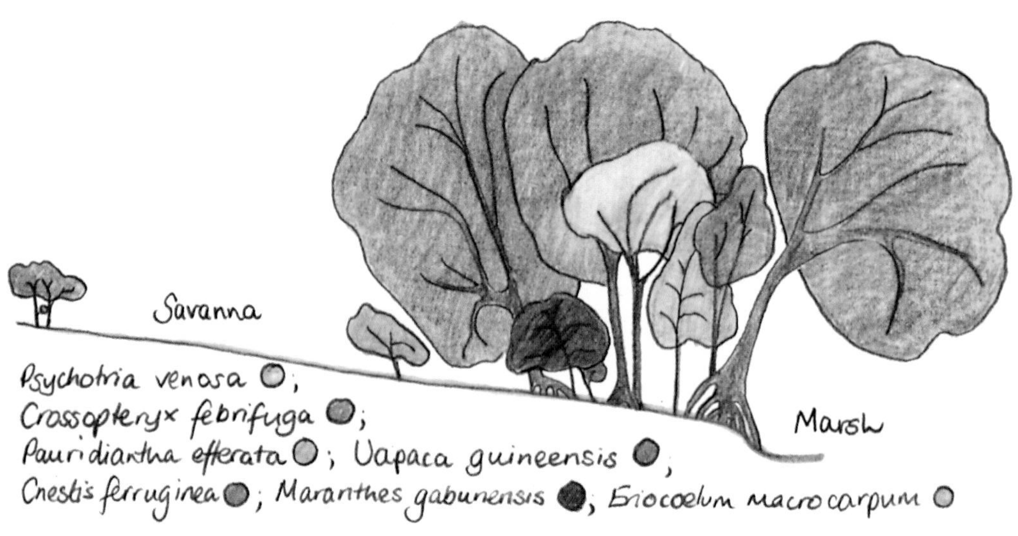

A young gallery forest fringing a savanna marsh.

Seeds of forest plants are regularly dispersed into the savanna, either by the wind or by animals, which eat forest fruits and later deposit the seeds in their dung out in the savanna. Most forest species are unable to grow in the hot, open conditions of the savanna and their seeds either fail to germinate, or are soon dried out. However, some species do survive, particularly on the edges of galleries and bosquets. Each year thousands of small plants begin to develop, only to be killed by the dry season fires. If fires become less frequent, or stop altogether, the appearance of the savanna changes rapidly. Small shrubs become common and vegetation soon forms a dense thicket. Many of these shrubs have nutritious leaves and they are often severely browsed by buffalo, bush buck and sitatunga, resulting in a stunted, coppiced form; but they also provide ideal cover for hunting leopards!

Despite the frequent browsing, some shrubs and trees grow tall and cast shade and savanna plants are gradually starved of light and die out. Conditions on the ground begin to resemble those found in areas of treefall in the forest and more and more forest species are able to grow. The early colonisers include three species which can grow up to be large forest trees: Okoumé, *Aucoumea klaineana*, Azobe, *Lophira alata*, and Ozouga, *Sacoglottis gabonensis*. These trees sometimes form dense copses in unburnt savannas, like natural plantations. They gradually grow taller, in closely packed, even aged stands. When mature, individual trees seem disproportioned, rising to about 40 m tall, but with small crowns which are crowded on all sides by those of their neighbours. Little light penetrates the dense canopy and savanna species gradually die out, leaving a sparse, open ground vegetation.

Around the turn of the century the french colonial government in Gabon initiated a policy of resettlement, moving whole villages out of the interior of the country to major roads and rivers. At this time there were many villages within what later became the Lopé Reserve, and when these people moved out to live close to the Ogooué river, nobody remained to light the annual fires. Hunters probably still used the area occasionally, but fires became less frequent and much of the savanna that existed at the time began to be colonised. Because of this, there is a good deal of young forest in the Reserve. When you walk along trails in the forest look out for vegetation with a characteristic open understory, where there are many trees of the same species, all of about 50 cm diameter or less, but reaching up to around 40-45 m tall, where their small canopies are tightly packed. These areas were savannas about a century ago, in which villages were located. If you fly over the forest, or look down from a viewpoint, they are clearly visible because of their homogenous texture and dull colour, compared to the surrounding forest.

Right, profile diagrams showing the process of savanna colonisation:
a) 20 years after colonisation;
b) 50 years after colonisation;
c) 150 years after colonisation.

Crossopteryx febrifuga; Cnestis ferruginea; Antidesma vogelianum;
Aidia ochroleuca, Uapaca guineensis, Sacoglottis gabonensis,
Ongokea gore; Pauridiantha efferata, Lophira alata;
Cola lizae; Pauridiantha floribunda,
Aucoumea klaineana; Trichoscypha acuminata

a

b

c

Right:

Apocynaceae
a) Landolphia incerta (young fruit)
b) Landolphia cf. jumellei
c) Landolphia mannii
Linaceae
d) Hugonia planchonii
Loganiaceae
e) Strychnos congolana
f) Strychnos malacoclados

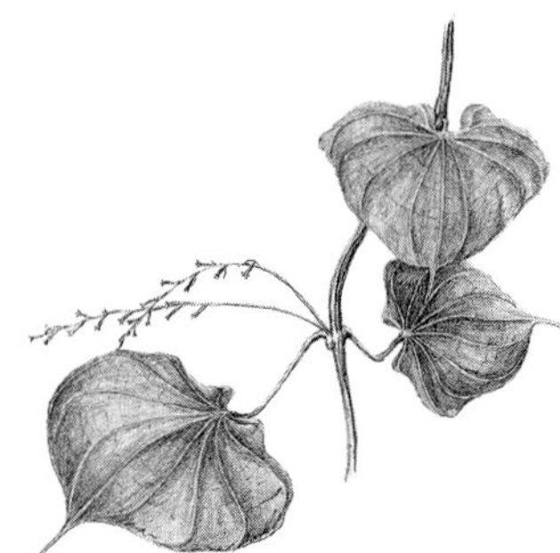

***Dioscorea sansibarensis*. (Dioscoraceae) - a wild yam. The tubers of several species of were once important food for humans and are still used by some cultures today.**

***Gnetum africanum* - a favoured vegetable in much of central Africa is one of the few representatives in Gabon of the Gymnosperms, a group of plants which dominated the rain forests of the world many millions of years ago.**

Lianes

APOCYNACEAE

For many years rumours have circulated of a dinosaur-like creature, half-elephant, half dragon, living deep in the vast Likouala swamp in central Congo, called *Mokele-mbembe* by local pygmies. These mythical creatures are said to slay elephants to make beds from their tusks, but to feed principally on the large fruits of a *Landolphia* liane, in the family Apocynaceae, which hangs down over the waters of the swamp. Several species of liane in this family occur in Lopé, some of which can be confused with species of some other families.

Landolphia incerta grows to about 5 m tall and is found throughout the forest in Lopé, particularly in open areas. Its characteristic opposite leaves (about 8 x 3.5 cm) with numerous, indistinct, parallel lateral nerves, facilitate identification. The delicate young leaves are red-pink. If broken, the leaf petiole exudes opaque white sap, typical of all Apocynaceae. The young fruits are white-green, with a wrinkled skin, maturing gradually from about July / August, and ripening in December / January. Ripe fruits are pale orange, about 5 cm diameter and are eaten by primates. ***Landolphia cf. jumellei*** is a small liane found in Marantaceae Forest in Lopé. The opposite leaves (10 x 5 cm) are indented at the base, with about 6 - 8 lateral nerves which form closed loops. The rubbery fruits are bright orange-yellow when ripe in March / April, and are eaten by gorillas. ***Landolphia mannii*** is a large liane, up to about 25 m high, found throughout the forest in Lopé, but which is more common in the forest-savanna mosaic and along rivers. The flower buds are yellow and open into scented, white flowers (7 mm across). The large, round fruits, about 20 cm diameter, are yellow when ripe. They have a leathery shell (about 1.5 cm thick) containing many large seeds (2 - 3 cm across) in a sticky, orange pulp. The fruits are eaten by gorillas, chimpanzees, mandrills, monkeys and elephants, and most resemble those said to constitute the diet of *Mokele-mbembe.*

LINACEAE

Hugonia planchonii is found mainly in the forest-savanna mosaic, growing to about 10 m. Its stems have woody hooks to help them cling to supporting vegetation. The alternate leaves (14 x 6 cm) have slightly serrated edges. The yellow flowers are about 2 cm across. The yellow fruits (1.5 cm diameter) ripen in July / August and are eaten by civets. Their seeds resemble small palm nuts.

LOGANIACEAE

Strychnos congolana is a liane up to about 35 m long, with a pale brown stem up to 10 cm diameter, which starts life as a clambering shrub. It occurs in all forest types in Lopé. The opposite branches and hooks can be confused with *Hugonia planchonii* but the leaves (10 x 4.5 cm) are opposite and have characteristic nervation, allowing the two species to be distinguished with ease. It has pale green flowers which are rarely seen. The fruits are pale green or yellow spheres (10 cm diameter), with an extremely hard shell about 4 mm thick, which can be mistaken for a small *Landolphia mannii.* The fruits contain numerous flattened, rubbery seeds (2 cm across). They have a have a powerful, sweet smell which can be detected from about 25 m and attracts elephants, which eat the fruit. ***Strychnos malacoclados*** is a smaller liane, up to about 25 m long, with a pale grey stem 1-2 cm diameter. The leaves have similar nervation to *Strychnos congolana*, but are only about 6 x 3 cm. The ripe fruits (2 cm diameter) are orange-red, with a single seed.

COMBRETACEAE

The species of Combretaceae lianes found to date in Lopé all have opposite leaves, about 10 x 4 cm. They occur in all forest types, but are particularly visible when in flower on the forest edge, during the long dry season. They are most easily distinguished by their bright blossom, and tend to go unnoticed when not flowering. They all have wind-dispersed, winged fruits.

Combretum paniculatum has vivid, scarlet, flowers obvious from a distance. It reaches about 25 m high. When growing within the forest the flowers are held above the supporting canopies and are generally only observed when fallen to the ground. The leaves are 50 % carbohydrate and 20 % protein and are cooked with other vegetables in many parts of Africa. *C. paniculatum* can be confused with ***Combretum cf. mannii,*** a species found on the savanna edge and along forest rivers, whose flowers are less striking (see drawing).

KA '94
b
c
d
a
f
KA '95
e

Right:

a) Combretum cf. mannii
b) Combretum paniculatum
c) Combretum platypterum
d) Combretum racemosum

Combretum platypterum is a liane or scrambling shrub, which can grow to about 30 m. It has orange-red flowers about 3-4 cm long, which produce large amounts of nectar and are often visited by sun-birds or sucked as sweets by children. The young fruits are bright, almost luminous, orange, with 4 - 5 papery wings. When ripe they dry to pale fawn and are easily confused with the fruits of *Petersianthus macrocarpus* (p. 171). These fruits are often found in the savanna, several hundred metres from the forest edge.

Combretum racemosum is found on the savanna edge, particularly in southern parts of the Lopé Reserve. Its crimson flowers are similar to those of *Combretum paniculatum*, but it also has modified white and bright pink leaves, creating a particularly spectacular display. Because of its vivid flowers it is considered a symbol of fertility and is often planted at the entrance to villages. Branches are sometimes hung over doorways to ward off spells.

CONNARACEAE

The Connaraceae lianes all have compound leaves and produce brightly coloured fruits, containing shiny seeds with vivid arils, which attract animal seed dispersers. Some species are very common. The Connaraceae are particularly important in Lopé because many species produce fruits in the long dry season. Several genera and over 20 species, have been found to date in the Lopé. The leaves of many species in this family are highly variable. Individuals of the same and of different species are easily confused and can often only be separated by a specialist, unless flowers and fruit are found. Many are large lianes, whose leaves and fruits are rarely seen, unless fallen to the ground. This is quite common when they have ripe fruits, which are dropped to the ground by animals. With leaves and fruit it is often possible to distinguish the species found in Lopé.

Cnestis corniculata

Agelaea paradoxa is a scrambling shrub or liane, which is sometimes common in the understory of mature forest. It can grow up to 40 m long. The leaves have 3 leaflets of variable size and nervation. It has small flowers on long stalks growing from the leaf axils, and a bright red fruit (3 cm long) containing a single shiny black seed with a bright orange aril. ***Agelaea pentagyna*** is very similar to *A. paradoxa*, but is generally found in galleries in the savanna. The two species can be distinguished by close examination of the flowers as *A. paradoxa* has sepals up to 2 mm long, whilst those of *A. pentagyna* are 2.5 - 5 mm.

Cnestis corniculata is a scrambling shrub or small liane about 5 m long, occasionally longer, found in all forest types. Its leaves are extremely variable in number and size of leaflets and may or may not be hairy. The flowers are in eye-catching bunches, with hundreds of blooms at any one time, each with 5 white petals about 6 mm long. The red fruits are variable in shape, but can be recognised by their dense covering of irritant hairs, which easily penetrate human skin, like the spines of a caterpillar. The leaves are eaten with food as a treatment for gonorrhoea. ***Cnestis ferruginea*** is one of the most characteristic plants of the savanna edge and younger vegetation types, although also found within the forest. It is a free standing shrub when small, developing into a liane. It has a whorl of leaves with small leaflets (4.5 x 2 cm) with a soft felt on their underside. The flowers are white stars about 5 mm across. The velvety stark red fruits open to reveal a single small black seed with a bright orange aril. This is juicy, though somewhat bitter and is widely used to clean and whiten teeth, leaving a refreshing taste in the mouth.

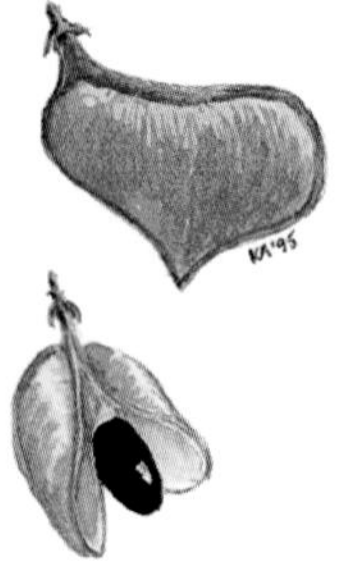

Fruits of *Connarus griffonianus*

Connarus griffonianus is a liane or lianescent shrub, common along the savanna edge and in galleries and bosquets, which can grow to about 15 cm diameter. It has 3 - 5 tough, leathery leaflets (10 x 3.5 cm) covered with soft brown hairs on their undersides. It produces large panicles of numerous, small flowers, with cream-white petals about 5 mm long, in August and September. The fruits are capsules covered in a copper-brown powdery coating of hairs. These open to reveal a single large seed with a bright orange aril.

Three species of *Manotes* have been found in Lopé, which can be recognised by the shape of their fruits. ***Manotes macrantha*** is a large liane common in the forest-savanna mosaic in Lopé, also found within the forest. It generally has 7 leaflets, each about 14 x 5 cm. The leaves appear smooth, but in fact are covered in a soft felt of hairs on the underside. The young leaves are burgundy and are the traditional source of ink in the region. If heated they produce a dark red liquid, which gradually turns black. The small flowers bloom from May to July. They are in large bunches and each flower has 5 red petals about 7 mm long. The pale orange fruits (1 cm long) ripen in August / October, opening to reveal a single seed covered in moist, yellow flesh.

a
b
c
d

Right:

a) Agelaea paradoxa
b) Cnestis ferruginea
c) Manotes macrantha
d) Rourea solanderi

Two other species of *Manotes* are found in the forest-savanna mosaic. ***Manotes expansa*** is a large liane up to 30 m long, with 7-12 leaflets typically about 6 x 2 cm. The underside of the leaflets has a sparse covering of pale brown hairs. The orange fruits are the same shape, but almost twice the size of those of *M. macrantha*, in small bunches. They each contain a black seed with a red aril. ***Manotes griffoniana*** is very similar to *M. expansa*, but its fruits are covered in quite long hairs.

Several species of *Rourea* occur in Lopé. They usually have leaves with 5 or more leaflets, like *Manotes*, with quite large fruits, similar to those of *Agelaea*. ***Rourea solanderi*** is a lianescent shrub, growing to be a large liane, which is common in the forest-savanna mosaic. Its leaves are similar to those of *Manotes macrantha* (see above), but are not hairy. It has beautiful, but delicate, flowers, with 5 thin, white petals each about 2 cm long, which fall after 1-2 nights. The orange fruit (3 cm long) is covered in soft velvet and opens to reveal a long, shiny black-brown seed, with an orange aril. Most of the other *Rourea* species can be distinguished by their fruits. ***Rourea calophylla*** is a large liane which occurs high in the canopy of mature forest. Its fruits are covered in a characteristic powdery coating of waxy ginger hairs. The fruits are about 2.5 cm long. Their seeds, with red arils, are usually missing when fruits are found on the ground. The leaves often have only 3 leaflets, so this species is easily mistaken for an *Agelaea*. ***Rourea minor*** is generally a small lianescent shrub or liane, found in young vegetation types and along old roads in Lopé; but can grow to be a large liane up to 25 m long and 15 cm diameter. It usually has 5-7 pale green leaflets (each 6 x 2.5 cm, or smaller). The pink-red fruits are about 1.5 cm long. ***Rourea myriantha*** is a very big liane up to 40 m long, found in mature forest. It has very variable leaflets. The fruits are generally only seen when fallen to the ground. They are orange when ripe, about 3 cm long, with a black, shiny seed and orange aril very like *R. solanderi*. ***Rourea parviflora*** is a large liane up to 35 m long and 15 cm diameter, found in the forest-savanna mosaic in Lopé. Its leaves are extremely variable. The fruits are yellow when ripe, 2-3 cm long, with a single shiny black seed with a bright red aril, eaten and dispersed by hornbills, monkeys and chimpanzees. ***Rourea thomsonii*** is a large liane found in all forest types in Lopé. It has orange fruits, about 3 cm long, each containing a shiny black seed with a red aril.

Unusually for the Connaraceae, ***Jollydora duparquetiana*** is a small tree, up to 8 m tall and 5 cm diameter, but usually smaller, found in the under-storey of mature forest (see p. 168). It produces hard, succulent yellow-orange fruits on its trunk from December to March.

DILLENIACEAE

When walking in the rain forest one occasionally goes quite long distances between sources of water. Forest peoples often cut sections out of large lianes and drink the copious amounts of clear, watery sap, with a fresh taste a little like carrot juice. Only a few species, commonly known as "water lianes", yield sap which is good to drink. Two species occur in Lopé, of which *Tetracera* is the more common.

Tetracera podotricha is a large liane which grows to about 30 m long and over 10 cm diameter, found throughout the forest in Lopé. It is particularly common in the forest-savanna mosaic. The bark has a regular pattern of roughly square fissures. The alternate leaves are about 11 x 6.5 cm, with sparse pale hairs on both sides. There are generally 8-10 bold lateral nerves, visible as indentations on the upper side. Young leaves are pink-red. The small white flowers, about 8 mm across, are in large, open bunches. The fruits are red capsules about 7 mm long, which open to display small black seeds with a bright orange, feathery aril eaten by birds.

Tetracera podotricha

VITACEAE

Cissus dinklagei is a large liane which is common in the forest-savanna mosaic, but which is also found within the main forest block. It can become extremely extensive, covering small trees along the savanna edge in dense, shiny green foliage. The stem is similar to that of *Tetracera podotricha*. The alternate leaves are shaped like spades or hearts (12 x 6 cm) with a stalk about 4-5 cm long. Flowering is extended, from December to July. The yellow fruits are about 2 cm long when ripe, from August to February. They have a sweet, succulent flesh around a single seed (p. 215). The fruits are eaten by many animals, including gorillas and chimpanzees. They have a sweet and pleasant taste, but after a minute or two cause a burning sensation similar to hot chilli pepper. This may be a special adaptation to discourage the same animal from eating too many ripe fruits at a time. The seeds of the fruits eaten before the burning sensation began would be dispersed, but others would remain for the next potential disperser, hence reducing the risk of the seeds all being dispersed to an unsuitable place, such as into the savanna.

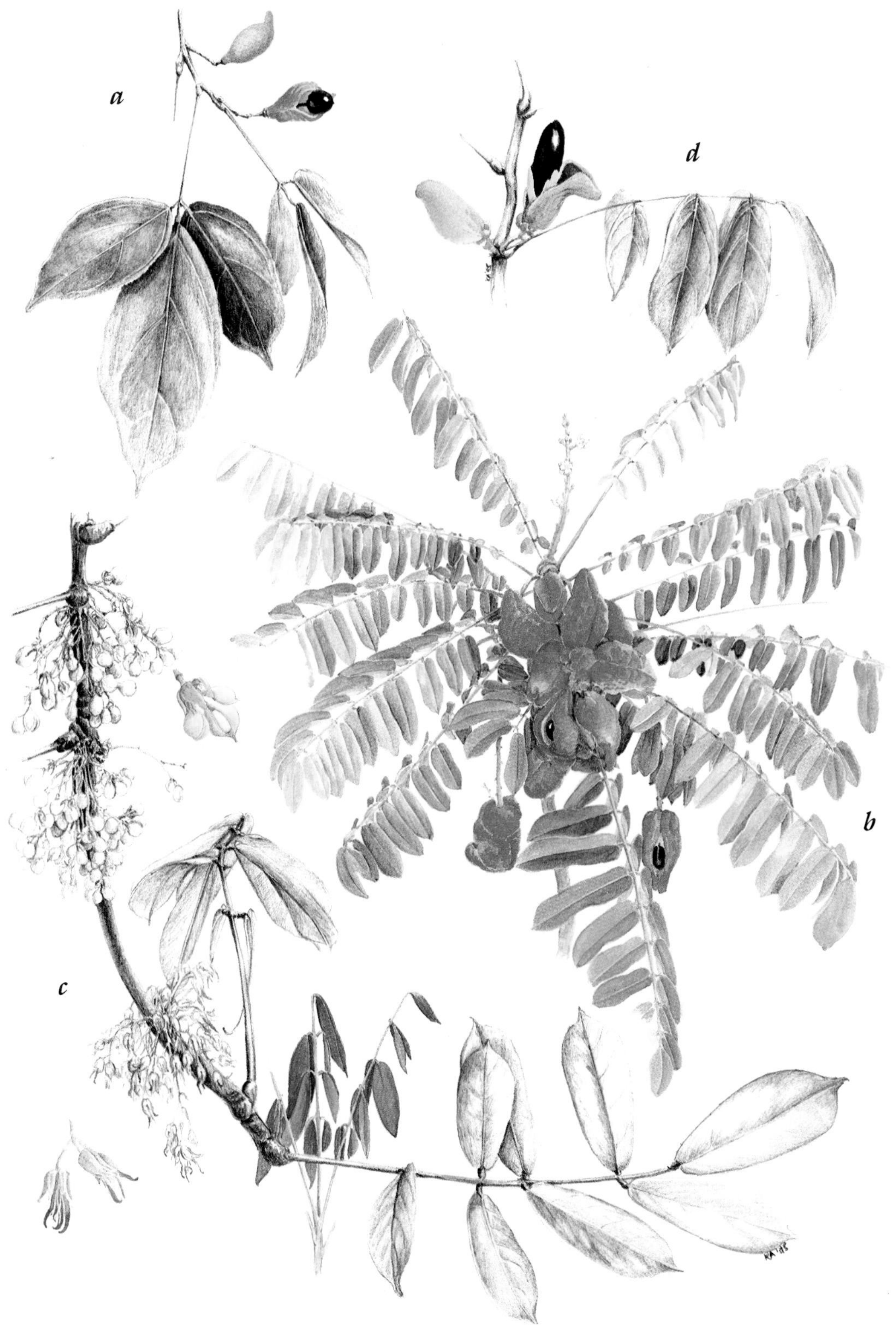
a
d
b
c

Right:

a) Tetracera podotricha
b) Cissus dinklagei
c) Cissus aff. barteri

Page 56:

a) Alchornea cordifolia
b) Macaranga gabunica
c) Manniophyton fulvum

Page 57:

a) Duparquetia orchidacea
b) Mezoneuron angolense
c) Entada gigas
d) Pseudoprosopis gilletii

Cissus dinklagei

A second species, ***Cissus aff. barteri***, is common in disturbed areas and along the savanna edge. It is quite a small liane, growing to about 5 m high, and is not used as a source of water. It has leaves similar to those of *Cissus dinklagei*, but its fruits are small red berries, about 5 mm diameter, eaten by birds.

EUPHORBIACEAE

Alchornea cordifolia is in fact a shrub but its long, scrambling, branches often give the impression of a liane. It is common in disturbed habitats, such as along old forestry roads, but can also be found in young forest types and on rock outcrops in the savanna. It forms a dense thicket along parts of the Ogooué which were disturbed during construction of the railway.

The alternate, serrated, leaves are rounded at the base, narrowing to a pointed tip, between 10-28 x 6-16 cm, on a long petiole of up to 14 cm. There are 2 small glands either side of the petiole at the base of the leaf. Like manyEuphorbiaceae, *Alchornea cordifolia* is a dioecious plant. The flowers are pale green and the long styles of the female flowers persist on the ripening fruit. The fruits hang in bunches of up to 30 or more, each one divided into two obvious sections. When ripe they turn red-pink and are about 1.2 x 1.5 cm. They have a firm green flesh, the texture of an unripe peach, and contain two pink seeds. These are mostly dispersed by birds, but it is possible that fish also play that role. The fruits make excellent bait for fish-hooks, so are obviously eaten, and fishes are known to swallow fruits of other species and later regurgitate the seeds, after having digested the flesh.

Macaranga gabunica is a liane which is most often found along old logging roads. It has tough, alternate leaves, with bold veination. They are about 8 x 7 cm, in the form of a rounded triangle. The small fruits are about 1 x 0.6 cm with an obvious division similar to that in *Alchornea cordifolia*. They are bright orange in colour and are covered in a layer of yellow powder.

Manniophyton fulvum starts life as a shrub, but as it grows it becomes a liane which may climb to over 10 m. The leaves have five distinct nerves at the base and are heart shaped, or are divided into three lobes. The leaves and stem are covered in stellate hairs and are rough and abrasive like sandpaper. When cut the stem secretes thick, red sap. The flowers are small, with white petals. The male flowers are arranged on a panicle about 25 cm long. The female panicles are shorter and flowers develop into a dry, hairy capsule with 3 deep lobes. When ripe this dehisces, throwing small seeds several metres. The seeds are occasionally eaten by gorillas. In some places they are used by people to treat intestinal worms and it is possible that gorillas have learnt to eat seeds of *Manniophyton* when sick.

The bark on the stem is particularly tough and was traditionally collected to make hunting nets. The bark is easily removed and when pounded becomes less abrasive and more easily worked. It was woven into nets about 1.5 m wide and many meters long. Traditionally each family had their own nets and the whole community would go out to hunt together. Men set the nets in a line, whilst women and children drove forest animals, mostly duikers, towards the trap by calling and beating sticks. The terrified animals run into the net, giving the men time to rush forwards and slit their throats.

LEGUMINOSAE; SUBFAMILY: CAESALPINIOIDEAE

The Caesalpinioideae is dominated by large tree species and contains very few lianes. However, there are two colourful exceptions to this rule in Lopé.

Duparquetia orchidacea is a liane found along the savanna edge, growing to about 15 m. Its compound leaves have 2 - 4 pairs and 1 terminal leaflet (12 x 4 cm) with 5, upcurving lateral veins. As suggested by its name, it has beautiful flowers resembling orchids. These bloom in November/December. Its dehiscent pods are about 10 x 1.5 cm.

Mezoneuron angolense grows to about 20 m along parts of the savanna edge and was not known to occur in Gabon until collected in the Lopé. It is a distinctive liane armed with formidable protective thorns. The stem is up to about 5 cm diameter and has many knobbles tipped by sharp spines. The leaves are bipinnate, with about 15 alternate leaflets on the pinnae (12 x 7 mm). The young leaves are bright red. Its yellow flowers open from August to about December. The young fruits are bright pink, but fade to green as they grow. When ripe they are about 8 x 3 cm, with a dry wing around the seed to aid dispersal by the wind.

a
b
c
KA '94

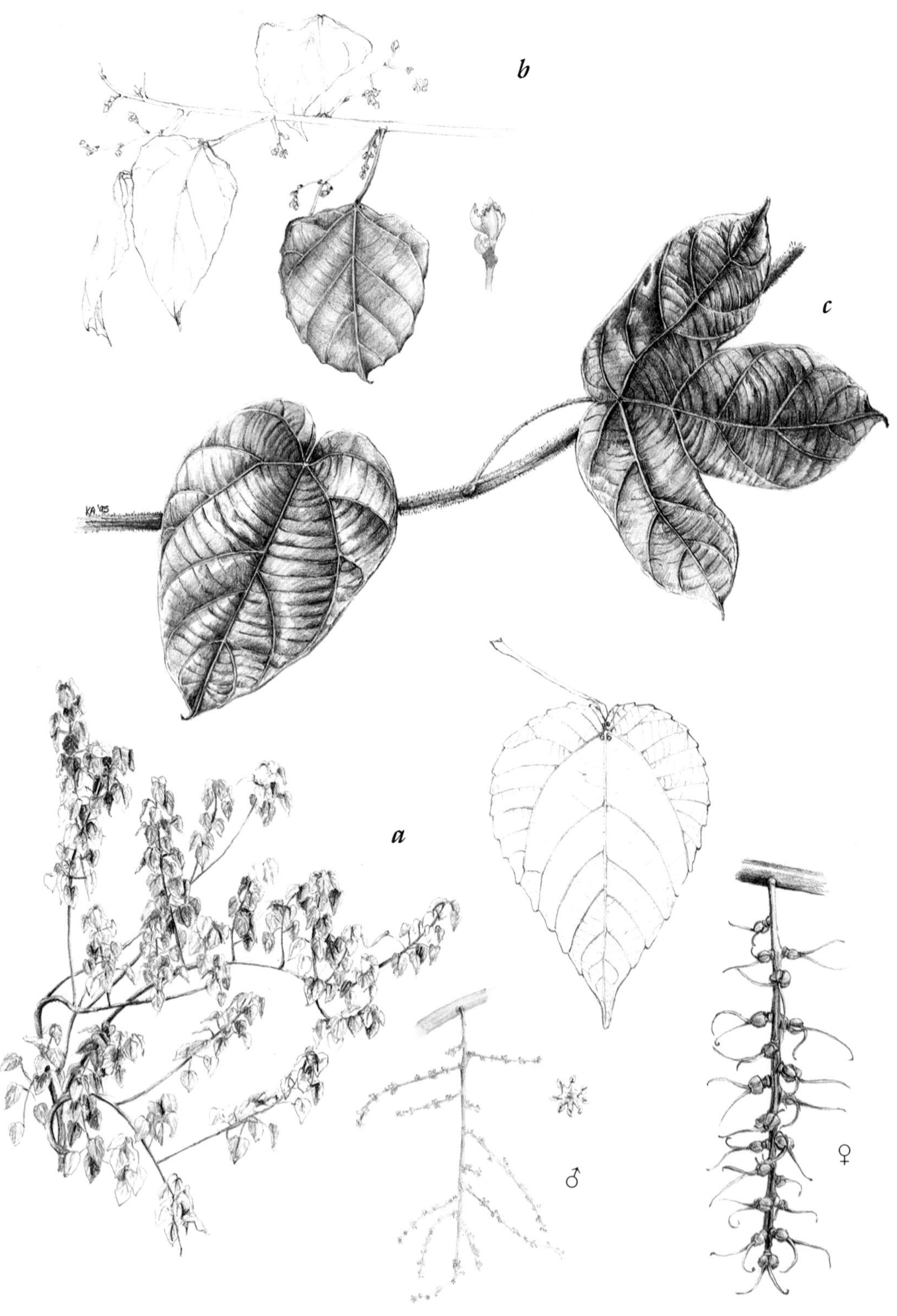
b
c
KA '95
a
♂
♀

a
b
c
d
KA '95

Right:

a) Baphia aff. maxima
b) Dalbergia aff. rufa
c) Dioclea reflexa
d) Leptoderris brachyptera

LEGUMINOSAE; SUBFAMILY: MIMOSOIDEAE

Like the Caesalpinioideae, the Mimosoideae is dominated by trees and shrubs, but contains a few species of liane in Lopé.

Entada gigas is found in Central America, Colombia, the Antilles and across tropical Africa. In Lopé it is found along the savanna edge and in galleries along rivers, particularly the Ogooué. It can grow to 30-40 m long and over 10 cm diameter. The compound leaves have 3-4 pairs of leaflets, which increase in size from the base to the tip of the leaf. The terminal pair are typically about 4.5 x 2.5 cm. All leaflets have an indented apex, with 9-13 indistinct lateral nerves. The scented yellow-green flowers are arranged on a spike which can exceed 20 cm long. The peculiar fruit is unmistakeable. It is a large, woody pod consisting of up to 12 valves arranged in a spiral. Each valve is about 10 cm across, containing a dark brown seed about 5 cm across (see p. 214). The stem is harvested for extraction of tough fibres in the bark, which can be used to make rope or hunting nets and *Entada gigas* is often planted at the entrance to villages to ward off accidents and danger. The needle-clawed galago, *Euoticus elegantulus*, eats gum obtained from the stem of *Entada gigas*, and in some places the distribution of this nocturnal primate corresponds exactly to that of the liane.

Pseudoprosopis gilletii is a medium sized liane found along the savanna edge and in gallery forest, growing to about 10 m tall. It has bipinnate leaves, with 3-8 pinnae, each with 11-16 pairs of opposite leaflets (14 x 5 mm). From a distance the foliage can be mistaken for *Pentaclethra macrophylla*, causing confusion if the liane is draped around the canopy of a large tree. The stem has large hooks, which help the liane to get a hold of supporting vegetation. The scented, white-yellow flowers are on a panicle up to about 50 cm long. It has small, dehiscent pods (8 x 1.4 cm) which throw the seeds a few metres when they split.

Hippocratea myrioneura **(Hippocratoideae) is a common liane on the savanna edge (see p.165)**

LEGUMINOSAE; SUBFAMILY: PAPILIONOIDEAE

The Papilionoideae contains many large lianes found within the forest in Lopé, including some which exceed 50 cm diameter. The family also contains many smaller cultivated species, such as peas and beans. In general the Papilionoideae lianes of Lopé remain poorly known, partly because it is difficult to collect the specimens of leaves, flowers and fruits needed to identify them; and partly because relatively few studies of the subfamily have been undertaken by specialists, so there are no good texts to aid identification.

Baphia aff. maxima is a liane which grows to about 15 m, found principally in disturbed areas and in river galleries. It has characteristic simple leaves (15 x 5 cm) with a stalk about 2 cm long. There are ginger hairs on the smaller stalks and on the midrib and lateral nerves on the underside of the leaves. The yellow flowers resemble those of a pea. The fruit is a dehiscent pod, about 8 cm long.

Dalbergia aff. rufa is a scrambling shrub on the savanna edge, but becomes a large liane within the forest (over 30 m long and up to 10 cm diameter). When large, it has a dark brown, deeply cracked stem. There are 6-12 asymmetric leaflets, which increase in size from the base of the compound leaf (7 x 3 cm). This species is particularly noticeable from about September to December, when covered in small white flowers. The golden fruits are dry, winged pods, which are sometimes carried several hundred metres by strong winds in December / January. The young leaves, flowers and bark are eaten by gorillas. Several other *Dalbergia* species occur in Lopé but have yet to be identified.

Dioclea reflexa is a scrambling shrub or liane found along rivers and streams in the forest-savanna mosaic in Lopé. Its compound leaf has an opposite pair and a single terminal leaflet, each about 14 x 7 cm, with sparse, silvery hairs on the underside and about 7 bold lateral nerves. The attractive flowers resemble those of the *Millettia* shrubs found on the savanna edge (p. 70). They have petals which are white at the base, darkening to pink-purple towards the tip. The fruits are wrinkled, woody pods which are swollen around 2-3 large, round seeds. The pods seem not to split, but fall into the water below and gradually rot, releasing the seeds. The seeds float and are carried away by the current. They are commonly washed up sand banks below the Lopé Hotel and are a familiar part of the flotsam that washes ashore on the beaches around Libreville.

Leptoderris brachyptera is a large liane found in the savanna-forest mosaic in Lopé, which is sometimes found creeping out into the savanna from the forest edge. It can be over 40 m long, with a diameter up to about 20 cm. It is easily identified by its characteristic compound leaf, with 2 opposite pairs and 1 terminal leaflet (12 x 7 cm) with a glossy, pale-gold underside. The fallen leaflets are often obvious amongst the leaf litter of bosquets in the forest-savanna mosaic. The small flowers are white and pink and the papery pod (14 x 4 cm) is dispersed by the wind. A second species, ***Leptoderris congolensis*** occurs in the gallery of the Ogooué and can be distinguished by its smaller leaflets (10 x 4 cm) which are glossy green-brown below, and its smaller fruits (9 x 2.5 cm).

b
a
c
KA'95
d
KA'94

Right :

a) Ficus elasticoides
b) Ficus mucuso
c) Ficus recurvata

Millettia barteri is a lianescent species of *Millettia,* a genus which also includes several common trees (p. 70). It is a large liane, climbing to 30 m or more. The leaves resemble those of *Millettia laurentii.* The flowers are pink-red, turning purple. They are arranged on a branched inflorescence up to 35 cm long, The dehiscent pods (7 x 2 cm), are covered in brown hairs.

Figs

MORACEAE

Figs are familiar to most people, partly because of the well known edible fig (*Ficus carica*) which grows in the Mediterranean region, and because several species are grown as ornamental house and garden plants. There are approximately 800 species worldwide, mostly restricted to the tropics. They range greatly in terms of life-form, including small shrubs, large forest trees, lianes and epiphytes, including the sinister strangler figs.

Figs are a classic example of co-evolution, where two species are dependant upon one another for survival. The fruits we know as figs start their lives as peculiar 'sacs', the inner sides of which are lined with numerous flowers. At the apex there is a narrow entrance protected by scales. For every species of fig there is a corresponding species of small fig wasp, each only about 1 mm long. There are three types of flower in figs: male flowers which produce pollen; female flowers in which seeds develop; and gall flowers, specially designed to accommodate the eggs and larvae of fig wasps.

Fig wasps fly around the forest searching for a flowering fig of the right species. When they find one they struggle through the scaly opening and lay their eggs on the gall flowers. One female can lay up to 300 eggs before she finally dies of exhaustion. The eggs develop into larvae which eventually hatch, releasing adult wasps into the fig's inner chamber. Wingless males mate immediately with females and die, never leaving the fruit. At this time the male flowers of the fig open, and the female wasps load pollen into special receptacles on their bodies. They then burrow their way out of the fruit and fly off in search of another flowering fig tree of the same species. At this time flocks of insectivorous birds, particularly swifts and martins, swarm above feasting on the newly hatched wasps. If the female finds the appropriate species in flower, she burrows in, fertilises the female flowers with the stored pollen from her previous home, and begins to lay eggs in the gall flowers, bringing the cycle full circle.

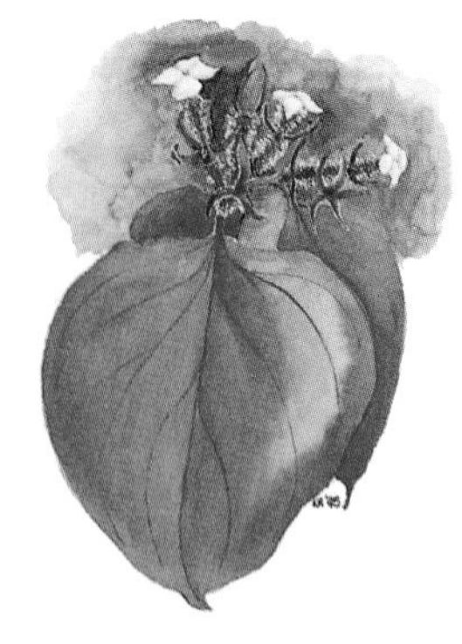

Mussaenda tenuiflora **(above) and** *Mussaenda erythrophylla* **(below) (Rubiaceae - see p.107)**

In Lopé there are at least 18 species of fig. The most spectacular is ***Ficus recurvata***, which starts its life as a small epiphyte growing on the trunk or in the branches of a forest tree. It sends aerial roots down to the ground and takes advantage of its lofty start to put branches above the canopy of its host. Once its roots reach the ground and begin to take up nutrients it grows rapidly, gradually covering the host with a tentacle-like 'trunk'. The fig begins to restrict the growth of its host tree, like a python squeezing the breath from its prey. In this way the 'strangler fig' finally kills its host, which gradually rots away, leaving the *Ficus recurvata* as a free standing tree in its own right, with high, intricate buttresses and large spreading branches.

Figs have characteristic leaves which can be used to distinguish between species. Other strangler figs you may see in Lopé include: ***Ficus barteri***, with leaves typically about 15 cm by 5 cm and small fruit about 1 cm diameter; ***Ficus cyathistipuloides***, the leaves of which have similar veination, but are only about 10 cm by 3 cm, with fruit about 3 cm diameter; ***Ficus elasticoides***, with leaves typically 15 cm by 8 cm, with numerous, tightly packed parellel veins and fruits about 2 cm diameter; ***Ficus thonningii***, with similar veination but smaller leaves, typically about 6 cm by 3 cm and a small fruit of about 1 cm diameter; ***Ficus ovata***, with a large leaf about 20 cm by 12 cm, which is velvety to the touch on the underside and has large figs about 5 cm diameter; ***Ficus polita***, which has similar sized fruits but a slightly smaller leaf, typically 15 cm by 12 cm, with similar veination but which is smooth to the touch on the underside; and ***Ficus subsagittifolia***, which has large leaves, often 30 cm by 15 cm or larger, with characteristic shape and veination with prominent stipules, and a fruit about 4 cm diameter.

There are fewer free standing and lianescent figs in Lopé. ***Ficus mucuso*** is an attractive, medium sized tree, with a smooth peachy bark. It produces large numbers of fruits on thick stalks which grow from the trunk and thicker branches.

Ficus sur, is a small tree rarely exceeding 5m found growing on rock outcrops in the savanna. It has distinctive toothed leaves, and produces fruits about 4 cm diameter on thick stalks, rather like *F. mucuso.*

c
a
b

Ficus variifolia is a large tree with high buttresses. Its bark is a favourite elephant food and the bark is always scarred to a height of 3 m or more. The leaves are typically 8 cm by 4 cm with a rough texture like that of sandpaper on both sides and small yellow fruits about 1 cm diameter. Its young leaves are eaten in large quantities by both gorillas and chimpanzees and it is not uncommon to find thirty or more chimp nests around a flushing *F. variifolia*.

Figs flourish in open habitats. In Lopé they are most abundant in gallery forests in the savanna and in river galleries in Marantaceae Forest, where most of the species mentioned above can be found. ***Ficus mucuso*** and ***Ficus sur*** are also common in the Ogooué gallery. ***Ficus kimuenzensis***, the only lianescent fig found to date in Lopé, is rare and seems to be restricted to Mature Forest.

Fig species fruit asynchronously - different individuals of the same species have flowers and fruits at different times of year. Therefore, fig fruits are available to some extent at all times of the year, including the dry season. Many species of frugivorous mammals and birds feed on figs, whilst others search out the fig wasp larvae hidden within. Figs are rich in calcium, a mineral which is critical for growth of strong bones and egg shells, and which is in scarce supply in the rain forest. So, not only do they provide a source of fruit in times of scarcity, but also contain key minerals. In forests where figs are abundant they become one of the most important foods for many animals, supplying a reliable, year round source of nutritious fruit.

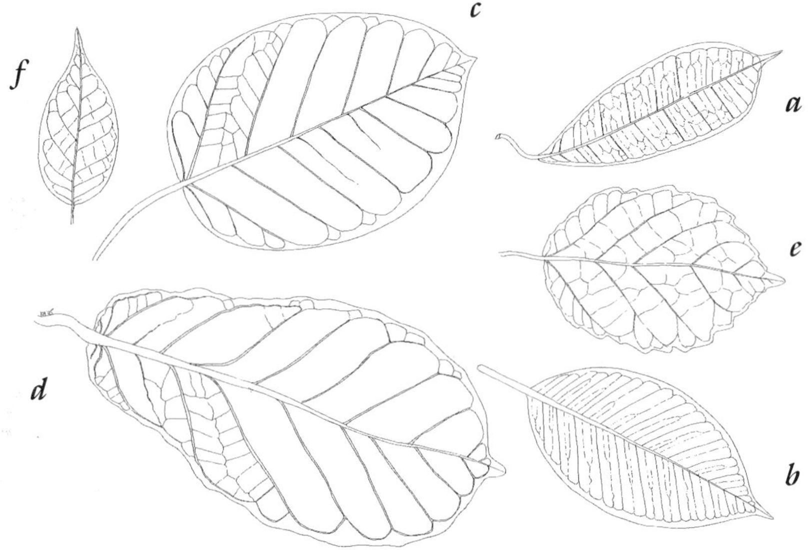

a) Ficus barteri
b) Ficus elasticoides
c) Ficus ovata
d) Ficus subsagittifolia
e) Ficus sur
f) Ficus variifolia

Parasites

LORANTHACEAE

The Loranthaceae is a family of parasitic plants which includes mistletoe, used as a Christmas decoration in many European countries. Their fruits are berries with sticky pulp eaten by birds, which disperse the seeds. Birds pass the seeds in dung and if they happen to be perching in a tree or shrub, the seed is sometimes deposited on a branch. It germinates, producing suckers which penetrate the branch of the host. As the parasite grows it uses these suckers to obtain nutrients from its host. They can sometimes grow to dominate the crown of the host tree and may eventually lead to its death. They are often obvious amongst the foliage of the host, but are occasionally a source of confusion when trying to identify a tree which happens to contain a parasite. Each different species of Loranthaceae tends to have one, or a few host species on which it is able to grow. If deposited on the wrong species or on the ground they cannot grow. They have opposite leaves which are easy to identify as belonging to the Loranthaceae but which rarely allow species identification. The flowers are often very colourful.

Right:

a) Agelanthus djurensis
b) Engleria cf. gabonensis
c) Helixanthera mannii
d) Phragmanthera cf. batangae
e) Phragmanthera capitata
f) Phragmanthera sp.

e
d
c
a
f
b

Right:

a) Laccospermum secundiflorum
b) Elaeis guineensis
c) Laccosperma laeve
d) Raphia sp.

Engleria cf. gabonensis is found in *Uapaca guineensis* (p. 23) trees on the forest edge in Lopé. Its leaves (7 x 4 cm) are typical of many Loranthaceae, with characteristic but relatively indistinct veination. It can easily be identified when flowering because of its unusual white flowers tipped with deep red-purple.

Helixanthera mannii is found within the main forest block as a parasite on *Plagiostyles africana* (p. 128). It flowers in December / January, producing eye catching bunches of cream coloured flowers. The white berries, about 5 mm long, ripen in March / April.

Phragmanthera aff. batangae occurs along the savanna edge as a parasite on several species of *Xylopia*. Its abundant, bright yellow-orange flowers bloom in August.

Phragmanthera capitata is one of the commonest and most versatile of the Loranthaceae in Lopé. It is found in the savanna on the shrubs *Bridelia ferruginea* and *Crossopteryx febrifuga* (p. 42), along the savanna edge on *Uapaca guineensis* (p. 23) and in villages on *Citrus* trees (p. 211). It flowers in August and December, giving a colourful display of yellow and pink blooms.

Phragmanthera sp. is found along the Ogooué gallery and is easily recognisable by its vivid red and white flowers.

Palms

ARECACEAE

These characteristic plants are familiar to everybody. Perhaps the best known is the coconut palm, *Cocos nucifera*, which has been introduced to some of the villages in the north of the Lopé, but which is generally associated with sunsets and tropical beaches. Several species of palm occur naturally in Lopé, and most of them are put to a wide range of uses by people.

The genera *Ancistrophyllum, Calamus, Eremospatha* and *Oncocalamus* are climbing palms known collectively as "rattans". Their stems are collected by humans, split, and used for weaving baskets or made into cane furniture.

Calamus deërratus has leaves about 1 m long, with numerous leaflets, up to 30 x 2.5 cm. The leaf sheath is armed with formidable protective prickles which surround the stem. The long flagellum is fixed close to the base of the leaf and is covered in small, curved prickles. Different plants are either male or female, bearing inflorescences on the cirrus. The fruits are about 1.5 cm long, with 16-21 vertical rows of yellow-orange scales.

Laccosperma secundiflorum is a climbing palm, found particularly along the edge of the savanna and in galleries along rivers. Its stems scramble over trees, growing to 35 m or more long. *Laccosperma secundiflorum* can be identified by its large leaves, about 1-2 m long, with many regular, divided leaflets, up to 60 x 2.5 cm. The leaves end in a prickly stem, the cirrus, about 2 m long. The cirrus has large, characteristic hooks, about every 10-15 cm along its length, which help the palm cling to surrounding vegetation. The flowers are in a large panicle at the end of the stem, which develops into a cluster of red fruits, each about 1.5 cm long, covered in 15-18 vertical rows of closely-packed, shiny scales. These attract large numbers of hornbills, their major seed disperser, when ripe. Elephants occasionally pull them down and eat the stems.

A second, rarer species, ***Laccosperma laeve***, is smaller, with leaves up to about 1 m long, with a cirrus up to about 50 cm long at the end, as for *Laccosperma secundiflorum*. The leaflets are typically about 15 x 3.5 cm. The cirrus has a series of small curved prickles, as for *Calamus deërratus* and large hooks, as on *Laccosperma secundiflorum*. Prickles are sparse or absent on the leaf sheaths around the stem. The inflorescences grow from the leaf axils and the orange fruits, about 1.5 cm long, have 12 vertical rows of shiny scales. Each fruit contains a single characteristic, prickly seed (p. 215) eaten and dispersed by chimpanzees and gorillas, as well as by hornbills. Gorillas, chimpanzees and elephants also eat the stem pith.

Raphia sp., known locally as bambou, occurs as stands and occasionally as isolated individuals in marshes in savannas and some forest galleries. Neither flowers nor fruits have yet been collected by botanists working in the reserve, so this species has not yet been fully identified. However, its leaves, which exceed 5m in length, and its characteristic form make it immediately recognisable. *Raphia* has many varied uses. Its sap is tapped to make palm wine; when young, its leaflets can be woven into into cloth, ropes or hammocks; or once mature the leaflets are plaited into roof tiles; and the leaf mid ribs are used in construction and to make furniture.

a
a
b
c
d
KA'93

Right:

Euphorbiaceae
a) Antidesma vogelianum
Malvaceae
b) Urena lobata
Myrtaceae
c) Psidium guineensis
Rubiaceae
d) Psychotria vogeliana
Oleaceae
e) Linociera mannii
Tiliaceae
f) Clappertonia ficifolia
g) Triumfetta cordifolia

Oncoba brachyanthera **(Flacourtiaceae) is a savanna edge shrub whose fruits are eaten by elephants.**

Aidia ochroleuca

Coffea eketensis

Elaeis guineensis, the oil palm, is a species of west African origin, now grown in plantations throughout the tropics, for its oily fruits. It is a characteristic species of the forest-savanna mosaic and Marantaceae Forest in Lopé, but is absent in mature forest. The 'trunk' of the oil palm, and in fact of all palms, is formed by the fusion of the bases of the leaf petioles. Hence, the diameter does not broaden with increased age. Rather, the width of the trunk at any height reflects the health of the tree when that part was formed. The trunks of oil palms in the forest in Lopé often start very thick, but as you look up they become spindly. These trees began life in open conditions in which oil palms thrive, such as on the edge of a gallery, but were later overtaken by the advance of the forest. The leaves, which are generally about 3 m long, are in a terminal crown. The flowers and fruits are hidden amongst the leaves and are rarely visible from the ground. However, the bright red-orange fruits are eaten by many animals and are often found on the ground under the tree. Fruiting is throughout the year, so palms become particularly important in the dry season when other fruits are scarce. At this time of year chimpanzee dung is often turned orange by large quantities of palm nut fibre. The fruits are also eaten on the tree by monkeys and birds, including the spectacular palm nut vulture, and on the ground by duikers, pigs and civets. They were particularly important for Stone Age and Iron Age peoples living in Lopé, and large quantities of carbonised palm nut shells have been found by archaeologists excavating pre-historic settlements. The nutritious oils extracted from the fibrous, oily flesh of the fruit and from the seed by the pre-historic inhabitants of Lopé are still widely used today. In addition the sap of the oil palm is tapped to make palm wine, an alcoholic drink much appreciated throughout tropical Africa.

Two small palms occur in the understory of mature forest, but are rare in Lopé. ***Podococcus barteri*** is an elegant palm of the forest floor. It is generally less than 1 m tall, with 6-9 leaves, typically about 70 cm long, bunched at the end of the slender stem. The leaflets are rhomboid, straight on the lower edges and with jagged teeth towards their tips. They are about 15 x 6 cm. The orange-red fruits, about 2.5 cm long, are on a central stalk about 30 cm in length. ***Sclerosperma mannii*** forms clumps of fronds, each about 2 m tall, similar in form to *Aframomum* (p. 99). The flowers and fruits are on stalks about 15 cm long, which grow out of the ground amongst the leaves.

Shrubs

A number of species of shrub of several different families are typical of the interface between savanna and forest in the Lopé. In areas where annual fires are hot, maintaining a sharp boundary between forest and savanna, these species are restricted to the forest edge. In places where fires rarely reach the forest edge a belt of scrub develops in which these species dominate. They are amongst the early colonisers when annual fires cease, allowing forest species to establish in the savanna and are also often found along logging roads.

EUPHORBIACEAE

Antidesma vogelianum is a common shrub along the savanna edge, which grows up to 5 m or more tall. They fruit twice a year, from September to December and from March to May, and flower as, and shortly after, the fruits ripen. The small, sweet, red-black fruits ripen a few at a time and are designed to be eaten and dispersed by birds. However, the fruits also attract many species of forest mammal out to the savanna edge. During the *Antidesma* fruiting seasons gorillas occasionally make nests out of savanna grasses and sleep out under the stars. Elephants are surprisingly delicate, plucking the tiny fruits without damaging the shrub itself.

MALVACEAE

Urena lobata has a large pink flower commonly seen in unburnt savannas. It is sometimes cultivated for its fibres, known as 'Congolese jute', which can be plaited into rope. The leaves are eaten by elephants.

g
a
e
d
f
c
b

Right:

a) Millettia mannii
b) Millettia griffoniana
c) Millettia sanagana
d) Millettia versicolor
e) Millettia laurentii **(see p. 144)**

MYRTACEAE

Psidium guineensis (wild guava) is a small shrub generally only about 1 m high. It becomes common in parts of the savanna which are rarely burnt. It fruits twice a year, at the same time as *Antidesma vogelianum*, and is eaten by many species of mammal and bird. When guavas are ripe elephants spend many hours out in the savanna feeding on the fruits. The flavour is better than that of domesticated varieties of guava, but if you are lucky enough to find ripe, yellow fruits leave some for the gorillas and chimpanzees!

RUBIACEAE

Aidia ochroleuca is a large shrub or small tree up to about 10 m tall, easily recognised by its characteristic fruits. *Aidia* is derived from the Greek word for 'everlasting', referring to the durability of the wood, which is used to make axe handles.

Coffea eketensis is a species of wild coffee. It is most noticeable in August and September when covered in cream-green flowers. It is important to conserve wild populations of close relatives of commercially valuable plants, because they can sometimes be used to improve qualities such as disease resistance in cultivated species.

Psychotria vogeliana is another species which fruits twice a year at the same time as *Antidesma vogelianum*, further increasing the attraction of the savanna edge for forest animals. Chimpanzees eat the tiny berries by wadging fruit into their mouth, sucking out the soft flesh and juice, spitting out a characteristic 'wadge' of skins and seeds.

OLEACEAE

Linociera mannii is a shrub or small tree growing up to about 10 m tall. Oleaceae derive their name from the Latin "olea" meaning 'olive', which is another member of this family. It also includes the jasmins, *Jasminum* spp. from tropical Asia, cultivated for their white of yellow, fragrant flowers. The flowers of *Linociera* have a strong, sweet scent like coconut and sugary fruits resembling olives.

TILIACEAE

Clappertonia ficifolia has a large pink flower which is at its most attractive in the early morning sunshine, since its delicate petals shrivel during the course of the day. The obvious red young fruits are covered in soft spikes.

Triumfetta cordifolia has pliable leaves which are the traditional toilet paper in the Lopé region. The bark is tough and fibrous and can be used as string. Its hooked seeds stick to the fur (or clothes!) of passing animals to drop off later, but are also dispersed by elephants, who ingest them by accident when feeding on foliage.

Cassia mannii
(Caesalpinioideae - see p.146)

LEGUMINOSAE; SUBFAMILY: PAPILIONOIDEAE (see p.58)

There are several species of *Millettia* found in the Reserve; three shrubs found on and close to the forest edge; one shrub along the banks of forest streams and rivers; one large forest tree; and at least one liane (p. 58). They all have compound leaves and flat, dehiscent pods. When flowering they can easily be distinguished by the different forms of the flower panicles.

Millettia mannii is a shrub growing to about 3 m tall, found singly, or in small populations, along the savanna edge. It generally has about 6 pairs and one terminal leaflet, each about 12 x 5 cm, with a characteristic, narrow-pointed ('caudate') tip. When flowering they are easily distinguished from other species of the same genus by their dark purple flowers and navy blue buds, the tips of which are covered in gold powder.

Millettia sanagana can be distinguished from the other two Millettia species growing on the forest edge by its large, wavy-edged leaflets, up to 20 x 9 cm. There tend to be only 3-4 pairs plus a terminal leaflet. The flowers are variable in colour; in some plants they are pale pink and purple, but others are almost white. The hairy pods are quite small and thin (10 x 2.5 cm).

The most attractive *Millettia*, ***Millettia griffoniana***, is found along forest rivers. Unlike the other species its flowers, which bloom in July/August, hang down from the branches, forming stunning pink-purple curtains. They have a strong scent which attracts hundreds of bees to each flowering shrub. The small pods, about 8 x 2.5 cm, are covered in a felt of soft hairs. The leaves have 3-4 pairs and a terminal leaflet. These are small, about 8 x 3 cm, and lack the strong nervation of the other Millettia species. Gorillas break its branches and eat the bark in the dry season and grey cheeked mangabeys split the smaller branches in search of insects.

b
e
c
d
a

Right:

a) Ceiba pentandra
b) Fagara macrophylla
c) Vitex doniana

Millettia versicolor is the commonest of the shrubs found on the savanna edge. It is also found fringing rock outcrops in the forest. It tends to be a shrub up to about 3-4 m, but can occasionally grow to be a tree of 15 m. It has about 5 pairs and one terminal leaflet, each about 15 x 6 cm. The underside of the leaf is covered by fine, silky hairs. The pink-purple flowers are held erect at the end of the stem and develop into obvious, flat pods, about 15 x 4 cm, covered in stiff, grey-brown hairs. These split with a sharp crack, firing seeds up to about 15 m. One or both curled valves often persist on the shrub for some time after they have split. Considering its means of dispersal it is surprising that *Millettia versicolor* is so common around isolated bosquets, or sometimes in small patches, in the middle of the savanna. The seeds are eaten by some animals, including mandrills, but there are no known dispersers. How then do the seeds arrive in isolated areas beyond the reach of their explosive pods? The answer lies with humans. The hard wood of *Millettia versicolor* is resistent to insect attack and traditionally was a favoured building material. When cut stems are planted in the ground they often take root and put out new foliage, forming a living post. When a village is abandoned the *Millettia* posts bush out to form shrubs. This may actually be the origin of some bosquets where the *Millettia* stand provided protection from savanna fires, allowing forest species dispersed in to the thicket to grow.

Millettia versicolor

Characteristic trees of the forest-savanna mosaic

A number of striking tree species, which are common in the forest-savanna mosaic, are rare or absent within the main forest block. These species are particularly adapted to the open conditions of the savanna and the forest edge.

***Ceiba pentandra* and *Trichoscypha abut* (Anacardiaceae - see p.114) in a bosquet.**

b
a
c
KA '95

Right:

Ricinodendron heudelotii

BOMBACACEAE

Bombacaceae is the family of the huge baobabs, one of which, *Adansonia digitata*, is occasionally planted in Gabon. The name of the family is derived from the Greek "bombus", meaning "silk", a reference to the abundant silky 'Kapok' obtained from the fruits of many species of Bombacaceae.

Ceiba pentandra (the cotton tree) is an impressive tree which can reach 65 m tall and over 3.5 m diameter. It is a native of tropical America but now occurs throughout the tropics. It may have been introduced to Africa a long time ago, but some people believe that its seeds could have been transported by the wind across the Atlantic. In many places it is considered a sacred, magical tree and is rarely cut, so is common around villages. In Gabon two *Ceiba pentandra* trees are often planted in front of a house where twins have been born. In Lopé it is restricted to the forest-savanna mosaic.

It has a long, pale grey, or occasionally bright pink, cylindrical trunk, with large buttresses up to 8 m high and huge, spreading branches. Young individuals have sharp spines on the trunk and buttresses, which gradually disappear as the tree grows larger, but persist on the branches. The compound leaves are 'digitate', with 8-10 leaflets up to about 15 x 4 cm long. Tender young leaves are eaten by many monkeys and if a branch or two are thrown down to the ground, make excellent salad. Black colobus, in particular, will move long distances to feed in a flushing kapok and once in the tree may stay there for up to a week, alternating between feeding and sleeping. The flowers have yellow-grey petals about 3 cm long and are covered with soft, silvery silk. They are pollinated by bats. The fruit is a capsule up to about 20 cm long, superficially resembling a cucumber. It splits into 5 sections, releasing a large ball of soft, grey-white kapok, containing numerous small black seeds. The kapok often remains in the open pod, high on the tree, until blown away by the wind. Strong winds, which often precede tropical storms, can carry balls of kapok several kilometers, dispersing the seeds far and wide. The soft kapok fluff is collected around the world to stuff pillows, cushions and mattresses. It is remarkably buoyant and is used in life-jackets and emergency rafts. In addition it burns well and can be used as tinder and in the manufacture of fireworks. The seeds are edible and contain 22-25 % 'kapok oil', which is used to make soap, ointments and paint, as well as being a good replacement for olive oil in cooking.

EUPHORBIACEAE

Ricinodendron heudelotti (Essessang) bears a striking resemblance to *Ceiba pentandra*, and is found in the same habitat. However, it generally lacks buttresses, its leaves contain only 3-5 leaflets and it has a fruit about 2.5 cm long, with 2-3 lobes.

Fruits of *Fagara macrophylla*

RUTACEAE

Fagara macrophylla (Olonvongo) has characteristic tufts of long, compound leaves, at the ends of the branches, rather like *Trichoscypha* (p. 114) and a grey, spiny trunk, a little like a young *Ceiba pentandra*. It grows to be about 20 m tall and is common in the savanna-forest mosaic, although also found in the main forest block. The leaves are up to 1 m long, with 15-20 alternate pairs of leathery, asymmetrical leaflets (14 x 4 cm). Young leaves are pink and can be mistaken for flowers. The flowers themselves are burgundy, on a large, spiny inflorescence on the ends of the branches above the leaves. The small fruits are reddish berries.

VERBENACEAE

Vitex doniana is common along the savanna edge and occasionally in moist parts of the savanna, as well as along the banks of the Ogooué. It is often the first tree species to establish as gallery forests evolve in low lying areas in the savanna. It has grey-brown, flakey bark and a rounded canopy. The characteristic digitate compound leaves have 5 rounded leaflets, between 6-12 x 3-6 cm, with about 10 pairs of prominent lateral nerves. Leaves are lost from December to February and the canopy is covered by pale new leaves from February to March. Bunches of white flowers develop in March - May, attracting many bees, as well as sun-birds. The fruits develop slowly over the long dry season. They begin to ripen, turning black, in August and persist on some trees until December-January. The fruits are eaten by gorillas, chimpanzees and monkeys, and are said to be edible, although they are not consumed by people in the Lopé area.

Other trees

Xylopia aethiopica

Xylopia parviflora

ANNONACEAE

Several species of *Xylopia* are common in galleries and bosquets and to a lesser extent in Marantaceae Forest and disturbed areas. They all produce fruit during the long dry season and, consequently, are particularly important for many species of bird and small monkey, which feed on the arils. The arils are difficult to remove and the seeds are small enough to be swallowed and dispersed by many species of mammal and bird. Hence they are perfectly adapted to be dispersed into isolated galleries and bosquets, where *Xylopia* is one of the dominant genera.

Xylopia aethiopica (Okala, or Ethiopian pepper) has a distinctive, fissured, silvery and orange bark, which is used in parts of Gabon to make the walls of huts. It is generally a small to medium sized tree, but can exceptionally reach about 60 cm diameter and almost 50 m in height. Its angular branches typically curve upwards towards their tips. There is little variation between the flowers of different *Xylopia* species. They are pale yellow, with long, thin petals. Flowering is staggered throughout the year except in the long dry season. The thin, green, sausage-like fruits of *X. aethiopica* grow in bunches of 20 or more and ripen at various times of the year, including the dry season. When ripe, the fruit splits along its inner side, opening out to reveal bright red inner walls and black seeds with a striking pale grey aril. *X. aethiopica* is a fast growing species which thrives in open conditions and which is often abundant along old logging roads. Its diameter increases at about 1 cm a year, so the time since logging can easily be estimated.

The seeds of *X. aethiopica* can be used as pepper to flavour food (they were exported from Africa to Europe in the Middle Ages as a 'pepper'), or to add kick to snuff; the young leaves are eaten as a vegetable, like spinnach, or added to palm wine to increase its intoxicating effect; and the wood is excellent for cooking. The seeds also have various medicinal properties. Crushed seeds are said to relieve headaches if rubbed into the forehead, and the fruits are often incorporated into mixtures applied for pain relief or given to women who have just given birth as a tonic.

Xylopia quintasii (Mvouma) is easily recognised by its angular branching, and brown, flakey bark, which takes on a shaggy appearance in older individuals. Older individuals have narrow buttresses. It becomes particularly common in some bosquets, but also occurs in most forest types. It flowers between February / April and its fruit ripen towards the end of the dry season. The fruits are smaller than those of *X. aethiopica*. They are red-green in colour and there are only four or five in a bunch. The seeds are enclosed in a delicate orange aril.

Xylopia hypolampra (Ndong eli) is a medium sized tree which occasionally reaches almost a metre diameter. Its herring bone pattern of smaller branches is particularly noticeable. These are tipped with young, pale green leaves and seem to constantly shimmer in the wind, particularly when it grows on the forest edge. The underside of the leaf is covered by soft, shiny hairs. The pale brown fruits are much fatter that those of the previous two species, but open in the same way to display seeds covered in a pale grey aril and red inner walls. Individuals fruit asynchronously and ripe fruit is available all year round. If you find fallen fruit break them open and smell the characteristic Annonaceae aroma.

Xylopia parviflora is relatively common in some galleries and can be distinguished from the other species by its smooth, pink bark and large bunches of red fruit which develop in the long dry season. These are particularly eye catching when they split to reveal more red on their inner walls.

Xylopia staudtii (Ntsua) is a rarer species generally found in mature forest. The trunk and branches resemble *Xylopia quintasii*, although the bark is paler, but it is easily distinguished by its stilt roots, resembling those of *Santiria trimera* (p. 120). Its fruits are large and fleshy, as those of *Xylopia hypolampra*, with typical bright red colouration on the inner-side of the valves when ripe (see p. 169).

One species easily mistaken for *Xylopia aethiopica* is another Annonaceae, ***Pachypodanthium staudtii***. The local Okandé name, "Egnanghoa ghama" means 'mother of *Xylopia aethiopica*'. It thrives in seasonally flooded areas, such as those along the Ogooué River and can sometimes form pure stands, as on the trail 'Super Jolie'. Its characteristic, conifer-like fruit, which is pale pink when ripe, persists on the ground, is the best way to identify this species (see p. 76).

Right:

a) Xylopia aethiopica
b) Xylopia quintasii
c) Xylopia hypolampra
d) Xylopia parviflora

a
a
b
b
c
c
d
d
b
Kalay

APOCYNACEAE

These trees are found most often close to the savanna edge and in younger forest types. They all have opposite or whorled leaves and opaque white sap. One species, *Funtumia elastica*, which is very rare in Lopé, is the native African rubber-tree. Several Apocynaceae trees have been introduced to Gabon, the most familiar being white and red frangipani, *Plumeria alba* and *P. rubra* respectively, which originate in tropical America and grow in urban gardens.

Holarrhena floribunda is a small tree growing up to about 15 m, which is common along the forest edge and in abandoned habitations. The bark is smooth and grey. The shiny leaves are typically 10 x 4 cm and are shed in the long dry season. It has dense clusters of small, perfumed white flowers from August / November. The fruits are thin pods about 30-40 cm long, which hang in pairs. These split down one side when ripe, releasing flattened seeds about 1 cm long, suspended from a parasol of silky brown hairs, which are carried long distances on the wind. The seeds are collected to stuff pillows. The dried pods often persist on the tree until the following flowering season, making *Holarrhena* quite easy to identify.

Picralima nitida is generally rare, but occurs in most forest types. It is a small bushy tree growing to about 15 m tall, with smooth, greyish bark. It has a dense crown of glossy, leathery leaves (20 x 8 cm) with about 20 pairs of faint lateral nerves and a slightly rolled margin. Different individuals flower and fruit asynchronously through much of the year. The white flowers are about 0.5 cm across. The large fruits, about 15 cm long and 12 cm diameter, usually hang in pairs, each weighing about 1 kg. When ripe they are yellow, with an overpowering sickly-sweet smell, which attracts elephants, the only seed dispersers. The fruits have a thick, tough skin enclosing numerous yellow seeds about 2 cm across, embedded in sticky pulp. Elephants chew the fruits, noisily squelching the seeds and pulp out of the husk, which they spit out. The name *Picralima* is derived from the Greek for 'bitter'. All parts of the plant have a bitter taste like that of quinine and it has many varied medicinal uses, including treatment of malaria and other fevers, abscesses and venereal disease.

Rauvolfia macrophylla (Esoma) is a medium sized tree, growing to 25 m, found most often along the forest edge and in young vegetation types. It has rough, pale grey bark, with many white lenticels. The large leaves (30 x 8 cm) have characteristic shape and veination, facilitating identification. They are arranged in whorls of 4. The small white flowers make the canopy stand out in January / March, developing into small berries. Bark fibre was traditionally used to make bow strings.

Rauvolfia vomitoria is a small tree or shrub which rarely exceeds 10 m, found in the same habitats as *R. macrophylla*. The angular branches are arranged in marked whorls. The papery leaves (12 x 5 cm) which are arranged in tufts of 4 - 6, have distinct lateral nerves. The small, scented, creamy-white flowers are arranged on stalks which branch repeatedly, ending in bunches of 3 flowers. The numerous fruits are bright red-orange berries, about 1 cm diameter, which are eaten by birds. It is particularly attractive when in flower and fruit and is often planted as an ornamental shrub. The bark and sap are extremely bitter to taste and can provoke vomiting, hence the scientific name. The bark and roots have many medicinal uses in different parts of Africa, including treatment of madness, leprosy and dysentry and to alleviate hair loss. In Gabon the leaves are heated in oil made from the seeds of *Baillonella toxisperma* (p. 184), and applied as an ointment to sooth rheumatism.

Pachypodanthium staudtii

BIGNONIACEAE

Kigelia africana (the sausage tree) occurs across much of Africa and is a very variable species. In Lopé it tends to be a scrambling shrub no more than 5 m tall, but elsewhere it can become a tree up to 25 m, with a large, spreading canopy. In some places it is planted as a shade tree. In Lopé it is found on the forest edge and in young vegetation. It has compound leaves with 3-6 pairs of opposite leaflets (14 x 6 cm). It tends not to be noticed unless flowering or fruiting. The red-orange flowers hang down in attractive panicles up to 1 m long. The fruit is the shape of a large German sausage, up to 45 cm long and 15 cm diameter, which is eaten by elephants. *Kigelia* is no longer found in parts of Rwanda where elephants have been eliminated by hunting, presumably because there is no other seed disperser. Elsewhere it is eaten by rhinoceros, which may also disperse the seeds, but this species is similarly threatened by hunting. The fruit has many associations with fetish in Africa and is also added to local beer during fermentation to improve its intoxicating effects. It is said that squirrels are fond of the fruit and that the sap they drink as they gnaw through the skin makes them drunk.

Right:

a) Holarrhena floribunda
b) Picralima nitida
c) Rauvolfia macrophylla
d) Rauvolfia vomitoria

b
a
d
c

Newbouldia laevis

Newbouldia laevis is a small tree reaching 20 m tall and about 30 cm diameter. In Lopé it tends to occur close to rock outcrops. The bark is yellow-brown with obvious vertical fissures. It has shiny, dark green, compound leaves, the stalks of which are swollen at the point of attachment of each pair of leaflets. There are 3 - 5 pairs of slightly toothed, opposite leaflets (13 x 5 cm) with a number of glands visible at their bases. The characteristic, trumpet-shaped, purple and white flowers are often observed fallen to the ground from July to September. The fruits are dark brown pods about 30 cm long, packed with winged seeds, about 4 cm across, which are dispersed by the wind. *Newbouldia laevis* can grow in savanna as well as in forest and is often planted as an ornamental species or as a live-fence. It is easily propagated from cuttings. In addition the bark is used to prepare an infusion taken to treat headaches and which can be gargled to relieve toothache.

Spathodea campanulata, the Gabonese tulip, is a medium sized tree growing up to 25 m tall and about 80 cm diameter. It is most common on the savanna edge and along rivers in the forest, but elsewhere in Gabon is common in and around villages. It has been introduced into many tropical countries and lines some of the main roads in several large cities around the world. It has pale brown bark, which flakes off in irregular patches. The crown is compact, with quite short branches. The compound leaves have 4-8 pairs of opposite, asymmetrical leaflets, each about 10 x 4 cm, with glands as in *Newbouldia laevis*. The distinctive flowers are orange, with a wide, ruffled corolla about 10 cm long, emerging from a leathery, boat shaped calyx, which is covered in brown felt. The black fruits are large pointed capsules, about 20 cm long, which stand upright above the leaves. These open to release numerous small winged seeds to the mercies of the wind.

Right:

Spathodea campanulata

Kigelia africana

BURSERACEAE

Aucoumea klaineana (Okoumé) is probably the most widely recognised plant in Gabon. Okoumé has long been the prime species exploited by foresters in Gabon. Traditionally it accounted for over 90% of timber exports and today, despite diversification of the industry, it accounts for well over half of Gabon's production, being ideal for the manufacture of plywood. Since the forestry industry is the major employer in Gabon, many people's livelihoods depend upon this one tree species. It is everywhere; peoples' houses are made of its wood, the goods trains which pass daily down the railway line are loaded down with its trunks and it is the commonest tree species within the forest over much of the country. The Post Office has issued stamps made of Okoumé wood in recognition of its economic importance and it features in Gabon's coat of arms.

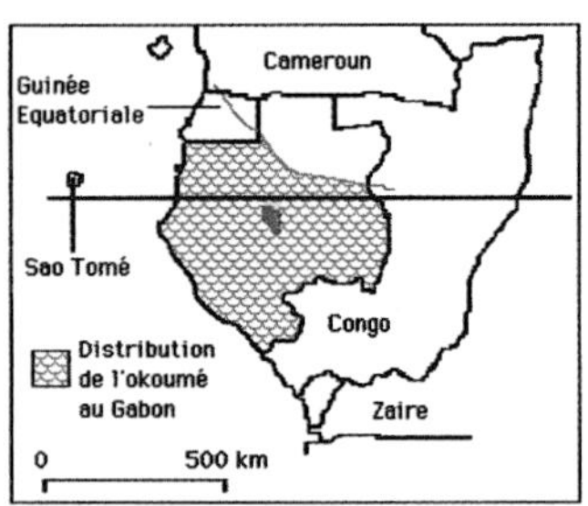

Distribution of Okoumé in Gabon

Okoumé is a species which is restricted to the southern two thirds of Gabon, although it just crosses the frontiers with Congo, Cameroun and Equatorial Guinea. It is the dominant large tree in much of the Lopé Reserve and some younger forest types are characterised by almost pure stands, reflecting past savanna colonisation (see p. 45). It is an easy tree to recognise. The trunk is often somewhat swollen immediately above the large buttresses. The bark is dark orange-grey in colour and detaches in roughly rectangular scales, particularly close to the base. If injured the bark exudes a sticky, clear, aromatic resin, which solidifies in the air to produce a hard, white, protective layer. This resin burns vigorously. It used to be collected in large quantities and burnt as a light source and it makes a perfect fire lighter when camping out in the forest. The compound leaf generally has one terminal and five opposite leaflets. When viewed high above in the canopy the long petiolules cannot be seen and the leaflets seem to float in thin air next to the petiole. The small white flowers develop after the long dry season. The fruits are unlike those of any other Burseraceae in Gabon. They are dry capsules which ripen from January to March, opening into five sections, each of which releases a single winged seed which can travel several hundred metres from the parent tree in a strong wind.

One aspect of Okoumé's biology is particularly fascinating. It tends to grow in stands and one often finds several trees quite close together. The root systems of these trees are often joined below the ground and nutrients are exchanged between individuals. These connections are sometimes visible where buttresses of neighbouring trees have fused. In Lopé one occasionally finds stumps, of Okoumé trees felled up to 25 years ago, which are still alive, nourished by their neighbours. It is thought that particularly large Okoumés are nourished by smaller trees all around and that if these are cut, without damaging the remainder of the stand, another individual will grow rapidly to take over the dominant position.

A few monkey species eat the flowers of Okoumé, but otherwise it does not provide much food for forest animals. However, each year around Christmas, Okoumés are attacked by the caterpillars of the moth *Sylepta balteata*. In some years almost all of the Okoumé trees lose the majority of their leaves to this infestation, taking on a sickly appearance which can last three or four months, before pink young leaves are produced. Many species of primate and bird feast on the caterpillars and in this way they probably protect the Okoumé trees from even worse damage.

In many ways Okoumé seems to be a species which is ideally suited to logging: it regenerates well in open conditions, such as in old plantations or savannas, so it should not be negatively affected by logging damage; it is thought to grow quite quickly - about 1 cm per year; and its communal nature may result in particularly fast regeneration. Unfortunately it is indicative of our scant knowledge of tropical forest systems that we know very little even about the biology of an important species like Okoumé. New evidence collected in the Lopé suggests that growth, particularly in smaller individuals, is not as fast as was thought by foresters. You may also notice that whilst there are many small Okoumés in younger forest types, there are no seedlings and saplings in Marantaceae or Mature Forest. It seems that most of the Okoumé trees in Lopé, and perhaps all of Gabon, are the result of savanna colonisation and forest disturbance in the past and that there is very little natural regeneration of Okoumé within the forest. This has wide ranging implications for the logging industry in Gabon. We do not know if control of insect pests by animals, such as the monkeys and birds which eat the plague of caterpillars in Lopé, is vital for the healthy development of Okoumé trees, and therefore, what the true implications of over-hunting may be. Nor do we know whether repeated removal of all the tallest, straightest trees by foresters will result in long term genetic deterioration of Okoumé. Until there are answers to these questions, management of Gabon's prime renewable resource will depend upon intuition.

Right:

Aucoumea klaineana

KA'95

HUMIRIACEAE

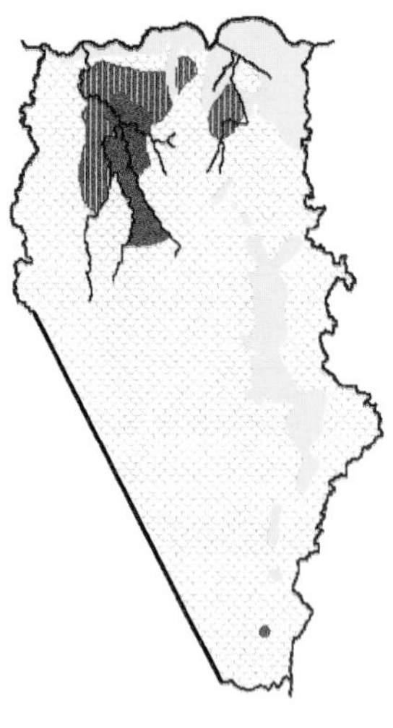

— Rivers
Savanna
Sacoglottis forest
Sacoglottis present
Forest without *Sacoglottis*

Distribution of *Sacoglottis gabonensis* in the Lopé Reserve.

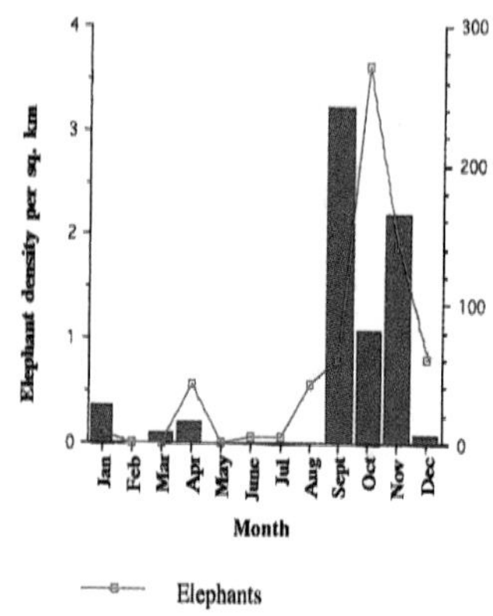

Elephants
Sacoglottis fruits

Relationship between *Sacoglottis gabonensis* fruiting and elephant density in the Lopé Reserve.

Right:

Sacoglottis gabonensis.

Sacoglottis gabonensis (Ozouga) is the only African representative of a family which is more common in tropical America. It is one of the dominant trees in the coastal rain forests of both west and central Africa, including Gabon, but is rare outside this zone. The fruit of *Sacoglottis* contains a hard stone in which there are numerous resin filled chambers. These act as a flotation device if the fruit falls into the sea. *Sacoglottis* seeds remain buoyant and viable for up to 4 years and can be transported many thousands of kilometers by ocean currents. Seeds of the South American species, *Sacoglottis amazonica,* are known to have floated from the Amazon or Orinoco rivers as far as the West Indies, and even to the shores of southern England. It is thought that *Sacoglottis gabonensis* evolved from seeds which arrived on the West African coast from South America in this way. If you search through the flotsam along the coast in Libreville you will probably find the characteristic warty seeds of *Sacoglottis* along with those of other species such as *Dioclea reflexa* (see pp. 214 - 215).

Sacoglottis is a good savanna coloniser and is common in some younger forest types and along parts of the forest edge in Lopé. In some places, particularly around savannas enclosed in the forest, *Sacoglottis* trees dominate the forest edge forming an almost pure stand. They are ideally suited to this habitat, since their branches form huge arches, which grow out over the savanna, casting shade on the ground below, hence cooling annual savanna fires which might otherwise scorch their trunks.

They have thick, leathery leaves, with characteristic rounded serrations. These accumulate on the ground under the crown, forming a dense layer of leaf litter which smothers other vegetation. In some places *Sacoglottis* has formed small pockets, or occasionally quite large stands, by gradually advancing into the savanna. These forests have an open appearance reminiscent of a European wood. Larger trees quite a long way from the savanna edge often reflect the process of colonisation and forest advance in their branches, all of which arch over towards the long disappeared savanna edge.

Young trees close to the savanna edge often have multiple trunks because they have coppiced after being broken by elephants, which feed on their leaves and bark. *Sacoglottis* can grow to be a large, rain forest tree, up to 60 m tall, with a trunk over 2 m diameter. Larger individuals have shaggy, red-brown bark which flakes off in long strips and their trunks are deeply furrowed and twisted, giving the tree a tortured appearance.

They flower from December / March producing eye catching bunches of small white flowers. The green fruits develop slowly over the long dry season, ripening in October / December, when even quite large branches bow under their weight. They are about the size of a plum and consist of a moist flesh around a hard, irregular stone. They are typical of fruits which are adapted for dispersal by elephants. They remain dull green even when ripe (elephants are colour blind); they have a strong, yeasty smell; and they abscise and fall to the ground as soon as they are ripe, rather than remaining attached until plucked by an arboreal frugivore. During the fruiting season, in places where *Sacoglottis* is common, the forest begins to smell like a large brewery as thousands of fruit gradually ferment on the ground.

Sacoglottis is one of the elephants' favourite foods. A single elephant can eat several thousand in a day, given the chance, and many people tell stories of seeing elephants staggering around late in the day, drunk from eating too many fermented *Sacoglottis* fruits (the fruit used to be used by people in Gabon to make an alcoholic drink!). Elephants rely greatly on their sense of smell, both to detect danger and to find food. When you meet them on a savanna tour it is never long before their trunks rise to scent the air, even if you are several hundred meters away. We can smell the fallen fruits under a *Sacoglottis* tree from 40 m or more, so imagine what they smell like to a hungry elephant. The fruit flesh is sweet, tasting a little like banana bread.

In the centre of the Lopé Reserve there is a large area where Sacoglottis is one of the dominant large trees. When these fruit, elephants arrive from all around, travelling 50 km or more to feed on the *Sacoglottis* fruits. Elephant densities reach up to six per square kilometer, meaning that you meet them every 1 - 2 hours in the forest. This illustrates how important fruits are in the diet of Lopé's forest elephants. In turn, the elephants are the only dispersers of *Sacoglottis* seeds in Lopé, depositing them in new savannas and along logging roads, to begin the colonisation process again. *Sacoglottis* does not occur between Lopé and the coastal sedimentary basin, about 120 km to the east. Given that seeds can take up to a week to pass through an elephants' digestive system, it is possible that this species arrived in the stomach of an elephant that had walked to Lopé from the coast.

KA'96

Uapaca gabonensis **(Euphorbiaceae -** **see p.23)** **is common in galleries and bosquets.**

IRVINGIACEAE

Klainedoxa gabonensis (Eveuss) is a species which, despite its name, occurs right across the rain forest belt of Africa from Sierra Leone to Uganda. In Lopé it occurs in most forest types, but it is perhaps most prominent in the galleries and on the forest edge. Here the characteristic rounded canopy and large leaves are visible from afar. If you look closely at the canopy you will see unmistakable large, erect stipules, which are in fact modified leaves growing from the base of the petiole. Many species of plant posess stipules, but rarely are they so well developed and prominent. *K. gabonensis* is a good example of plasticity of tree form. When growing in the open, light conditions on the edge of galleries, it is a medium sized tree, rarely exceeding 30m. However, when growing within the forest its form changes. It becomes a very large tree growing to 50m or more in height with large, spreading branches.

Its flowers develop between February and May. They are small and pale, but are highly visible because of the bright pink stalk on which they are borne and their long, fluffy, white stamens. The large fruits develop slowly, ripening in November / December. When mature they are about the size of an apple, with four or five distinct lobes, each surrounding a stone, shaped like a large garlic clove, containing a seed. The dry, fibrous fruits are green, with a purple hue, and without odour. When ripe they taste a little like sugar cane. They are eaten by many of the frugivorous mammals, but only yellow-back duikers, elephants and occasionally silver-back gorillas disperse their large triangular seeds. The seeds can be extracted from the hard stone and pounded into a paste which is used in cooking, like peanuts.

Klainedoxa seedlings and saplings are quite common, often occuring in clumps where they were deposited in a pile of elephant dung. They have distinctive tough, leathery leaves with numerous fine lateral nerves, which can be up to 40 cm long by 10 cm wide. In younger individuals the trunk is covered in long, sharp spines, but these gradually disappear as the tree exceeds about 15 cm diameter.

When you see the tree up close the bark is purplish-grey. Older individuals have several large thin buttresses which extend quite high up the trunk, resembling those of *Desbordesia glaucescens* (Alep), another Irvingiaceae, found in Mature Forest (see p. 132). Leaves of mature individuals are smaller than those of young plants, typically about 15 by 5 cm, but with similar texture and veination. Leaves turn yellow as they senesce and these are often visible on the ground amongst older, grey litter. Fallen stipules are also prominent on the ground and there are often also fruit remains and seeds.

A second variety of *Klainedoxa* occurs in Lopé. This has a similar trunk to *K. gabonensis*, but the leaves are smaller and more clumped and fruit are about half as big as those of the commoner form. Elsewhere in Africa, trees with leaves and fruit which are intermediate between the two Lopé forms occur. Some plant taxonomists class these two races as the same species, but in Lopé we have noticed that as well as the physical differences, the time of flowering and fruiting differs. It is possible that these biological differences will prove to be the best way to distinguish two closely related species, which are not currently recognised as being different.

This emphasises a fundamental problem for biologists, namely that of distinguishing regional variation within a species from the difference between two separate species. Nowdays genetic methods are often used to aid in classification of species, but very little research of this kind has been undertaken in tropical forests, which contain about 80% of the world's plant species.

MORACEAE

Milicia (Chlorophora) excelsa (Iroko) is a large tree found most frequently in forest galleries in the savanna or in young forest types. It is known to grow to up to 55 m tall and 3 m diameter, but tends to be smaller. It has quite thick, low, rounded buttresses. The rough bark is pale grey, flaking off in large angular scales. The first branches are thick and leave the trunk at a common point, forming a fairly flat, airy, spreading canopy. Young trees are often deformed by frequent damage from gorillas feeding on their bark and leaves, and have stubby canopies with dense foliage.

It has large, long-stalked leaves (15 x 8 cm), with approximately 15 pairs of thick, parallel lateral veins, which are prominent on the underside. Particularly in young plants, the leaves are often attacked by an insect, *Phytolima lata*, resulting in large galls which are often eaten by monkeys and gorillas. From a distance the mature leaves appear metallic in the mid-day sun, making the canopy shimmer, as if made of platinum. *Milicia* is a deciduous species which tends to lose its leaves in the long or short dry season. Senescing leaves turn

Right:

Klainedoxa gabonensis

KA'94

Right:

a) Milicia excelsa
b) Musanga cecropioides
c) Myrianthus arboreus

Trees are dioecious, flowering and fruiting in January / May. The male flowers are white catkins up to 20 cm long which hang down; and green female flowers are short fat spikes about 4 cm long. The green fruits (6 x 2 cm), which contain numerous small seeds, resemble a plump green caterpillar. The flesh is sweet and is eaten by many birds and primates.

In the dry season, when there is little fruit around, *Milicia* becomes extremely important for gorillas. Whole groups, including the large silver-back, can sometimes be seen high in a *Milicia* canopy, stripping and eating the bark of the smaller branches and twigs. This is a crucial food at a time when little else is available. It is only eaten in the long dry season, suggesting that it is not a favourite food, or perhaps, that gorillas are sufficiently intelligent to save it for a time of need. Iroko is a precious wood, which is sometimes called 'African oak' or 'African teak'. It is heavily exploited by foresters, so gorillas living in logged forest will have many fewer trees to feed in during the long dry season, and may therefore suffer greatly, even when overall damage levels due to logging are not too high.

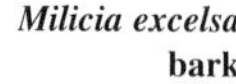

***Milicia excelsa* bark**

A mature *Milicia excelsa* (above) and a typical young tree, deformed by repeated feeding by gorillas, who break the branches to eat the bark (below).

Musanga cecropioides (Parasolier or umbrella tree) is one of the most familiar trees of the African rain forest for most people. It is, in fact, a species which grows only in disturbed areas, such as around villages, along roads or, occasionally, in large gaps in the forest. Within Lopé it is rare, perhaps because it needs richer soils, or perhaps because the large number of elephants in the Reserve eat both young plants and mature trees. It can reach about 20 m and occasionally exceeds 60 cm diameter. The smooth bark is pale grey. It has a straight trunk with high stilt-roots. The branches are thin but spread widely in the form of a candelabra, with a flat crown. Its characteristic leaves are unmistakeable. These are 'digitate', with 12-15 segments, each up to 45 x 10 cm, radiating in a circle. They have a stout stalk up to 60 cm long. The pink male flowers resemble those of *Myrianthus*. The female flowers develop into flattened, green, succulent fruits up to 10 cm across, with numerous tiny seeds, which are eaten by primates, bats, birds and humans.

Myrianthus arboreus is quite common along rivers in Marantaceae forest in Lopé. It is closely related to *Musanga* and resembles it to some extent. It grows to 15-20 m tall. The bark is smooth and greyish and most trees have stilt-roots. It has spreading branches and the leaves are digitate, with 5 leaflets, resembling those of a European horse chestnut. The leaflets have sharp, prominent, forwards pointing teeth along their margins and are up to 45 x 15 cm, with a stalk up to 45 cm long. Male flowers are dull yellow, arranged along branched stalks. Female flowers are arranged in small heads about 2.5 cm across. They develop into large, yellow fruit with numerous polygonal sections, each containing a seed surrounded by fibrous flesh, full of refreshing, sugary juice. The fruits are eaten by most primates and by elephants and their characteristic seeds (p. 215) and seedlings (p. 4) are often found in old dung piles.

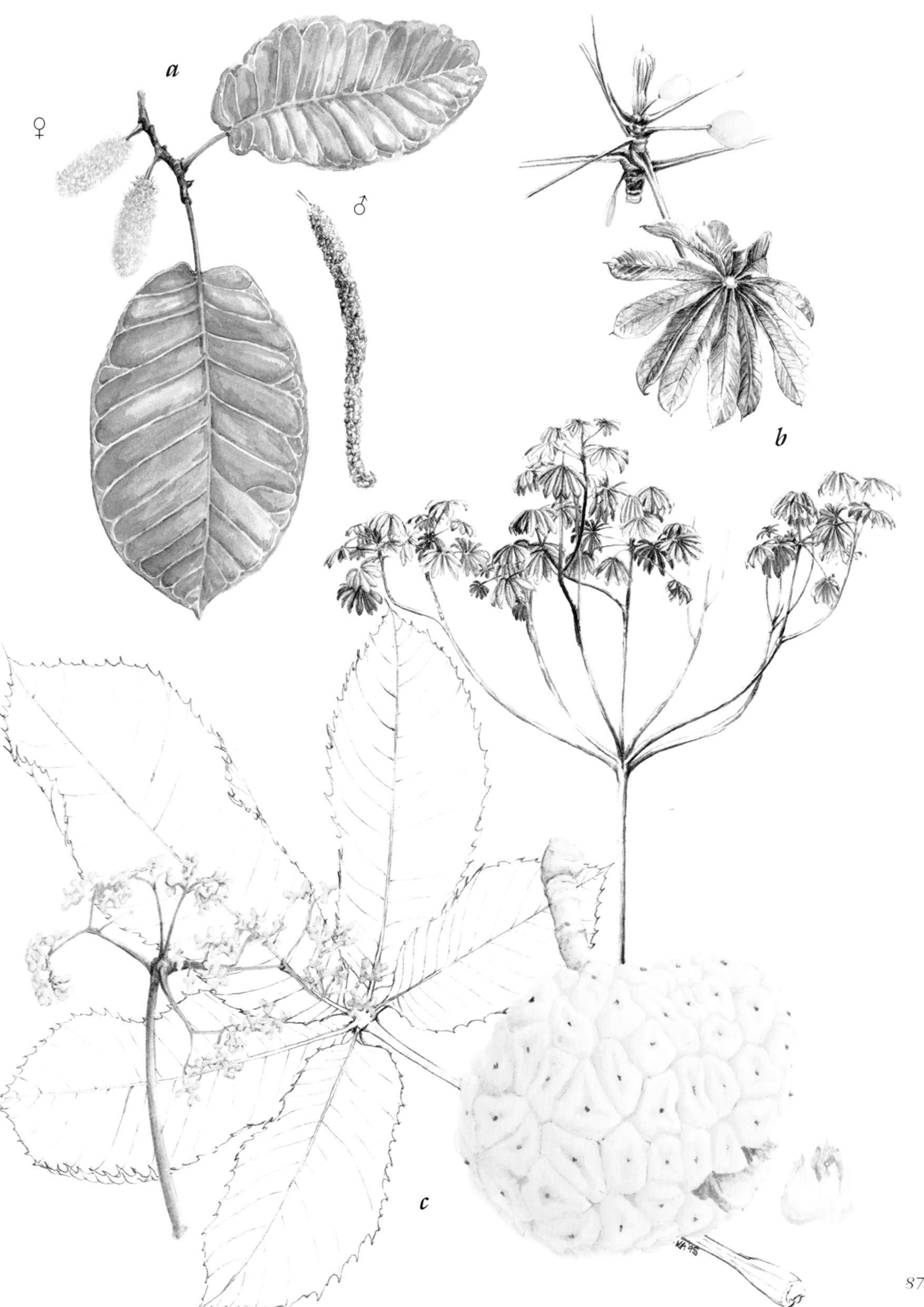
a
♀
♂
b
c
KA 95

OCHNACEAE

Fruits of *Lophira alata*

Lophira alata (Azobé, or iron wood) is one of the characteristic large tree species of the Lopé. Like *Sacoglottis gabonensis* and *Aucoumea klaineana*, it is an excellent savanna coloniser, if protected from fire. It is a dominant component of much of the younger forest in the Reserve, as well as of many galleries, including those along the Ogooué.

Its form varies greatly depending on where it grow: within the forest it becomes a large, impressive tree, occasionally reaching 60 m in height with a diameter of 150 cm or more. The bark is brown-orange and peels off in irregular flakes. A characteristic layer of bright yellow powder is sometimes visible where bark has recently peeled away. The trunk is tall and cylindrical, but in larger trees is slightly fluted near the base, with indistinct, thick, rounded buttresses. The boughs are twisted and the branches end in erect bunches of tough, leathery leaves. These are up to 35 x 10 cm, with a fine lattice of parallel secondary nerves. They often have numerous, roughly spherical, distortions, or 'galls', caused by insects. Around December *Lophira alata* leaves yellow and fall, leaving them bare for a brief period, before they flush with a spectacular display of bright red young leaves. These gradually fade to pink, through peach, and yellowy green, to pale green and finally darken to the deep green of mature leaves. In some years this is highly synchronised and hundreds of trees flush in the same week, whilst in others it is staggered, lasting up to two months.

Right:

Lophira alata

As the new leaves unfold the flowers open. These hang in big bunches about 15 cm long, their large white petals offset against the flush young leaves. The flowers are about 3 cm across, with a large yellow rosette of stamens at the centre. They have a powerful perfume, as rich as the finest rose. The fruit is a small conical capsule about 3 x 1 cm, with two wings; a large one up to 10 x 3 cm and a smaller one about 3 x 1 cm. These wings are bright red when young and fade to brown as they ripen in late January / March. The capsule contains a single, bright green, seed. Once the fruit is released the wings cause it to spin in the wind, prolonging the time it is in the air, hence increasing the potential dispersal distance. On a windy day the seeds can travel several hundred metres before falling to the ground. In some places the seeds are collected to make an edible oil.

Azobes that have grown in more open conditions than those experienced in the forest, such as on the forest edge or in a savanna, tend to be much shorter and to branch low. These trees can sometimes resemble a European oak in form, with large round canopies and many thick branches, starting just a few metres above the ground. This demonstrates the striking effect of environment on tree form. Had these individuals grown in the forest they would have had a tall, branchless trunk. The tropical rain forest is, in many respects, a perfect plantation, which ensures that the tallest trees have long straight trunks, ideal for processing by modern machinery. As soon as one attempts to grow most tropical trees in plantations one runs into problems. This is demonstrated by the natural plantations of *Lophira alata* that you will notice in areas protected from annual burns. Here small *Lophira* trees are popping up in dense stands. Often they are no more than a single trunk a few centimeters diameter, with a whorl of leaves all the way to their tips. The leaves on these young plants are larger than on adult trees, sometimes exceeding 70 cm in length, and the last few tend to be red, giving the saplings a fiery crown. In young forest types one can see how these early colonisers branch low and have crooked trunks. It is the next generation, which grow up in their shade, which will be tall and straight. Azobé is a hard, durable wood used to build bridges and from which the sleepers of the 'transgabonais' railway were made.

PASSIFLORACEAE

Barteria fistulosa (ant tree or, locally, the adultery tree) is a common small tree, up to about 15 m tall, in young and disturbed forest types. The bark is smooth and reddish. Its large, alternate leaves are generally about 30 x 12 cm. They are arranged along long wavy branches, which can be mistaken for compound leaves, giving a characteristic open form which never develops into a true canopy. It flowers in December. The flowers have large white petals about 3 cm long, arranged around a prominent yellow stigma. They form an eye catching display arranged in a long row in the axil of each leaf. The dull green fruits, each about 3 cm in diameter, resemble passion fruits (which are in the genus Passiflora of this family). They contain numerous small, dimpled seeds surrounded in a moist, yellowish, sugary flesh.

Barteria fistulosa

Barteria fistulosa is an excellent example of coevolution. It is in your interest to notice that it is almost always inhabited by large, fierce, black ants. These ants, *Tetraponera aethiops*, commonly known as '*Barteria* ants' can only survive on *Barteria* trees. Like all social insects, they produce 'queens', which move away to form new colonies. Queen *Barteria* ants are winged and, having mated, they fly in search of a young *Barteria fistulosa*. She burrows into one of the hollow branches, which are specially designed to give shelter to these ants, and begins to lay eggs. The worker ants which hatch are extremely aggressive. These ants move out onto the stem and leaves of the young *Barteria*, and attack any other animals they find there. They soon clear off any other ants, or caterpillars and once this job is done they conduct regular patrols to defend their host. Meanwhile, within the hollow branches, they farm small scale insects. These feed on the sap of the *Barteria* tree and, in turn, secrete a honeydew liquid which feeds the ants.

Barteria trees without ants tend to appear sickly and are host to many parasites. These bear witness to the efficiency of the ants. As the tree grows the ant colony goes from strength to strength and they begin to travel further afield. Whilst some ants remain on the tree to defend it directly, others climb down to the ground and begin to gnaw through the stems of plants growing around its base. They gradually clear a roughly circular patch, preventing other plants from growing up to compete with the *Barteria* for light and nutrients. Partly because of this, *Barteria fistulosa* can sometimes form quite extensive stands.

Right:

Barteria fistulosa

KA'93

Fruits of *Eriocoelum macrocarpum* (Sapindaceae - see p.152)

You only have to touch the branch of a *Barteria* tree lightly with a stick to appreciate the ferocity of its ants. They come streaming out from the hollow branches and search the trunk, branches and leaves for an intruder. If they find any foreign object they attack without hesitation. More ants rush down the trunk, or drop from the canopy, to search the ground below. If they find something they latch on with their jaws and probe with their abdomen, searching for sensitive tissue to sting. Their sting is like that of a wasp and is painful for a day or more. It is said to be able to penetrate an elephant's skin. In the past, local Okandé people attached women accused of adultery to the tree, to force them to reveal their lover's identity.

How then is *Barteria* pollinated and its seeds dispersed ? When it is flowering the ants seem to become less aggressive, as if they understand that they have to let insect pollinators visit the flowers. When fruit are ripe one sometimes sees monkeys hanging by one arm from a neighbouring tree, reaching down in an attempt to pluck a fruit without disturbing the ants. However, the main seed dispersers are bats. The ants are not active at night and fruit bats land on the branches to feed on the fruit. They swallow the small seeds and pass them in their dung, ensuring that there will be more young *Barteria* trees for the next generation of queen *Tetraponera aethiops* ants.

The bark of the *Barteria* tree is used to treat tooth ache. If you have a rotten tooth you collect some bark and pack it into the carie. If left overnight the bark supposedly causes the tooth to shatter, hence curing the problem by eliminating the tooth. In some places pregnant women traditionally eat a mixture of leaves and peanuts.

Mandrills deserve special mention. Only they seem to be brave (or perhaps stupid) enough to eat the ants themselves in Lopé; although elephants sometimes feed on the leaves, and in northern Congo gorillas eat both the ants and the bark.

Trees found in marshes

Marshes in the savanna are often fringed by forest containing tree species typical of gallery forests. They sometimes also contain the forest trees *Mitragyna (Hallea) ciliata* and *Nauclea vanderguchtii* (see p. 204), both of which can grow with their bases in water. Two other species are typical of this habitat.

LOGANIACEAE

Anthocleista vogelii is a small tree typically up to 10 m tall and 15 cm diameter, although it can grow larger. It has a characteristic form, consisting of a few, widely spreading, crooked branches, with tufts of large leaves (30-40 x 10 cm). The smooth bark is pale grey-brown and there are usually small spines on the trunk and particularly the branches. The flowers are cream or orange-brown on conspicuous, upright, branched inflorescences. The flowers never open fully. The fruits are green spheres, about 2 cm diameter, containing numerous tiny seeds dispersed by bats. Extracts from the roots are commonly used in homeopathy, and are said to cure gonorrhoea, leprosy, elephantiasis of the scrotum and menstrual problems, amongst other afflictions.

A second species, ***Anthocleista schweinfurthii,*** closely resembles *A. vogelii* but is found principally in disturbed areas and can be distinguished by its fruits, which are on a stalk which droops downwards (see p.210).

PANDANACEAE

Pandanus candelabrum ("screw pine") is a small tree which grows in swamps. It is up to 10 m tall and about 15 cm diameter. The straight trunk is yellowish-grey, covered in numerous small thorns, with aerial roots at the base. There are a few, upwardly curving branches, which end in bunches of long, strap-like leaves, arranged in spirals. The leaves are V-shaped in cross-section, with many forward-pointing thorns along their margins. The leaves often appear broken in the middle and droop downwards. Male trees have flowers on densely crowded fat spikes up to 30 cm long. In females the flower spike is shorter and develops into a large cone-like fruit about 20 x 12 cm. *Pandanus* often forms dense thickets in swamps and marshes, which can only be penetrated along muddy channels opened up by elephants, which eat the leaves.

Right:

***a) Anthocleista vogelii* (a young tree)**
b) Pandanus candelabrum

a
b
KA'95
KA'94

5/ MARANTACEAE FOREST

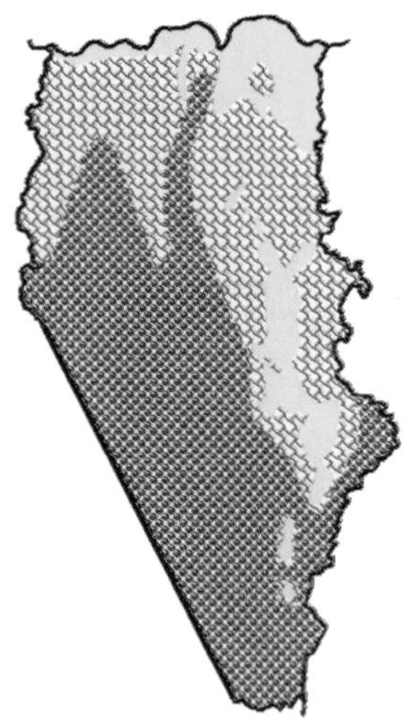

Savanna

Young forest and Marantaceae forest

Mature forest

Simplified vegetation map of the Lopé Reserve.

This is one of the dominant vegetation types in Lopé. It is characterised by a dense ground vegetation made up of free standing and lianescent species of herbaceaous plants, mostly wild gingers and Marantaceae (arrow roots). These form an almost impenetrable thicket about two metres tall, but which occasionally climbs up to a height of 10m or more, forming towers which engulf small trees and dead stumps. The only way to penetrate this forest is along well worn elephant trails. Because of the dense herbaceous vegetation little light reaches the ground, so few other young trees and shrubs are able to establish. This results in Marantaceae Forest having an unusual structure for a tropical forest. There are very few small and medium sized trees, so once you have your head above the ground vegetation the forest appears open and you can often see monkeys in the canopy far away. Perhaps the high density of elephants also contributes to this, for they can push over medium sized trees to feed on their leaves or fruit.

Marantaceae Forest develops from the tightly packed vegetation which forms after savanna colonisation. All of the early colonisers which grew up in savanna are about the same age, so there comes a time when they all begin to die. Because they are tightly packed when one tree falls it often brings down several of its neighbours, forming large gaps in the canopy which allow light to penetrate. These provide ideal conditions for the growth of Marantaceae species, which explode to fill the gap on the ground, whilst trees close to the gap are finally able to spread their branches out. So, the remaining pioneers gradually change their form, branching out after years of confinement. However, their seeds which were so successful out in the savanna are not adapted to the shady conditions of the forest floor and new tree species begin to grow up and compete with the early colonisers. In younger Marantaceae Forests the canopy is still dominated by the colonisers, but as time progresses, it becomes more diverse. This process gradually results in an increase in the diversity and structural complexity of the forest. There comes a point when the trees above begin to shade out the Marantaceae below. As ground vegetation becomes less dense more and more trees establish, and the Marantaceae Forest gives way to Mature Forest (see p. 163).

Marantaceae Forest

Aucoumea klaineana ●, Diospyros dendo ●; Lophira alata ●
Dacryodes buettneri ○; ▭ Marantaceaes and zingiberaceaes

Marantaceae Forest occurs in a band up to about 20 km wide around the Lopé savannas. Its presence shows us that several hundred years ago much of this area was savanna. In fact, up to about 1400 years ago almost half of the Lopé may have been covered by a mosaic of savanna and gallery forests, like those that remain in the north of the Reserve today. The area was densely populated by Iron Age peoples, whose pottery, iron furnaces and rock engravings are still visible today. For reasons we can only guess, these people disappeared. Perhaps there was an outbreak of a particularly infectious and deadly disease, which killed many people and caused the survivors to leave the area. There was a major population crash, which affected much of Gabon, as well as parts of surrounding countries. Between the sixth and eleventh centuries AD there is no evidence of people surviving in the Lopé.

During this period there were major changes in the vegetation. Savannas were no longer burnt regularly and were gradually colonised and replaced by forest until, about 800 years ago, the ancestors of the people who currently live in the Lopé area arrived from the north. Their arrival can be dated quite accurately from carbon dates of charcoal found in sites of past habitation, in association with pottery decorated in their characteristic style. With their arrival regular fires once again raged through the grasslands, establishing a new equilibrium between forest and savanna.

During the long dry season, when little fruit is available, many animals move into the Marantaceae Forest to feed on the leaves and stems of the abundant arrow roots and gingers. For many species, particularly large mammals like elephants and gorillas, they are an important part of the diet all year round. Because of this, Marantaceae Forest supports exceptionally high densities of many species. The density of elephants is about three per square kilometer, which means that we see them on average every 7-10 km walked. In fact, no tropical rain forest in the World is known to have a higher density of mammals than the Marantaceae Forest in Lopé.

A fungus growing on dead wood

Plants without Flowers

The plant kingdom can be divided into two broad categories: the plants without flowers, comprising Fungi, Algae, Lichens, Mosses and Ferns; and the remainder, the plants with flowers, with which this guide is principally concerned.

Fungi, the mushrooms, are immediately recognised by most people. They include a great diversity in the tropical forest, but are difficult to identify and poorly known, with the exception of certain edible species, such as the chantarelle, *Cantharellus ciberius*, which is found in galleries in Lopé in close association with the tree *Julbernardia brieyi* (p. 202). *Cantharellus* is an ectomychorhizal fungus, whose hyphae cover and grow between the cells in the root system of *Julbernardia* in a symbiotic relationship. The fungus helps the tree obtain nitrogen necessary for protein production and in turn receives nutrients.

Algae are essentially marine plants and are rarely noticed in Lopé. Exceptions are the blooms of microscopic blue-green *Spirogyra*, sometimes found in marshes or in slow flowing rivers in the dry season. In some parts of Gabon these are eaten in large quantities by bongo, *Tragelaphus euryceros*, a large forest antelope. Lichens are formed by a union of fungi and algae and are common on rocks, tree trunks, where they sometimes create vivid patterns, and on leaves. Lichens of the genus *Usnea* grow like a beard on the branches of trees on some of the higher ridges in Lopé. Mosses form small green carpets on rocks, on the ground, on rotting wood and on tree trunks, particularly in moist areas. To date 15 species have been identified in Lopé, but collections are at an early stage and many more remain to be identified.

The Ferns are by far the most striking of the non-flowering plants and occur in a great variety of shapes and sizes in Lopé. To date almost 70 species have been found in various habitats. Ferns can often be identified by means of the form and arrangement of their leaves. At certain times of year powdery brown or black spots, or lines, appear on the underside of the leaf. These consist of numerous tiny sacs, called sporangia, which contain spores. When released, the spores give rise to new ferns, like the seeds of flowering plants. The pattern of these sporangia is sometimes necessary to allow, or confirm, identification of some fern species. Many species are found within the forest, some of which are illustrated.

Platycerium stemania
or «stag-horn», an epiphytic fern.

Bolbitis gaboonensis is a fern found on the ground in mature forest, in which the brown sporangia completely cover the underside of the leaf. **Bolbitis heudelotii** occurs on rocks along streams and rivers in all forest types in Lopé. This species has two very different forms depending on whether its leaves are held erect above water, or if they are drifting in the current.

Cyathea camerooniana is a small tree fern, growing to about 2 - 3 m tall, found mainly in moist valleys in mature forest in Lopé, although it is occasionally encountered along rivers in Marantaceae forest. The rhizome grows up above the ground like the trunk of a tree, and the large leaves, which can be over 2 m long, are bunched towards the top of the stem, rather like a palm. In some montane regions of Africa other species of tree ferns occasionally exceed 5m tall.

Marattia fraxinea is a large fern found along water courses in mature forest in Lopé, particularly at higher altitudes. It has erect fronds up to 2.5 m high, with two distinctive lines of sporangia.

Microgramma owariensis is a small epiphytic fern with leaves about 8 cm long, found on trees, and sometimes on rocks, throughout the forest in Lopé.

Triplophyllum vogelii, has its leaf in 3 distinct sections, a characteristic of the genus *Triplophyllum*, which includes several other species found in Lopé.

Below:

a) Bolbitis gaboonensis
b) Bolbitis heudelotii
c) Cyathea camerooniana
d) Marattia fraxinea
e) Microgramma owariensis
f) Triplophyllum vogelii

Marantaceae

The Marantaceae (Arrowroots) is a family of large-leaved herbaceous plants with underground rhizomes. The rhizome of *Maranta arundinacea*, a South American species introduced to Gabon, provides an edible flour known as arrowroot, which lends its name to the family as a whole. The Marantaceae is one of the most important families in the Lopé. Species of Marantaceae dominate the under-storey in much of the Lopé, particularly in Marantaceae Forest, where they form dense, almost impenetrable thickets, along with several Zingiberaceae species (p. 99).

Many species of Marantaceae provide food for large mammals such as elephants, gorillas, chimpanzees, mandrills and monkeys. Because they are available all year round, unlike fruit, they represent a dependable fall-back food in times of scarcity, such as in the long dry season. At this time buffalo eat large quantities of some Marantaceae species, even though they tend to ignore them during the rest of the year. It is probably because of the abundance of Marantaceae and Zingiberaceae species in Marantaceae forest that this vegetation type has the highest density of large mammals ever recorded in a tropical rain forest. Several species of Marantaceae can be recognised by their form and fruits in Lopé. They are found in most habitats in Lopé, but here we divide them into aquatic (see p. 198) and upland species.

Megaphrynium macrostachyum

MARANTACEAE ON WELL-DRAINED SOILS

Ataenidia conferta has an erect, branched, succulent stem and leaves similar to *Marantochloa* (p. 198) or young *Haumania* plants (but the latter have dry stems). However, it can easily be identified by the presence of persistent, red-purple bracts, which sometimes contain delicate white flowers. The leaves are of variable size (up to 40 x 20 cm) usually with a purple-red underside. *Ataenidia* tends to grow in moist areas, though not in water, and may form dense stands. It is used in Gabon in magic spells cast, to provoke quarrels within families or villages.

Haumania liebrechtsiana is the dominant species of Marantaceae in Lopé and is quite variable in form. In the under-storey of Mature forest, it generally has an erect, branched stem, similar to that of *Ataenidia conferta*, with 1-10 small leaves (15 x 7 cm). In light gaps it becomes lianescent, with 30 or more slightly larger leaves. In Marantaceae Forest a single stem can be over 20 m long, with over 100 leaves (up to 30 x 15 cm). Here *Haumania* forms thickets, which can only be penetrated on elephant paths and covers small trees in dense vine towers. The delicate white flowers emerge from green bracts and are pollinated by bees. The fruit is a hard, dry, spiny, three lobed capsule, which splits to throw the seeds a few metres. The main form of reproduction is by vegetative propogation and this sometimes results in distinct 'fronts' of *Haumania*, where it is advancing into young vegetation types. The young leaves and leaf buds are eaten by gorillas, chimpanzees and mandrills, leaving feeding sign which sometimes allows their progress to be tracked. The damaged stems soon oxidise and blacken, so even freshly eaten shoots can appear quite old at first glance. Elephants uproot and eat the underground rhizomes and occasionally clear quite large patches within the Marantaceae Forest. This gives seedlings of forest trees, which cannot grow in the shady conditions under a dense cover of *Haumania* leaves, a chance to grow. The seeds are eaten by gorillas and chimpanzees, who crunch them up with relish - they taste a little like hazel nuts found in European forests.

Hypselodelphis violacea is a climbing liane which is often inter-twined with stems of *Haumania liebrechtsiana* in vine towers. Its leaves are similar in size to those of *Haumania*, but can easily be distinguished by their arrangement on a long stem. The smaller bracts and triangular fruit are also distinctive. Young leaves and buds are eaten in the same way as for *Haumania*, but *Hypselodelphis* shoots do not turn black when broken and so are easily distinguished on fresh feeding trail. A second species, ***Hypselodelphis hirsuta***, is rare, but can be distinguished from *H. violacea* by its hairy stems and fruit with three rounded capsules.

Two species of *Marantochloa* occur on dry land. ***Marantochloa filipes*** has the same branched form as the aquatic species (see p. 198) but has a thin, dry stem and small, dark green leaves (7-15 x 3-7 cm). It occasionally becomes common in humid areas, but is never aquatic. ***Marantochloa mildbraedii*** is very similar to *M. cordifolia*, but grows on dry land, either on steep valley sides or in disturbed areas. It can also be distinguished by its hairy stem and leaf margin.

c
d
e
b
a

Megaphrynium macrostachyum is similar in form to *Halopegia azurea*, but is much larger and grows on dry ground. Numerous stems emerge from a tussock. The petioles are up to about 3 m long, with a single spade-shaped leaf of variable size, generally between 30-60 x 12-30 cm, but occasionally up to 90 cm long. The upper side of the leaf is dull green. Yellowish flowers are borne on a stalk which grows off the leaf petiole. The ripe fruits are red or black capsules in 3 sections. They contain 3 seeds with a sugary white flesh. The fruits are eaten and dispersed by apes, mandrills and elephants. Apes and mandrills also eat the base of the rolled, young leaves, which are tender and taste a little like cucumber. The leaves are put to many uses by humans. They are collected in large quantities for use as roof tiles, as food wrappers and as 'ecological tin foil', which is wrapped around food to be cooked in the embers of a fire. A second very similar species, **Megaphrynium velutinum**, is usually somewhat smaller, with petioles about 1.5-2 m long and leaves about 30-50 x 15-30 cm. The upper surface of the leaf is shiny, not dull. Young leaves and fruits of this species are eaten by animals, but the leaves are not used by humans.

Left:

*a) **Ataenidia conferta***
*b) **Haumania liebrechtsiana***
*c) **Hypselodelphis violacea***
*d) **Marantochloa filipes***
*e) **Megaphrynium macrostachyum***

Wild gingers

ZINGIBERACEAE

The Zingiberaceae are broad-leaved herbs with underground rhizomes. If you crush the leaf or break the stem of plants in this family there is usually a strong aromatic smell, somewhat like that of ginger. In the case of ginger, *Zingiber officinale*, introduced to Gabon from Asia and the Pacific, the rhizome is used as a spice, as is the root of *Curcuma longa*, saffron, the principal ingredient in curry powder. Another species, *Phaeomeria magnifica*, the porcelain rose, is cultivated for its large, fleshy, pink flowers. The most familiar species in this family in Gabon is ***Aframomum giganteum***, whose fronds reach up to 6 m tall. This species invades the edges of forest roads forming dense, impenetrable thickets. The genus *Aframomum* is represented by about 20 species in Gabon.

The commonest species in Lopé is ***Aframomum sericeum***, named in 1997 from collections made at the Lopé and probably endemic to a small region centred on the northern savannas of the Reserve. The abundance of this rare, new species in the Lopé is truly remarkable. In young vegetation types it reaches densities of over 5,000 stems per hectare. It is a light loving species which thrives in gaps in Marantaceae Forest. The stems are up to 3 m long, curving over to form half-arches. The underside of the leaves is covered in a down of soft hairs. Stems and roots are eaten by elephants and the stem pith is consumed by apes and mandrills, who leave characteristic feeding sign. They flower and fruit throughout the wet season. The flowers are delicate pink trumpets, about 7 cm high, borne on the surface of the soil, on thick stems which grow off the rhizome. They develop into bright red, ridged, fruits, up to about 8 cm long. These contain numerous small, shiny black seeds in a white, tangy pulp, which is excellent to eat. The seeds are peppery if crunched. You have to be very observant to find a tasty ripe fruit intact, as their empty red shells are common along gorilla, chimpanzee or mandrill feeding trail, but if you are lucky they make a refreshing snack.

Aframomum sericeum

Two other species of *Aframomum* are relatively common. ***Aframomum leptolepis*** is similar to *Aframomum sericeum*, but its leaves are not hairy and it has a smooth red fruit. It is most abundant along old forestry roads in mature forest and attracts animals onto the roads where they are more easily seen. ***Aframomum longipetiolatum***, has smaller fronds which rarely reach 1 m long. It is easily identified by the large red spots and white, powdery, coating on the leaves. Its flowers and fruits are held up to about 30 cm above the ground on fleshy stems and the red fruit have a smooth skin like *A. leptolepis*.

Costus albus and ***Costus lucanusianus*** both have leaves arranged in characteristic spirals. *Costus albus* is easily recognised by its twisted stems, in the form of a helix. The stems are generally 1-2 m high, with leaves every 5 cm or so. The large, fleshy inflorescence grows on a separate stem and produces 1-2 flowers at a time, over an extended period. The flowers are delicate white trumpets about 6-7 cm long, with a yellow patch towards the tip. Many small fruits develop within the inflorescence. *Costus lucanusianus* has straight stems up to 3 m long, with leaves about every 2 cm. Stems are often bowed over under the weight of their characteristic large terminal inflorescences or fruits.

Aframomum longipetiolatum

a
b
c

Renealmia cincinnata and ***Renealmia macrocolea*** have similar form to *Aframomum*, but the leaves are held more vertical. The two *Renealmia* species are easily distinguished because the underside of the leaves of *R. cincinnata* are red whilst those of *R. macrocolea* are green. Many small white flowers develop on a common stalk growing off the rhizome. The fruits are about 1-1.5 cm long, containing about 20 small seeds with delicate arils. *R. cincinnata* has red fruits with yellow arils and those of *R. macrocolea* are red-orange with orange arils. The stem pith is occasionally eaten by gorillas and chimpanzees, but is a favourite for mandrills, which leave characteristic shredded feeding remains.

Other herbs

Few herbs can live in the gloom of the under-storey, particularly in areas with dense cover of Marantaceae and Zingiberaceae, and it is a rare treat to find bright flowers. However, herbs become relatively common where light penetrates to the forest floor, along the banks of forest streams, in light gaps and close to old roads.

Left :

a) Costus lucanusianus
b) Costus albus
c) Aframomum sericeum

Renealmia macrocolea

Renealmia macrocolea

Right:
Acanthaceae of the forest
- ***a) Acanthus montanus***
- ***b) Anisotes macrophylla***
- ***c) Asystasia macrophylla***
- ***d) Hypoestes verticillaris***
- ***e) Justicia insularis***
- ***f) Pseuderanthemum tunicatum***
- ***g) Rhinacanthus virens***

The Acanthaceae family includes many small flowering forest herbs. ***Acanthus montanus*** has tough, prickly leaves like those of a thistle. ***Anisotes macrophylla*** is covered in spectacular pink flowers in July / August, which look like shrimps. Gorillas occasionally eat its leaves. ***Asystasia macrophylla*** is a shrub growing to 3 - 4m tall which is common along some rivers. The other species illustrated are all small under-storey herbs with delicate flowers. ***Hypoestes verticillaris*** is common along some old roads in the forest. All of the Acanthaceae have small capsular fruits which dehisce when ripe, throwing seeds a short distance from their parents.

Amongst other families represented in the under-storey, ***Thonningia sanguinea*** (Balanophoraceae), is a curious species, without leaves, which lives as a parasite on the roots of other plants. The prickly red flower is used to stop young boys urinating in their beds. ***Commelina capitata*** (Commelinaceae) and ***Aneilema beniniense*** are small herbs related to the Marantaceae and Zingiberaceae, which are sometimes eaten by gorillas and chimpanzees. ***Calvoa monticola*** (Melastomataceae; one of several species known locally as "l'oseille") is generally found on rock outcrops. Its succulent leaves can be eaten raw, but are more usually cooked with fish as an equivalent of sorrel. ***Geophila afzelii*** (Rubiaceae) is a common creeper which covers the forest floor in some places. ***Geophila obvollata*** ressembles *Geophila afzelii* but is distinguished by its bright blue fruits. ***Pseudosabicea mildbraedii*** is an unusual Rubiaceae. One of its opposite leaves is stunted, and can easily be mistaken for a stipule.

Anchomanes difformis **(see p. 15)**

b
a
f
d
e
g
c

g
e
h
i
f
b
c
d
a

Lianes

ANNONACEAE

Lianes are not very abundant in the Lopé, perhaps because many of them are eaten by elephants, which are extremely abundant. The Annonaceae contain several genera of lianes and lianescent shrubs, some of which produce important fruit foods for animals.

Artabotrys cf. crassipetalus is a relatively small liane, with a stem about 6 m long and 3 cm thick, found in Marantaceae Forest in Lopé. The leaf is about 13 x 6 cm. The fruits are about 5 cm long and were unknown to science until a specimen was collected in Lopé in 1993. ***Artabotrys thomsonii*** is a large liane found in gallery forest in Lopé. It can reach 30 m long and has a dark, circular stem up to 20 cm diameter. The leaves (14 x 7 cm) have a midrib which is hairy on both sides and about 9 pairs of bold lateral nerves. Its fruits are about 2 x 1.5 cm when ripe in October / November.

Monanthotaxis congolensis is a small shrub to about 3 m high, which is somewhat lianescent when large. It is common in rocky areas in the forest and in some galleries in the savanna. It is easily identified by its leaves, which are green above and silver below. It has small yellow flowers, about 8 mm across, and furry pink fruits which are about 1 cm diameter, when ripe from April to July. These contain a single, characteristic seed (p. 214), with a sugary flesh, eaten by elephants, gorillas and chimpanzees. ***Monanthotaxis diclina*** is a common liane which grows in all forest types in Lopé and which can exceed 20 m long and 10 cm diameter. The stem is dark and smaller branches are covered in ginger hairs. The leaves are typically about 12 x 5 cm, green above and grey-green below, with about 10-12 lateral nerves. The underside is covered in soft, ginger hairs. The flowers and fruits are in eye-catching bunches on the stem and twigs. The seeds resemble small bullets and are often found in the dung of chimpanzees, gorillas and elephants in November / February. ***Monanthotaxis aff. klainii*** is a small liane generally about 5 m long, found in galleries in the savanna. The leaves (13 x 6 cm) are green above and grey-green below, with about 8 lateral nerves. The flowers are similar to those of *Monanthotaxis congolensis* and the fruits are in small bunches, turning red when ripe in October / December.

Uvaria klaineana is a large liane found in mature forest. It has characteristic small, leathery leaves (3 x 1.5 cm). These are dark green above and are covered in a soft, pale brown felt below, with lateral nerves which are barely visible. The fruits are in remarkable bunches, with long, thin pedicels about 4 cm long. ***Uvaria psorosperma*** is a small liane found in gallery forests which was known only from one specimen until found in Lopé. The leaves are quite small (7 x 3 cm) with about 8 prominent lateral nerves. The fruits ripen in April / May and are similar to those of *Uvaria klaineana*, but the pedicels are only about 1 cm long. ***Uvaria cf. scabrida*** is a large liane up to about 20 m long and 10 cm diameter. It occurs in all forest types in Lopé. The large leaves (18 x 8 cm) are densely covered on the underside in brown, stellate hairs, with the texture of coarse velvet. The large, yellow flowers have petals up to 2 cm across. The fruits are brick-red in colour, about 5 x 2 cm. The flesh around the seeds has a pleasant, sweet flavour like pineapple when ripe and is eaten by many forest animals in March/April. ***Uvaria versicolor*** is a small, scrambling shrub, up to about 2 m tall, found close to rock outcrops in the forest. Its leaves (8 x 3.5 cm) are dark above and pale green-brown below. It flowers in May/June and fruits ripen in August / September.

RUBIACEAE

The Rubiaceae contains relatively few lianes compared to its large diversity of shrubs and small trees. Most of the lianes found in Lopé are quite small and are most common in Marantaceae forest, the forest-savanna mosaic or in areas disturbed by logging.

Atractogyne gabonii reaches about 5-10 m, with stems about 2 cm diameter. The spade-shaped leaves (11 x 6 cm) have a stalk about 4 cm long and 4-6 pairs of upcurving lateral nerves. The flowers are pale green with a little purple on the 5 lobes of the corolla, about 1.5 cm long. The fruits, which are said to relieve sore throats, are like thin, pink sausages about 7-15 cm long. They contain white pulp, which tastes like cough mixture and are eaten by many animals, which disperse their numerous, tiny black seeds.

Commelina capitata **(Commelinaceae)**

Left:

Balanophoraceae
a) Thonningia sanguinea
Commelinaceae
b) Aneilema beniniense
Melastomataceae
c) Calvoa monticola
d) Warneckea yangambensis
Oxalidaceae
e) Biophytum talbotii
Rubiaceae
f) Geophila afzelii
g) Lasianthus batangensis
h) Pseudosabicea mildbraedii
Sterculiaceae
i) Leptonychia echinocarpa

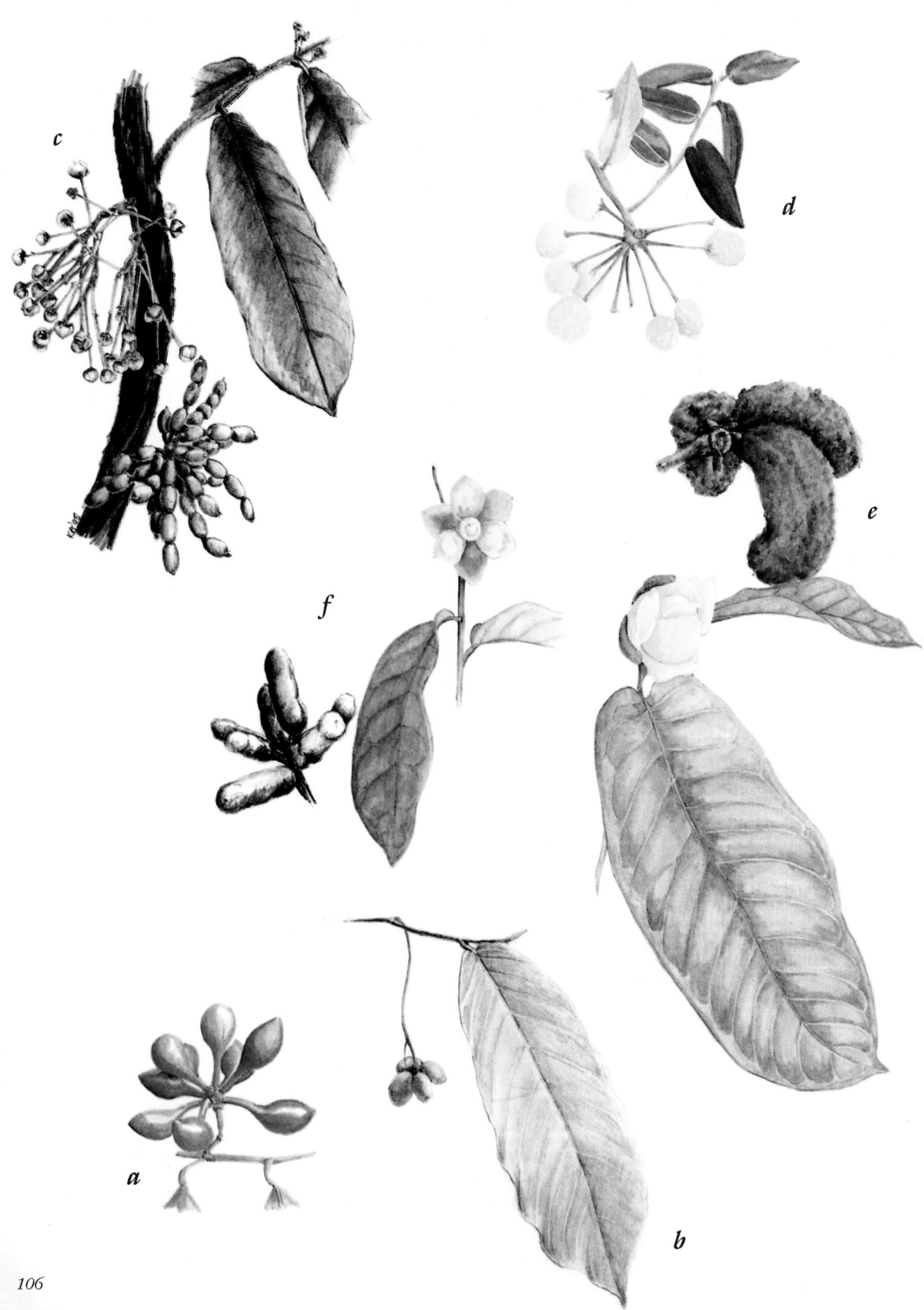
c
d
e
f
a
b

Bertiera cf. letouzeyi reaches about 3 m tall. The leaves (8 x 5 cm) are sparsely hairy on their undersides, with about 8 lateral nerves. It has small, white flowers, about 7 mm long. The red fruits, about 11 mm diameter, are slightly hairy, and contain 40-55 tiny, brown-black seeds.

Morinda morindoides grows to about 15 m, its leaves (10 x 5 cm) have about 6 lateral nerves. It has fragrant white flowers and a characteristic green, lobed fruit, which is often found on the ground some distance away, causing some confusion as to where it has come from.

Mussaenda debeauxii is a liane up to about 5 m high. Young stems and leaves are covered in dense brown hairs. The leaves (8 x 4.5 cm) have 8-10 lateral nerves. The flowers are in groups of 10-20. Each green and yellow flower is about 3-6 cm long. The orange fruits, about 2.5 cm long, are also covered by brown hairs. They contain numerous tiny seeds, are quite sweet and are eaten by gorillas. Two other species, ***Mussaenda erythrophylla*** and ***Mussaenda cf. tenuiflora*** (see p.60) are lianes to about 10 m tall. They are particularly eye catching when in flower as they have bright, leaf-like sepals about 10 x 5 cm. *Mussaenda erythrophylla* has scarlet sepals with white flowers and *Mussaenda cf. tenuifolia* has bright white sepals and yellow flowers.

Polycoryne fernandensis is found in the forest-savanna mosaic in Lopé. It has large rounded leaves (14 x 9 cm) with petioles about 4 cm long. The strongly perfumed white flowers smell like jasmine. The spherical green fruits turn yellow when ripe, with a diameter of 4-5 cm. The fruit skin is often marked by brown, leathery patches.

Rutidea pavettoides grows to about 5 m, with characteristic asymmetrical leaves (8 x 5 cm) are covered in long, ginger hairs on both sides. The stems are also densely covered in ginger hairs. It has fragrant white flowers and yellow-red fruits with a crown of persistent sepals.

Uncaria africana grows up to about 5-6 m, occasionally higher, with a well protected thorny stem. The leaves are typically about 11 x 4 cm. The strongly scented, pale, yellow flowers form large balls about 5 cm across. The sphere of fruits is about 10 cm diameter. The fruits dry to black and open releasing tiny seeds with two opposite wings, each of about 3-4 mm, which are dispersed by the wind.

Shrubs

AGAVACEAE

Two shrubs in the Agavaceae, ***Dracaena aubryana*** and ***Dracaena thalioides***, occur within the main forest block. They grow to about 2 m tall and can be distinguished by the leaf shape: the leaves of *D. aubryana* (28 x 7cm) have a petiole about 7cm long and those of *D. thalioides* (26 x 5cm) have a petiole 25cm long. ***Dracaena fragrans*** is a large tree found occasionally on high ridges in Lopé. It is commonly known as the Dragon Tree, reflecting the Greek meaning of the generic name, which is "female dragon", apparently because some species have red sap like dragon's blood. It grows to about 30 m tall and almost 1 m diameter. It has flakey, yellow-brown bark and is fluted at the base. The canopy is unmistakeable, consisting of tufts of long, leathery leaves about 125 x 4 cm. In some parts of Africa, particularly in montane regions, this species is planted as a fence to demarcate fields. In parts of Gabon it is planted beside trails leading to burial grounds, or as a talisman to protect villages from evil spirits. Hence it is often a good indicator of past human habitation.

Sansevieria trifasciata is a herbaceous plant found on rocks. It has leathery leaves up to about 75 cm long with alternating bands of light and dark green. These leaves give plants of the genus *Sanseviera*, which are common house plants, their English name, 'mother in law's tongue'. The white flowers are observed in March and April.

RUBIACEAE

There are a great diversity of shrubs of the Rubiaceae family in Lopé and in many places they are the commonest plants in the forest under-storey. However, they are difficult to identify, even for a specialist, and tend to go unnoticed except when flowering or fruiting. Only those more likely to catch your attention are presented in this guide.

Bertiera aethiopica grows to about 2-3 m tall. The twigs and both sides of the leaves are covered in a dense pelt of soft, pale hairs. The leaves (9 x 3.5 cm) have 7-12 lateral nerves. The green flowers are about 1 cm long, on a stalk of about 15 cm. The fruits are small, bright blue berries which are eaten by the terrestrial sun-tailed guenon, *Cercopithecus solatus*, a monkey which is only found in the Lopé Reserve, and in the Forêt des Abeilles, to the east.

Left:
Annonaceae lianes (see p. 105)

a) Artabotrys cf. crassipetalus
b) Monanthotaxis congolensis
c) Monanthotaxis diclina
d) Uvaria klaineana
e) Uvaria cf. scabrida
f) Uvaria versicolor

Page 108 :
Rubiaceae lianes

a) Atractogyne gabonii
b) Bertiera cf. letouzeyi
c) Morinda morindoides
d) Mussaenda tenuiflora
e) Polycoryne fernandensis
f) Uncaria africana

Page 109:

a) Dracaena fragrans
b) Dracaena thalioides
c) Sansevieria trifasciata

e
b
c
d
a
f

c
a
b
KA'05

Right:

a) Bertiera aethiopica
b) Bertiera racemosa
c) Oxyanthus unilocularis
d) Pavetta puberula
e) Rothmannia whitfieldii
f) Tricalysia cf. oligoneura

A second species, ***Bertiera racemosa var. elephantina*** occasionally grows up to about 8 m. The large leaves are typically about 24 x 8 cm, but may exceed 35 cm in length. The pale green flowers are about 1.5 cm long. There are usually small nests made of mud in amongst the flowers, occupied by aggressive ants of the genus *Crematogaster*. The green fruits are about 1 cm diameter when ripe, with numerous small black seeds.

Leptactina cf. arnoldiana grows to about 6 m tall and is most often seen along old logging roads. It has large leaves, up to 45 x 18 cm, with up to 25 pairs of bold lateral nerves, which are eaten by elephants. Its striking white flowers are up to 12 cm long.

Oxyanthus unilocularis grows along the forest edge, in young vegetation types and along the Ogooué in Lopé, reaching up to 8 m tall. It has large, asymmetrical leaves (35 x 17 cm) with 14-16 pairs of lateral nerves. Leaves are covered in abrasive hairs on the undersides, producing a texture like sand paper. The white flowers are up to 20 cm long. The green fruits are about 2.5 cm diameter when ripe, containing numerous small seeds.

Pavetta hispida is a small shrub growing to about 1 m tall, found in mature forest in Lopé. It produces eye-catching bunches of white-cream flowers in January / February. A second species, ***Pavetta puberula***, is found throughout the forest, particularly in disturbed areas. It grows to about 5 m tall occasionally reaching over 10 cm diameter. It has smooth, pale bark and leaves (20 x 8 cm) which are eaten by gorillas and elephants. The perfumed white flowers bloom in September / October and the small fruits remain green when ripe.

Psychotria peduncularis is a small shrub, similar to *Psychotria vogeliana* (p. 68), but found mostly within the forest. It can be distinguished from *P. vogeliana* by its hairy leaves and stems, by the leaf shape, and by the fruits, which are bright blue, not white, when ripe.

Rothmannia whitfieldii is typically about 2-5 m tall and is found most often along the forest edge, or occasionally close to rock outcrops within the forest. Its leaves (15 x 7 cm) are arranged in groups of 3, with about 10 lateral nerves and a distinct network of secondary nerves. The flowers are about 20 cm long and develop into a characteristic ridged, green fruit about 7 cm long, which bears a slight resemblance to that of *Massularia acuminata*.

Tricalysia cf. oligoneura grows to about 3 m tall. The leaves (12 x 5 cm) have 6-7 pairs of lateral nerves. Small white flowers, about 8 mm across, line the branches in August. The fruits are small, bright red berries about 6 mm diameter, containing 3-4 seeds. Its flexible wood is used by hunters in Gabon, in snares set to trap small mammals like duikers.

Leptactina cf. arnoldiana

a
d
c
e
b
f

Trees

ANACARDIACEAE

Antrocaryon klaineanum (Onzabili or «antelopes' buttons») is a large tree found most often in mature forest in Lopé. It reaches about 45 m high and 1 m diameter. The base is always swollen by elephant damage. The bark is smooth in part, with tiny rounded scales 2-3 mm across, called lenticels, and elsewhere is cracked and rough, flaking off in roughly rectangular scales. The compound leaves are about 45 cm long, bunched at the ends of the branchlets in star-like whorls. They have 5-8 pairs of opposite leaflets (10 x 3 cm). It has small white flowers which are rarely seen. The ripe yellow fruits are about 3 cm across and hang in bunches and are one of the rare succulent fruits to ripen in the dry season. They consist of a thin, sugary flesh around a flattened stone which looks like a button (p. 214). The fruit has an acidic taste, but is pleasant to eat. However, the slippery flesh is extremely difficult to remove from the stone so the seed is easily swallowed by mistake, despite its relatively large size. This is a character common to many animal dispersed fruits. It is in the trees' interest that animals swallow their seeds whole and deposit them in dung at a later date, thereby dispersing them away from the parent tree. However, this represents a 'cost' to the animal, who fills its stomach with woody, indigestible seeds instead of nutritious food. This is more of a problem for smaller animals, who have smaller stomachs and prefer to spend more time preparing and sorting food, to maximise the digestibility of what they eat. Hence, monkeys tend to spend time sucking and chewing the flesh from around the seed, which they spit out, whilst gorillas, chimpanzees, and particularly elephants, are excellent seed dispersers, because they swallow most fruits whole.

The characteristic, pitted, stone (see p. 214) has five more or less well defined lobes, within which there are five seeds. These are oily and edible, but are difficult to extract because of the thickness of the nut-shell. Carbonised fragments of *Antrocaryon klaineanum* stones have been found in excavations of rubbish pits located around Iron Age villages in Lopé, dating to about 2,300 years ago. A closely related species, with a larger stone, *Antrocaryon micraster*, is known to burst if put in hot cinders. Pre-historic inhabitants of the Lopé area may have collected *Antrocaryon klaineanum* fruits to eat their flesh and seeds.

Lannea welwitschii is a medium to large tree found in galleries and Marantaceae forest, particularly in areas with thin soil. It occasionally reaches 35 m tall and 80 cm diameter. The trunk has no buttresses. The bark is smooth, with numerous lenticels. Highly characteristic pits, where bark has flaked off, are irregularly scattered up the trunk. The compound leaves, about 10-25 cm long, are arranged in sparse, star-like, clusters. They have 1-4 pairs of opposite, asymmetrical, leaflets, with about 10 pairs of prominent lateral nerves. The leaves turn yellow as they age. The tiny flowers are yellowish green, developing into small brown-purple fruits, about 6 mm long. They hang in conspicuous clusters below the leaves and have thin, edible, acidic flesh and small seeds. They are typical of fruits dispersed by birds, and many species eat them in large quantities. The bark can be used to produce a saffron dye.

Pseudospondias longifolia (Ofoss) is a medium sized tree with slight buttresses and yellow-brown, flakey bark. It has compound leaves up to about 50 cm long, with 6-12 pairs of asymmetric, alternate leaflets (15 x 6 cm). Twice a year, in February and July/August, eye-catching panicles of small, greenish-white, flowers grow at the ends of the terminal branches. The plum-like fruits ripen in July/August and in November. They are dark purple, about 4 x 2 cm and when fully ripe are excellent to eat, if a little tart, and are sometimes sold in villages beside the road. The seed is an irregular stone (p. 214). *Pseudospondias longifolia* is quite rare in Lopé, so those trees which fruit in the long dry season become a centre of attention for frugivorous monkeys, apes and birds.

Pseudospondias microcarpa is a medium to large tree, common along watercourses. The crooked, irregular trunk often leans out over the water, with low, spreading buttresses which can extend several metres. The bark is pale and cracked. The leaves are similar to those of *P. longifolia*, but are only about 30 cm long, with 4-7 pairs of leaflets. Leaves are replaced throughout the year and the canopy usually contains soft, pink new leaves and yellow senescing leaflets, as well as mature foliage. The flowers are similar to *P. longifolia*. There are two periods of flowering, in August/November and February/April. The resinous, red-purple, fruits are about 2 x 1 cm when ripe and are edible. They are eaten by many species of animal and bird and are the only tree in which the red-fronted parrot, *Poicephalus gulielmi*, is regularly observed. Like some other plants that grow beside water, their seeds float and are probably dispersed by water as well as by animals. They make good fish bait.

Right:

a) Antrocaryon klaineanum
b) Lannea welwitschii
c) Pseudospondias microcarpa
d) Pseudospondias longifolia

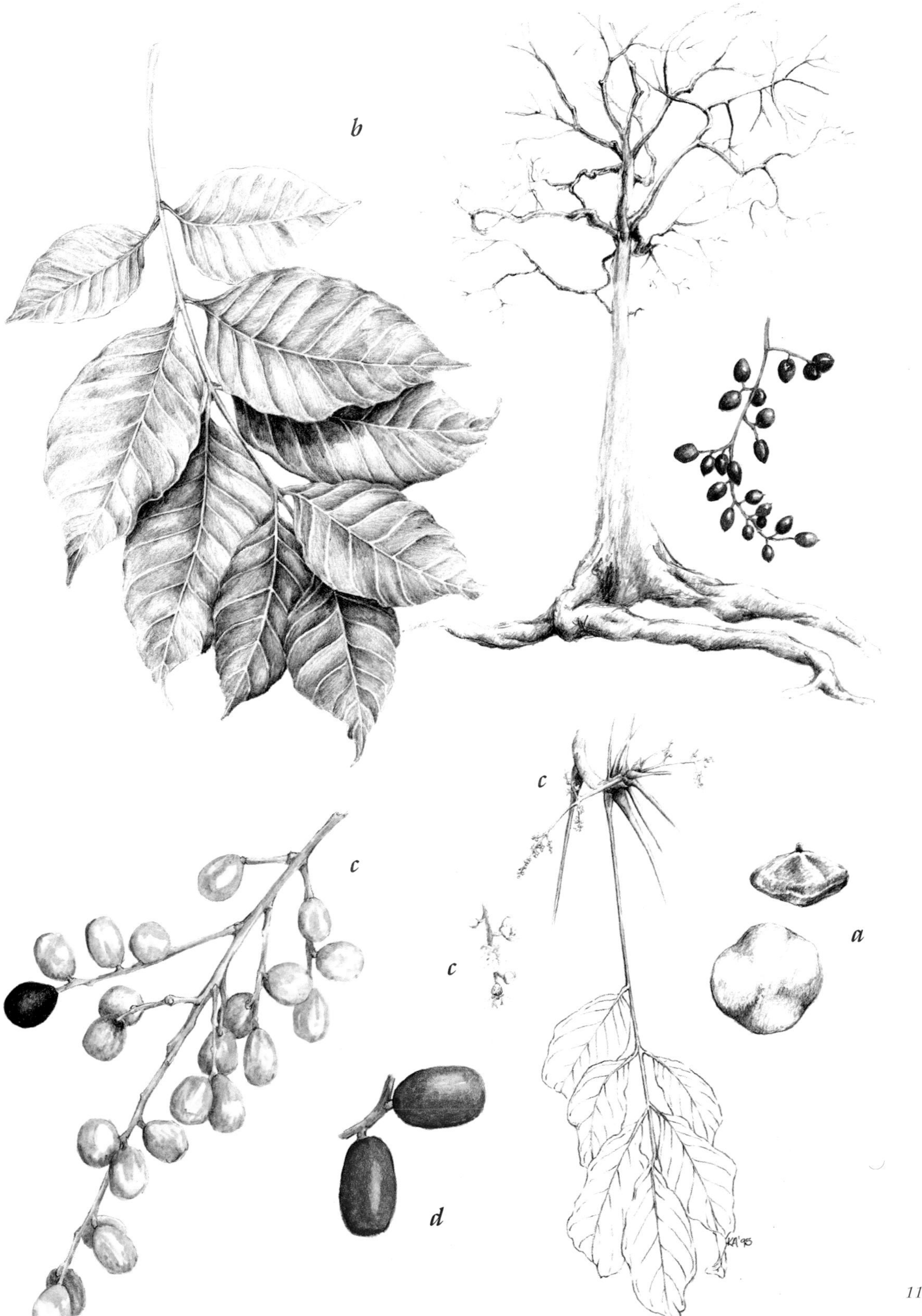
b
c
c
c
a
d
KA'95

Right:

a) Trichoscypha abut
b) Trichoscypha acuminata

Trichoscypha abut & Trichoscypha acuminata are known collectively as the «Raisins du Gabon» (grape of Gabon) or amvout. They are both medium sized trees found in all forest types in Lopé. They can be up to 20 m tall with a diameter of up to about 50 cm. Both species have easily recognised dark brown, fissured bark, with numerous large knobbles from which the flowers grow. There are few, if any, branches and the large compound leaves are arranged in tufts at the end of the trunk.

The leaves of *Trichoscypha abut* are about 2 m long, with about 20 pairs of slightly asymmetrical leaflets (20 x 8 cm). Because of its branching and leaves it resembles a palm tree. The long petioles persist on the ground under the tree and both they and the underside of the leaflets are covered in brown hairs. Flowers develop from the knobbles on the trunk in January. They are in large, drooping, red panicles each with hundreds of small flowers. These develop into dense bunches of cream fruits, which become pale pink as they ripen around Easter. They are much sought after by all the frugivores and are highly appreciated by humans. They are about 7 x 4 cm, with velvety skin and a soft, bright red, fibrous flesh, full of sweet juice, around a large seed (p. 214). They can be eaten directly, but also make excellent juice and ice cream. However, it is quite a rare event in the Lopé to find more than the remains of ripe fruit on the ground, since the numerous forest animals rarely miss such a delicious bonanza.

Trichoscypha acuminata is the commoner of the two species. Its form and trunk are very similar to those of *Trichoscypha abut*. However, it is easily distinguished by its smaller, hairless leaves. The leaves are up to 1 m long, with 6 - 12 pairs of slightly asymmetrical leaflets (15 x 5 cm). Flowers develop from about June onwards. The fruits are similar, but are smaller, about 5 x 2.5 cm, and turn wine red when they ripen in January. They are equally sought after as those of *T. abut*. The bark is sometimes used to treat constipation in infants.

Enantia chlorantha

ANNONACEAE

These are all medium sized trees of the forest understorey. They all have simple, alternate leaves and tend to have branches perpendicular to the trunk.

Annonidium floribundum is a rare tree found only in Gabon, which occurs in mature forest in Lopé. It grows to about 20 m tall and has smooth, dark bark. It has large leaves (25 x 12 cm) with about 12 bold lateral veins. Characteristic large yellow flowers grow on the trunk and larger branches. The fruits are unknown to science. A closely related species, ***Annonidium mannii***, which has not been found in Lopé, has large yellow fruits, up to 50 x 30 cm, which resemble pineapples, with a pleasant sweet-sour taste, much appreciated by humans and animals alike.

Enantia chlorantha is a fairly common tree in Lopé, growing to about 20 m tall and 40 cm diameter, occasionally larger. The smooth, black bark is silvered by lichens, creating an attractive marbled effect. If cut, the unique, vivid yellow inner bark is revealed. The branches grow perpendicular to the trunk, curving down towards their tips and the crown is tall and thin, rising to a point. The leaves (15 x 5 cm) have indistinct lateral nerves. Pale, green-white new leaves are often present at the ends of the branchlets. The flowers resemble those of *Xylopia* (p.74), with yellow-green petals about 2-3 cm long. The fruits are in small bunches amongst the leaves. They are red when ripe from November to February, about 2.5 x 1.2 cm, on a stalk about 2.5 cm long, with a single characteristic seed (p. 214). Chimpanzees eat the resinous fruits, and often nest in *Enantia* trees in the fruiting season, perhaps so they can wake up to a breakfast of fresh fruit.

The wood is often used to make paddles for canoes, and the bark contains quite high concentrations of an alkaloid called Berberine and has many medicinal uses, including treatment of ulcers and malaria. In some parts of Africa this species is becoming very rare, due to the demand for its bark for homeopathic remedies. It is also said to have aphrodisiac properties: the bark is left to soak overnight in a bottle of water and the resulting solution is drunk to improve male sexual performance.

Neostanthera robsonii is a rare tree found only in Gabon, which is restricted to the higher slopes of some mountains in mature forest in Lopé. It grows to about 15 m and 25 cm diameter. The trunk is dark and fissured. The leaves (20 x 7 cm) are olive-green above and paler below, covered in soft, blond hairs. There are about 16-20 pairs of highly visible lateral nerves. The persistent fruits, which grow on the trunk and larger branches in bunches of 30-40, resemble those of *Uvaria klaineana* (see p. 105). They are about 1 cm long, on a stalk of about 3 cm and are covered in brown hairs.

a
a
b
a
b
KA'94

Right:

a) Annonidium floribundum
b) Enantia chlorantha
c) Polyalthia suaveolens
d) Uvariastrum pierreanum

Polyalthia (Greenwayodendron) suaveolens is a common understorey tree within the main forest block, closely resembling *Enantia chlorantha*. There are two varieties, *Polyalthia suaveolens gabonica* and *P. s. suaveolens*, both of which are found in Lopé. The former is the commoner of the two. The marbling on its trunk is less vivid than in *Enantia*, being dark brown and grey-green, and the inner bark is pale brown, with a strong resinous odour. The leaves (15 x 6 cm) with bold lateral nerves, are covered in very short brown hairs on their undersides. They are similar to the leaves of *Beilschmiedia fulva* (p. 134). The green-brown flowers are similar to those of *Enantia chlorantha* and the fruits are spheres about 1.5 cm diameter, with characteristic seeds (p. 214). Small bunches of fruits are crowded along the larger branches and more sparsely distributed amongst the foliage. They become reddish as they ripen from November to March. The resinous pulp is eaten by several of the monkeys and by chimpanzees. The second variety, *P. s. suaveolens* is rare in Lopé, but occurs patchily in the main forest block. It is larger than *P. s. gabonensis*, reaching 40 m tall and 70 cm diameter and has small, hairless leaves (9 x 3 cm). The wood is very hard and resists insect attack, so is a favoured timber for construction and furniture making. The powdered bark is a remedy for stomach aches.

Uvariastrum pierreanum is common in young forest types, in the forest savanna mosaic and in Marantaceae Forest, but rare in mature forest. It grows to about 25 m tall and 40 cm diameter, but is generally smaller. The trunk is irregularly fluted, particularly in larger trees, similar to that of *Trichilia prieureana* (p. 148). The bark is grey-brown and flakes off in long, thin rectangles. The crown is tall and slender. The leaves (12 x 3.5 cm) have 9-12 pairs of looped lateral nerves and have a characteristic wavy edge. The flower buds are like small, grey pyramids on long stalks growing off the top of the trunk and the branches. They open in September and October into attractive yellow flowers, about 5 cm across, with a strong perfume. The fruits are in bunches of up to 5-6. They are yellow when ripe from January to March, about 8 x 3.5 cm, with a soft, velvety skin. The flesh around the seeds is a little tart, but excellent to eat. The characteristic seeds (p. 214) are found in large numbers in the dung of gorillas, chimpanzees and elephants, the major seed dispersers, but the fruits are also eaten by many other animals.

Uvariastrum pierreanum

BURSERACEAE

Like Okoumé (p. 80), the other Burseraceae trees have compound leaves and secrete sticky, resinous sap if injured. They also tend to have good quality timber. However, unlike Okoumé, which has dry, wind dispersed seeds, the other Burseraceae species have succulent fruits which are eaten by animals.

Dacryodes buettneri (Ozigo or wild Atanga) like Okoumé, has a limited distribution, restricted mostly to Gabon. It produces a soft, white plywood valued almost as much as that of Okoumé. It is one of the most striking and easily recognised large trees found in the forest. It can exceed 50 m tall and 150 cm diameter. The bark is sulphurous yellow and peels off the trunk in long, thin scales. The base of the trunk tends to be slightly fluted, with low rounded buttresses. The branches form a tangled crown which is particularly striking from below because of the coppery glow of the foliage. Its leaves have about 5-8 opposite leaflets, each about 12 x 3 cm. The leaflets are asymmetrical at the base and narrow to a long, pointed tip. Above they are dark and shiny, but the underside is covered by a golden down of short, soft hairs. The flowers are small and similar in colour to the underside of the leaf. They are held erect above the canopy, on panicles up to about 30 cm long. When *Dacryodes buettneri* flower from September to November their golden canopies stand out from afar. The fruits are also held above the canopy to display them to arboreal and avian seed dispersers. When young, fruits are pale green, ripening to shiny blue-black. They are the form of cocktail sausages, about 3-4 x 1.5 cm and contain a single, large seed of similar shape, enclosed in resinous, olive-green flesh. This flesh is excellent to eat when cooked, by soaking in boiling water for a minute or so and then dipped in salt.

Many animal species feed on the fruit. As their fruits ripen, *Dacryodes buettneri* trees attract huge, raucous flocks of African grey parrots, several species of hornbill and large mixed troops of monkeys. Chimpanzees also eat large amounts of the fruit and when they find a big tree with a good fruit crop they utter loud, excited vocalisations, to call in other members of their group to the feast.

a
c
d
b

Right:

Dacryodes buettneri

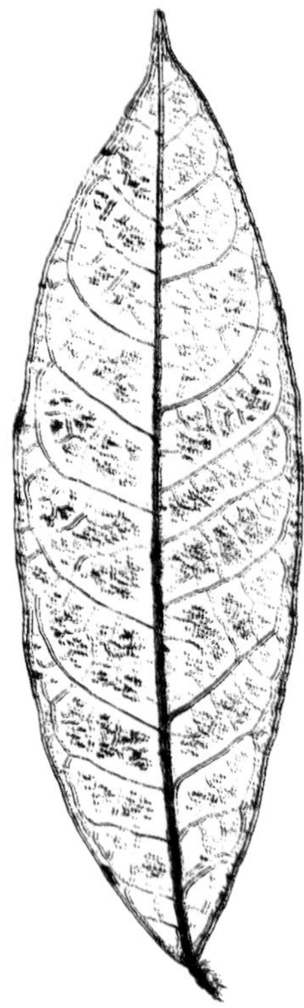

***Dacryodes normandii* leaflet**

Gorillas, on the other hand, never eat *Dacryodes buettneri* fruits. There are several species of bacteria which are only found in the digestive system of gorillas. These are thought to help gorillas digest some of the leaves and stems which they eat and it is, therefore, very important that the gorillas maintain a healthy 'gut flora'. The nutritious flesh of *Dacryodes buettneri* fruits is rich in oils, and it is thought that these may inhibit some of the bacteria and upset the workings of the gorillas' digestive system, rather like when we take antibiotics.

The fruit resembles that of ***Dacryodes edulis***, commonly known as 'Atanga', a tree species which is rare in Lopé's forests, but which has been domesticated and is grown in villages in much of west and central Africa. This species has conspicuous rust-coloured panicles of flowers and larger fruits, up to 7 x 3.5 cm, which hang in large bunches. These are bright pink when young, ripening to blue-black. They are prepared in the same way as *Dacryodes buettneri*.

When it becomes large, the trunk of ***Dacryodes normandii*** (Ossabel) is similar in appearance to *D. buettneri*. However, it is generally a medium sized tree of up to about 40 cm diameter on which the golden bark tends not to be particularly flakey. It has quite long compound leaves. The asymmetrical leaflets (20 x 5 cm) are larger than those of *D. buettneri*. They have long, sparse hairs on the underside, but lack the golden colouration of *D. buettneri*. The fruits are shorter and fatter. They have a sweet, succulent flesh, which tastes very like gooseberries and is eaten by most of the forest frugivores, including gorillas.

Canarium schweinfurthii (Aiélé) is a large tree found in most forest types in Lopé. It can reach 50 m or more in height and up to almost 2 m diameter. The trunk is usually straight and branchless. It has pale grey, scaly bark, with quite obvious vertical fissures which become more pronounced as the tree ages. If wounded it weeps clear resin which, as in other Burseraceae, smells like turpentine and sets in a hard, sulphur-yellow layer. This contains essential oils and is sometimes used as incense, burning with a smokey, lavender-scented flame. In some places the soot is collected to make ink or for use in body tattooing. During the Second World War the resin was used as a replacement for gum-mastic in making wound-dressings and in many parts of Africa it is used to treat skin complaints such as eczema.

The compound leaves are arranged in star-like whorls at the end of branchlets. They generally have about 12 pairs and 1 terminal leaflet (12 x 4 cm) with strong veination. *Canarium schweinfurthii* is a deciduous species, losing all of its leaves at one time and then flushing with a whole canopy of bright young buds. However, unlike trees in temperate regions which lose their leaves each winter, there seems to be no specific season for *Canarium schweinfurthii*, which can have young leaves in any month of the year in Lopé. The new leaves and branchlets are covered in short, rusty hairs.

The pale yellow flowers are about 1 cm long, on narrow panicles which develop among the leaves at the ends of the branchlets in March / June. The fruits ripen in October / November. These are similar to those of *Dacryodes buettneri*, another Burseraceae. They are black when ripe and are held above the canopy to attract their major seed dispersers, the hornbills. They are eaten by many other animals, including chimpanzees, which are their other major seed disperser. Their hard, pointed seeds are triangular in cross section (p. 214) and make attractive necklaces. In some places they are also strung and attached to calabashes to make musical instruments. In some parts of Africa the fruits are considered a delicacy, when softened in warm water. During the fruiting season, whole communities of people move into the forest to collect them. However, in Lopé they are rarely eaten, perhaps because the hornbills and chimpanzees devour most of the fruit on the tree. The seed-kernel is oily and can be eaten cooked or made into vegetable-butter used in cooking.

Santiria trimera (Ebo) is a medium sized tree found in mature forest and some galleries. It has characteristic thin, vertically flattened, arched, stilt roots and if you make a small cut in the bark it has a strong, resinous smell like that of young mangoes. It has umber coloured bark, which flakes off in irregular patches. The compound leaves have 2-4 pairs of generally quite large leaflets and a single terminal one with a longer stalk. It has small yellow-green flowers, about 5 mm across, on narrow panicles, which mostly develop from the leaf-axils. The flattened fruits are about 3 cm across, and resemble damsons. They are red-purple when ripe and contain a characteristic seed (p. 214) surrounded by a thin, sugary flesh. The fruits are eaten by many animals. They smell of turpentine, but taste like wine and are much appreciated by humans in Gabon. In some parts of Africa the tree is cultivated and its fruits sold at markets. The oily seed is also consumed by man in some places.

KA'95

Right:

a) Canarium schweinfurthii
b) Santiria trimera

CHRYSOBALANACEAE

The Chrysobalanaceae include about 450 species of tree and shrub, many occurring only in America. They are closely related to, and used to be classified within, the Rosaceae, which contain familiar trees such as apple, cherry and peach. There are several species of medium and large trees in Lopé.

Acioa pallescens is a large shrub or tree, to about 10 m tall, found most often on the edge of galleries. The alternate leaves are thick and waxy, about 12 x 6 cm, with a short, thick petiole and two small stipules. Two glands are visible on the underside of the leaf just above the petiole. It produces very conspicuous flowers in October / November in large bunches at the ends of the shoots. These have 5 white petals, each about 1 cm long with 5 sepals covered in a pelt of grey-green hairs. There are numerous fused green stamens, about 4 cm long, which project out of the flower and split at their apex to form a bushy tail. The fruits (4 x 2.5 cm) are brown with a sparse covering of long hairs and a dense undercoat, which penetrate the skin like the hairs of a caterpillar if touched.

Chrysobalanus icaco atacorensis (Icaquier), like *Symphonia globulifera* (p. 169) is one of the few species found both in Africa and the New World. In tropical and sub-tropical America it is often cultivated as an ornamental shrub. It is a shrub or small tree growing to just over 10 m, found in forest galleries in the savanna and along the Ogooué. The leaves (6 x 2.5 cm) are small and leathery, with sparse fine hairs on the underside and on the smaller branchlets. It has small white flowers and characteristic ridged fruits, about 2 cm long, with a thin, sugary, edible flesh surrounding its hard stone. The seed, rich in oil and sugar, is used by humans in some parts of Africa and tastes like a sunflower seed.

Licania elaeosperma is a tree up to almost 20 m high. It is found in galleries close to and along the Ogooué, generally in moist gulleys. It has a crooked, irregular, trunk with small buttresses, and drooping branches and foliage. The leaves are about 11 x 4 cm. The tree is most noticeable in July / August when covered in tiny green-white flowers, which develop into a characteristic warty, egg shaped, fruit about 5 cm long. This contains a nut about 3 cm long within which there is a single large seed. The seed is about 50 % 'po-yok oil', which can be used as a drying oil in paint manufacture. The oil is also used as a body perfume and as a conditioner in hair-dressing, which is said to stimulate hair growth.

Magnistipula zenkeri (Efot) is found in galleries within the forest, often overhanging the water. It is a medium-sized tree growing to about 15 m tall and 40 cm diameter. The rough bark is pale grey and the trunk twisted. The alternate leaves (12 x 4 cm) each have two fine stipules, about 5 mm long, at their base. When young the leaves are vivid purple. The white flowers are in small bunches at the ends of the shoots. These are pollinated by ants, which are attracted by a honey-like secretion from special glands in the flowers. The large potato-like fruits about 8 cm across. These are pale brown, with thick flesh around a single large seed. The flesh is eaten by pigs, duikers and mandrills, but it seems that the major means of seed dispersal is by water. The fruits fall into the water and float away downstream.

Maranthes aubrevillei is a large tree found principally in galleries and bosquets in the savanna, although it is also present in the main forest block. It grows up to about 40 m tall and about 1 m diameter. The characteristic blackish bark is marked by many patches of white lichen. The bark is smooth, with fine vertical fissures. The trunk is straight and without buttresses. The leaves, like many Chrysobalanaceae, have two glands on their short fat petioles. They are about 10 x 4.5 cm, with about 8-9 bold lateral veins and an intricate pattern of tertiary veins. The young leaves are bright red and when flushing in a gallery *Maranthes aubrevillei* is particularly striking. It has small white flowers and hard, dry, fibrous fruits.

Maranthes gabunensis (Afatouk) is a medium sized tree. It grows to about 20m tall and 60 cm diameter. The dark bark is smooth and often appears marbled by lichens. The large leaves (20 x 10 cm), with prominent lateral veins are similar to those of *Strombosiopsis tetrandra* (p. 182), but can be distinguished when found on the ground by their shorter stalk, with two obvious glands close to the leaf. The flowers are arranged in groups of 10-20 on a curved stalk about 15 cm long. They have an obvious receptacle, about 3 cm long. The white petals are about 1.5 cm long, with about 40 bushy, white, anthers which project about 3 cm out of the flower. The fruits are dry nuts with a thin green skin, which contain two small seeds. They are probably dispersed by monkeys and rodents.

a
b
KA'95
KA'95

Right:

a) Acioa pallescens
b) Magnistipula zenkeri
c) Maranthes aubrevillei
d) Maranthes gabunensis
e) Maranthes glabra
f) Parinari excelsa

Maranthes glabra (Ekoulebang) is a large tree up to about 40 m tall and 80 cm dimeter, common in mature forest. The flakey bark is yellow-brown and there are sometimes slight, low buttresses. It has dense, dark green foliage. The alternate leaves (9 x 5 cm) are tough and leathery and glossy above. There are two glands on the stalk, but these are sometimes indistinct. The flowers are white, about 1 cm across, in bunches held erect above the canopy. The dry, woody, brown fruits are about 4 x 2.5 cm. They contain two edible, oily, but well protected seeds. In some parts of Africa, but not in the Lopé, chimpanzees break into the seeds using stone tools, and red river hogs can crack the fruit open in their jaws. The main seed dispersers are probably rodents.

Parinari excelsa (Ossang eli or the Guinea plum) is quite a rare large tree, restricted to mature forest. It has rough grey-yellow bark, which flakes off in irregular scales. The base has slight buttresses. It has large, widely spreading, branches, with a distinctive golden-brown crown when viewed from below. The alternate leaves (8 x 4 cm) have a short stalk with two obvious glands on the upper side and are dark green above. There are 15-20 pairs of bold lateral veins and the underside is covered by a conspicuous golden-brown felt. It produces large numbers of highly visible, dirty-white, sweet-scented, flowers, which develop into large fruits about 5 cm long with a rough, brown, warty skin. The fruit has a soft, yellowish, edible, pulp with a flavour similar to that of an avocado. This is nutritious, containing about 40% sugar and can be fermented to make an alcoholic drink. The large stone is extremely hard and difficult to crack, but if opened contains two seeds packed in a cottony wool, which makes excellent fire-tinder. The oily kernel is also edible and is often roasted and added to other foods. As for many species with large seeds, the only seed disperser is the elephant.

CLUSIACEAE

Pentadesma butyracea (Agnuhé) is a medium sized tree which is most common in Marantaceae Forest. It grows to be over 30 m tall and can be up to 1 m diameter. The bark is dark brown, with a rough, flakey texture and the base is always swollen by elephant damage. The angular branches jut out perpendicular to the trunk, in a characteristic whorl. It has opposite leaves, as do all the Clusiaceae, which are quite leathery and typically about 11 x 4 cm. These are covered by a dense network of parallel veins and numerous translucent dots. Yellow sap, a characteristic of plants in the Clusiaceae, can often be seen oozing out of wounds on the trunk where elephants have fed. As the sap dries it darkens, becoming orange, then black. Be careful not to get it on your clothing, as it is a powerful dye which will leave permanent black marks. If you look closely you will probably find small yellow insects sheltering in crevices in the trunk. These seem to have evolved a camouflage which enables them to blend in with the *Pentadesma* sap.

Pentadesma butyracea

Large, cream coloured flowers bloom from March / September, held in bunches like chandeliers. Fallen flowers are generally evident on the ground below and when fresh these also ooze yellow sap. They are about 5 cm long, with fleshy petals, numerous bushy stamens and have a fresh odour. They produce large quantities of nectar, which is food for many of the primates, who are probably one of its major pollinators, but who also destroy many of the flowers. The first fruits ripen in September, but the bulk of the crop matures in October / December, with some trees retaining fruit into February. The large brown fruits measure about 15 x 10 cm and weigh up to about 1 kg. At their base they have a dark red-brown 'wig' of persistent stamens. Each fruit contains up to 10 large seeds embedded in a fleshy yellow pulp full of sticky sap. The seeds, which contain large quantities of oil, used to be consumed by humans and are eaten unripe by gorillas. When the fruit is ripe the flesh is sweet and quite pleasant to eat. It makes excellent sorbet. However, when under-ripe it is bitter because of the large quantities of tannins it contains. The fruits are eaten by several of the monkey species as well as by gorillas and elephants. During the fruiting season elephants open up large paths connecting all the *Pentadesma* trees, creating an intricate network of trails. Only they swallow and disperse the large seeds.

Gorillas are particularly fond of the ripe flesh of *Pentadesma*, although they also eat the seeds of unripe fruits. As a group of gorillas approach a fruiting tree they utter excited 'food grunts', and there is often an undignified rush as the tree comes into sight, since there will not be room for everybody up in the canopy. It is a mystery therefore why their close relatives, the chimpanzees, have never been observed to eat either the fruit or seeds of *Pentadesma*.

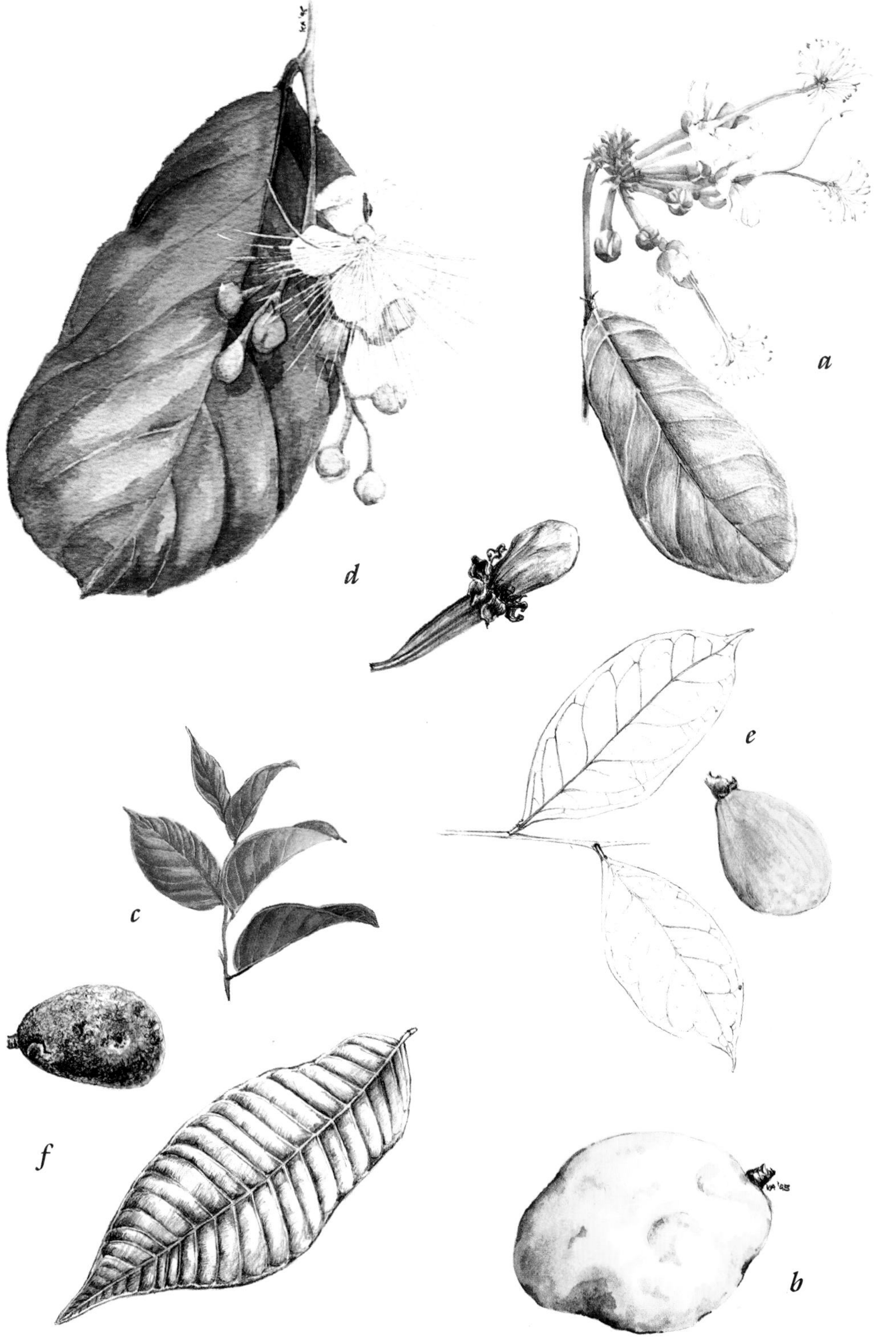
a
d
e
c
f
b

Right:

a) Pentadesma butyracea
b) Pentadesma grandifolia

A second species, ***Pentadesma grandifolia***, was recently found in the Lopé. This species, which is common in semi-montane forests on Mount Cameroon, had never before been found in Gabon. It can easily be recognised by its characteristic silvery-black bark, which has a regular pattern of square fissures. Otherwise it resembles *Pentadesma butyracea*, but is generally smaller. The leaves average about 8 x 4 cm; the flowers are 3 - 4 cm long, with fewer stamens; and the ridged fruit is about 7 x 8 cm, containing only one or two seeds. This species is found only on a few of the highest mountains in Lopé and is thought to be left over from a time when Africa's climate was much cooler, and montane forests extended to lower altitudes than today. *Pentadesma grandifolia*, like its larger relative, is dependant on elephants as seed dispersers, although its fruit has a dryer flesh with an unpleasant taste.

DIPTEROCARPACEAE

Today this family is a minor component of the African flora, although it is thought that it originated eastern Africa. In Asia large trees in the genera *Dipterocarpus, Hopea, Parashorea* and *Shorea* dominate the forest. In the forests of Indomalaysia and Indochina these genera often form pure stands. All of the Dipterocarpaceae are wind dispersed. Their seeds have wings and are quite small and light, in order to maximise dispersal distance. They lack large food reserves, so tend to germinate immediately, and have no mechanical protection to discourage potential seed predators. However, they have adopted a strategy to avoid having all of their seed crop eaten. They do not flower and fruit every year, but are somehow synchronised to do so in the same year. In this way there is a huge production which swamps the animals which eat seeds with a glut of food. They are unable to eat all of the seed crop, so some are left to germinate and grow. This is an good example of how animals, as well as weather, can affect the timing of flowering and fruiting.

Marquesia excelsa (Ntana) is the only Dipterocarp occurring in the African rain forest. It tends to occur in low lying areas close to rivers, where it sometimes forms small stands. It is a large tree which can grow to be 50 m tall and resembles *Sacoglottis gabonensis* to some extent (p. 82). The shaggy bark is dark brown. It has large, thin, buttresses which rise high up the trunk. The trunk itself is fluted and crooked and tends to branch low, into a rectangular canopy. The alternate leaves, about 10 x 3.5 cm, have quite strong veination. The fruits ripen in February / March and are unmistakable, with 5 dry wings each about 2.5 cm long. They are produced in large numbers and when the wind gusts they are released, revolving to the ground like a swarm of tiny helicopters.

LUXEMBOURGIACEAE

This family has only one African representative, although as for the Dipterocarpaceae, it is important elsewhere; in this case mainly in Brazil.

Testulea gabonensis (Izombé) bears a resemblance to *Lophira alata* (p.88), reflecting the fact that the Luxemburgiaceae family is closely related to the Ochnaceae. It is a large tree, found in the main forest block, which grows to up to about 50 m tall and just over 1 m diameter. The bark is yellow-brown and flakes off in irregular scales. It has narrow rounded buttresses which can rise quite high up the otherwise straight, cylindrical trunk. The leaves are about 20 x 5 cm and are bunched towards the ends of the branches. They resemble the leaves of *Lophira alata* from a distance but when viewed close up are easily recognised by their wavy edge and distinct nervation. The flowers have 4 pink petals and develop into characteristic air-filled capsules, about 4 cm long, with 2 valves. When young green fruit fall to the ground in January it is difficult to walk past a *Testulea* tree without making loud popping noises, as the capsules burst underfoot. The fruits dry and open along the join between the two valves, releasing small wind dispersed seeds about 2 cm long, which resemble those of *Hippocratea myrioneura* (p. 164) and are a favourite food of grey parrots. There is a high demand for the wood in Libreville for furniture making and carpentry.

EUPHORBIACEAE

The Euphorbiaceae includes a large number of tree species, some of which can become abundant in the forest understorey. Their leaves are almost always alternate and flowers are always either male or female and are often on separate plants. A well known species introduced from South America, *Hevea brasiliensis*, is the source of industrial rubber and is grown in plantations in Gabon.

Alchornea hirtella is a shrub or small tree up to 10 m tall, found on higher ridges in mature forest in Lopé. The leaves are typically about 13 x 5 cm. It is easily recognised by its characteristic fruits (see p. 213).

Alchornea hirtella

b
b
a

Right:

a) Marquesia excelsa
b) Testulea gabonensis

Page 128:

Conceveiba macrostachys,
a new species restricted to Lopé and the surrounding region

Page 129:

a) Duvigneaudia inopinata
b) Mareya micrantha
c) Mareyopsis longifolia
d) Phyllanthus diandrus
e) Plagiostyles africana

Sapium ellipticum

Duvigneaudia inopinata is a medium sized tree growing to about 20 m tall and 50 cm diameter. It is found close to water in the main forest block. The smooth bark is pale grey. The leaves are typically about 10 x 3 cm. The most distinguishing feature of this species is its large fruit (4 x 7 cm) with a warty, pale grey-brown skin on its hard outer shell, which splits into 3 sections when ripe.

Mareya micrantha is a small tree which grows to just over 10 m tall. It occurs in small populations within the main forest block, often close to water, but is generally rare. The pale bark is flakey. It has characteristic, slightly toothed leaves, which are dark above and pale below, with 4-8 pairs of upcurving lateral nerves and a well defined pattern of secondary nerves. The leaves (12 x 5cm) have a finely hairy stalk of about 2 cm. *Mareya* is most often noticed when in flower in September and October. The flowers are on slender spikes which can be over 30 cm long, growing from the leaf axils. Several tiny, cream coloured, fragrant male flowers are arranged around each female flower. Fruits are about 5 mm across, with 3 distinct lobes.

The generic name of ***Mareyopsis longifolia*** is derived from the Greek for "like *Mareya*". It is a small tree up to about 10 m tall, which becomes common in the understorey in parts of the mature forest in Lopé. It has dark brown bark and the smaller branches are finely hairy. The leaves (30 x 8 cm) have a stalk about 3 cm long and as many as 20 pairs of prominent lateral nerves, each running to a tooth on the leaf margin. The flowers are on slender stalks up to about 20 cm long. Female flowers are solitary, surrounded by dense clusters of tiny, red, male flowers. The fruits have 2 or 3 lobes and are about 1.2 cm deep and 2.5 cm across. They are pink when ripe in March, hanging in eye-catching bunches on the trunk and main branches.

Further south in the Lopé ***Conceveiba macrostachys***, a species similar in appearance to *Mareyopsis longifolia*, becomes common. Its leaves are similar, but can exceed 50 cm long, have a longer stem and are more coarsely toothed. It has wine-red flowers on long stalks and red fruits similar to those of *Mareyopsis longifolia*. This species was discovered in Lopé in 1988 and is the first African record of a genus which is common in South America. In some parts of the Reserve it dominates the middle canopy, with over 5,000 trees occurring per square kilometre, but it seems to be restricted to the southern half of the Lopé and the surrounding region. In fact, the distribution of this species is very similar to that of the endemic sun-tailed guenon, *Cercopithecus solatus* (see p. 107) and is further evidence that a forest refuge existed in the Lopé region during a dry climatic phase in the past.

Phyllanthus diandrus is a small tree to about 5 m or, more frequently, a coppicing shrub with numerous stems. Its bark is brown, with small, regular vertical fissures which are a good distinguishing feature. Its characteristic 2-3 lobed green fruits, about 1 cm across, dangle on thin stalks about 5 cm long. ***Phyllanthus polyanthus*** is a medium sized tree up to about 20 m tall and 50 cm diameter, found in the main forest block. It has pale, lenticelled bark. The papery leaves are about 6 x 4 cm, with indistinct lateral nerves and are arranged on small branchlets which can give the impression of long compound leaves. The fruits are green spheres about 1.5 cm diameter, also dangling on thin stalks about 4 cm long. A third species. ***Margaritaria discoidea***, previously known as *Phyllanthus discoideus*, occurs in the savanna-forest mosaic. It has unmistakeable, blackish-brown, flakey, fibrous bark. Its flattened fruits, about 1 cm across, on slender stalks about 0.5 cm long, attract large, noisy flocks of green fruit pigeons when ripe in the long dry season.

Plagiostyles africana is a medium sized tree up to 25 m high and 60 cm diameter. It has smooth, milk chocolate coloured bark, with patches of characteristic horizontal ridges, like elephant skin. It has a dense canopy. The slightly serrated leaves are about 12 x 4.5 cm, and turn bright yellow as they age, before falling from the tree. The sweet red fruits ripen on female trees in October / December and are eaten by both gorillas and chimpanzees.

Sapium ellipticum is a medium sized tree growing to about 35 m tall and 60 cm diameter. The bark is pale and smooth on young trees, but becomes dark brown and fissured on older individuals. The leaves (8 x 4 cm) turn bright red as they age. The leaf margin has shallow, wavy teeth and numerous, indistinct lateral veins, making fallen red leaves easy to identify. The tiny yellowish flowers are on spikes about 3-5 cm long, with both male and female flowers. The 2-lobed fruits, borne on slender stalks about 5 mm long, are about 8 mm across, crowned with persistent, coiled styles. They turn orange-red when ripe and are probably dispersed by birds.

a
b

KA97

b
a
c
e
d
KA'95
KA'94

Right:

a) Caloncoba glauca
b) Camptostylus mannii
c) Casearia barteri
d) Scottellia coriacea

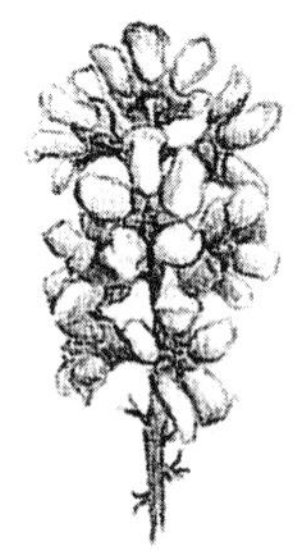

Homalium sarcopetalum

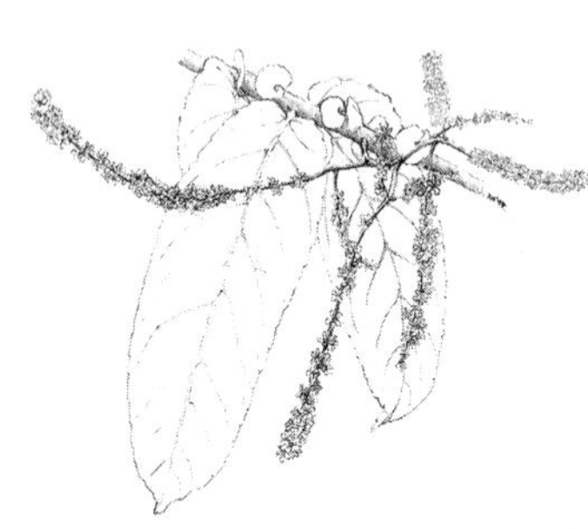

FLACOURTIACEAE

The Flacourtiaceae are mostly shrubs and small-medium sized trees, with simple, alternate leaves. Several species are found in Lopé.

Caloncoba glauca is a medium sized forest tree often found quite close to rivers and streams, particularly in Marantaceae Forest in Lopé. It has brownish bark and is generally less than 20 m tall. The leaf is typically about 20 x 6 cm, with open veination and a stalk about 5-6 cm long. The intricate flowers are large rosettes with about 10 white petals, each about 5 cm long and a mass of yellow anthers at the centre. These can be seen during much of the year. The young fruits are fluted and pointed, at the end of stout stalks about 5 cm long. When ripe they are yellowish, about 6 cm across, with a firm flesh containing numerous seeds. The fruits are said to be edible. The seeds contain an oil which used to be used to treat leprosy, and syphilis. Leaf sap is rubbed into the temples to relieve migraines in Congo.

Camptostylus mannii is a medium-sized forest tree growing to almost 20 m tall, although it often flowers when much smaller, particularly when growing close to the forest edge. The smooth bark is pinkish-brown. The leaves are similar to those of *Caloncoba glauca*, but have lateral nerves which form closed loops. The flowers and fruits also resemble those of *Caloncoba glauca*, but the white petals are only about 1.5 cm long and the fruits, which ripen in February / March, about 2.5 cm across.

Casearia barteri is a medium sized tree which grows to about 25 m tall and 50 cm diameter. It has smooth, golden bark covered in lenticels and irregular vertical fissures. The leaves are typically about 15 x 5 cm, resembling those of many *Beilschmiedia* species found in Lopé (p. 134), with which *Casearia barteri* is easily confused. The small flowers, about 6 mm across, lack petals but have 6 greenish-white sepals which persist on the fruit. The conspicuous bright yellow fruit are clustered along the length of the branches. They are about 5 cm long with three fleshy valves which open as the fruits ripen to reveal numerous seeds in a bright pink, rotten-smelling pulp.

Homalium letestui is the commonest of several species of *Homalium* which occur in Lopé. It is a medium sized tree which can grow to over 30 m tall and up to about 80 cm diameter. It is generally found in gallery forests in the savanna or close to rock outcrops in Marantaceae Forest. The bark is greyish to dark red-brown. It is smooth, with some vertical cracks and sometimes flakes off in patches. The base of the trunk is often damaged by elephant feeding and sometimes has high, irregular, buttresses. The branches tend to be short and the crown arranged in tiers high on the trunk. The characteristic large, leathery leaves (20 x 10 cm) have serrated margins. Leaves are shed in the long dry season and the crown flushes with garish red, new leaves. The pink-brown flowers form large, striking bunches, in January / February. The flowers have 5-6 petals, each about 8 mm long, which are characteristic of the genus as a whole. A second species, ***Homalium sarcopetalum***, is found along rocky galleries in savanna close to the Ogooué. It can be distinguished from *Homalium letestui* by its smaller leaves (15 x 7 cm) with small, ear like stipules, and by its flowers, which have small, green-white petals, only about 3 mm long.

Lindackeria dentata is a rare shrub or small tree found in young forest in Lopé. It is most easily recognised by its coarsly toothed, rounded leaves (13 x 9cm) on a stalk about 10 cm long and by its prickly green-orange fruits. The fruits open to reveal a few black, shiny seeds with red arils.

Scottellia coriacea is a medium sized tree which can grow up to about 35 m tall and 80 cm diameter, although it is usually much smaller. It occurs in most forest types in Lopé but is most common close to rock outcrops. It has smooth, pale, green-brown bark and is slightly fluted at the base in larger individuals. The branches curve down towards the ground, particularly in smaller individuals, rather like those of *Napoleona vogelii* (p. 170). The leathery leaves (8 x 4cm) are lightly serrated on the upper half of the margin. *Scottellia* produces numerous small white flowers, about 5 mm across, in December / January. The characteristic spherical fruits are about 8 mm diameter opening to reveal small seeds with thin, bright red arils. These arils are eaten by many of the monkeys. Rocky areas, where *Scottellia* is common, become a centre of attention when it is fruiting, from January to April and fruit remains litter the ground. The wood was used traditionally to make household items such as spoons and combs.

d
b
a
c
KA'95

Right:

a) Irvingia gabonensis
b) Irvingia grandifolia
c) Desbordesia glaucescens

Irvingia gabonensis

The forest elephant, *Loxodonta africana cyclotis*, has small rounded ears, tusks pointing down to the ground and is smaller than the savanna or bush elephant, *L. a. africana*

IRVINGIACEAE

Irvingia gabonensis (Andok, chocolatier or bush mango) is a large tree found in all forest types in Lopé. When viewed from afar it has dense, bushy, dark green foliage, which rises into numerous turret-like points in the crown. The base of the trunk is invariably scarred and swollen from elephant damage. It is often lightly fluted, particularly in larger trees, with slight buttresses. The bark is pale. In younger individuals it is smooth, but becomes flakey in older trees. When viewed from below the wide, spreading branches are enclosed in a dense crown of foliage. They have an unusual form, intertwined like the coiled serpents of medusa's hair. The pale young leaves are enclosed within a protective stipule. Mature leaves are up to 15 x 7 cm, but more typically are about 9 x 5 cm. It has small clusters of unremarkable, greenish flowers from September / November. The fruit is 5-7 cm long, somewhat resembling a mango. When ripe in January / February it has smooth, yellowish skin with sweet, fibrous pulp surrounding a large stone. This contains a single large seed, which is delicious when roasted. The seeds are highly appreciated throughout Africa, and each year many fruits are collected and cracked. They are an important source of income for many rural communities. The seeds are pounded into a block, which resembles chocolate - hence the tree's common name. In Gabon this is used to prepare a traditional dark brown sauce, particularly appreciated with game meat and fish.

The fruits are eaten by many animal species but only elephants and adult gorillas swallow the seeds. When there is a lot of fruit around both of these animals have diarrhetic dung, because of the large quantities of fruit they eat. Both pass the seeds undamaged in their dung. They are vital seed dispersers, since almost all seeds left lying under or close to the parent tree are extracted and eaten by red river hogs and rodents. In some parts of Ivory Coast, where all the elephants have been killed by poachers, *Irvingia gabonensis* no longer regenerates, except when planted by man around villages.

Irvingia grandifolia (Olène) is a large tree which can exceed 45 m in height. Larger trees have high, thick buttresses, but these are often distorted by elephant damage. It has thick, spreading branches, which give the crown a sparse, open appearance, particularly when viewed from below. The large leaves are up to 25 x 15 cm, with numerous parallel veins. They turn bright red when old. It is unusual to find a tree without a flash of red, unless the whole crown is flushing with pale young leaves. Its small white flowers form in September / October, arranged on spikes up to 15 cm long. The fruits ripen in December / January and are similar to those of *Irvingia gabonensis*, but are smaller, only about 2.5 cm long, and less sought after by humans. The noise of falling fruit is almost incessant when a large tree is fruiting nearby, making it difficult to detect approaching groups of elephants or gorillas, arriving to feast on this bounty falling from the canopy.

Desbordesia glaucescens (Alep) is an impressive and beautiful forest tree, which can exceed 50 m. It has rough, pale bark, with spectacular high, thin buttresses. In older trees the trunk tends to rot at the base and the tree is supported by the large buttresses. It generally has a high, branchless trunk and a relatively small canopy. The leaves are similar to those of *Irvingia gabonensis*, but are shiny above and dull on their underside and are noticeably clumped. Unlike the other Irvingiaceae, it has wind dispersed seeds and each winged fruit (10 x 4 cm), has one or two seeds. The young fruits and foliage are bright pink. In October / November, when the fruits are developing, *D. glaucescens* really stands out with its bright pink canopy. The fruits dry to a pale brown before being carried away on the wind. The wood is particularly hard and because of its long straight trunk 'Alep' is often used for bridge construction by foresters.

LAURACEAE

The Lauraceae family takes its name from *Laurus nobilis*, the Laurel or Bayleaf. This small shrub, whose aromatic leaves are used in cooking, has been introduced into Gabon from the Mediterranean. The name *Laurus* is derived from the Celtic word 'blawr', meaning evergreen. The french call it the 'Laurier d'Apollon' after Greek mythology. The God Apollo supposedly persued the mountain nymph, Daphne, who made so much noise when he caught her that Mother Earth came just in time to save her. In her place she left a laurel-tree and Apollo made a wreath from its leaves, to console himself. Later, similar crowns were made to adorn heros. The family also contains other familiar species, such as *Persea americana*, the avocado pear and *Cinnamomum cassia*, the cinnamon-tree, whose bark is used to flavour many cakes and desserts.

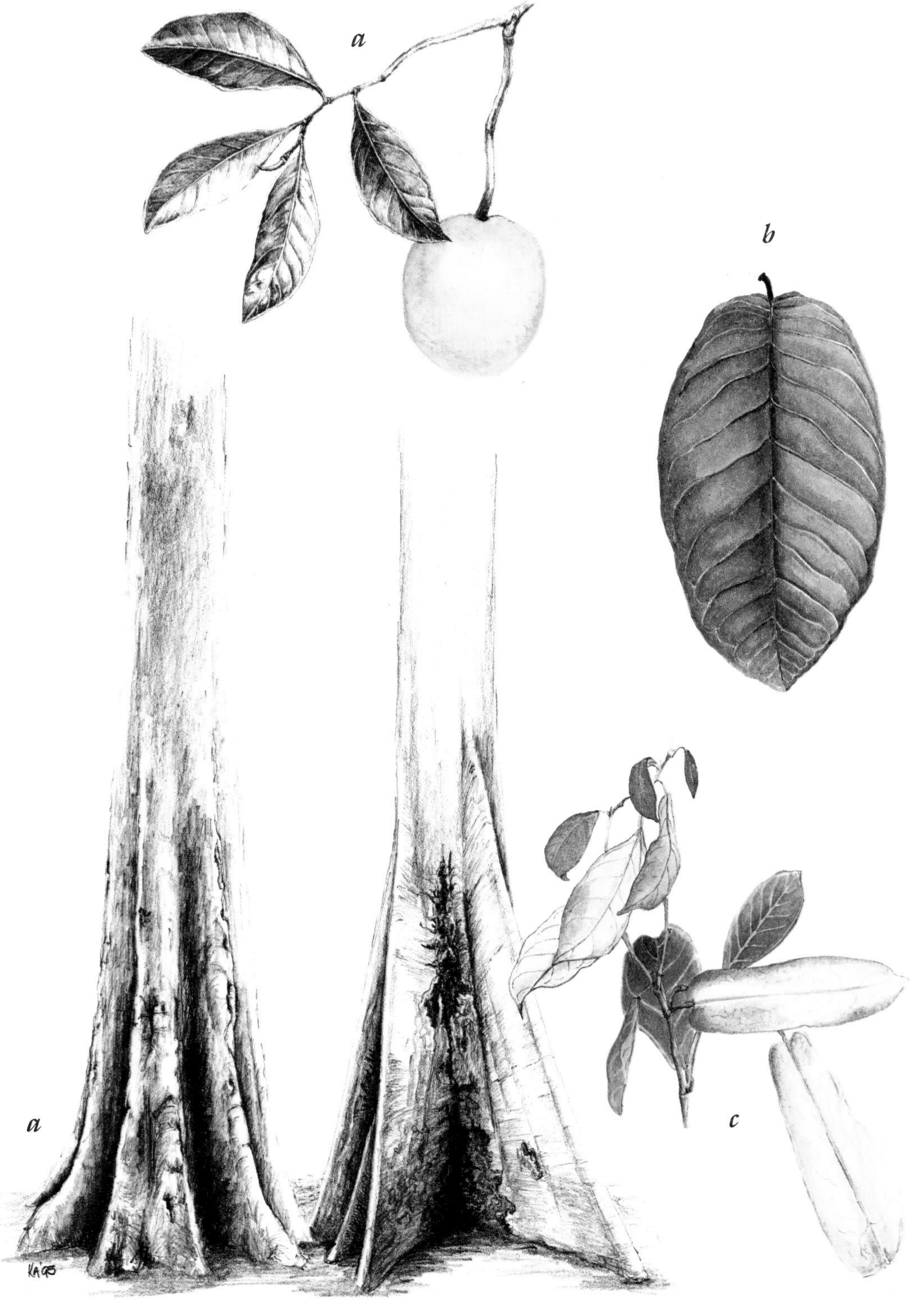
a
b
a
c
KA'95

Beilschmiedia fulva

Beilschmiedia fulva (Nkonengu) grows to be quite a large tree although it rarely exceeds 35 m tall or 70 cm diameter. The trunk is without buttresses. The bark is red-brown and flakes off in large patches, revealing numerous lenticels. The underside of the leaves (15 x 10 cm) has strong, characteristic, nervation and is covered in rusty hairs. The leaves yellow as they age and rapidly blacken having fallen to the ground. Like all *Beilschmiedia* species it has small, inconspicuous flowers. The pink fruits are egg-shaped, about 4 cm long. They have a strong resinous smell reminiscent of marzipan and are eaten by chimpanzees. The seeds are pale brown, about 2-3 cm long. They are variable in shape, some resembling small, pale brown, birds eggs, whilst others are elongated and pointed (p. 214). The foresters name for the tree is derived from the Fang name "Nkan-Ngui", meaning "pig's penis", presumably because of the form of the fruit.

There are probably 10 or more species of *Beilschmiedia* in the Lopé Reserve. *Beilschmiedia fulva* is easy to identify because of its characteristic leaves. The others have leaves which are difficult to distinguish. Partly because of their inconspicuous flowers, few have been collected by botanists and it is difficult to identify specimens, even if we manage to collect them. As illustrated by some of the new species you will read about in this guide, the flora of the rain forests of central Africa is poorly known. To identify plants collected in Lopé we refer to the Flora of Gabon, produced by the Natural History Museum in Paris. Unfortunately only about a third of plant families found in Gabon have been described to date. So, until further collections have been made, taxonomic studies undertaken and floras published, certain groups of species will remain extremely difficult to identify.

Hypodaphnis zenkeri is a medium sized tree rarely exceeding 15 m tall or 40 cm diameter. It occurs in the main forest block, as isolated individuals and occasionally becomes quite common in localised pockets. The form is twisted, rather like a European bay tree. It is easily identified from its distinctive alternate leaves, which are typically crowded towards the end of the branches. They are about 15 x 6 cm, with about 5 pairs of lateral nerves and numerous parallel tertiary nerves. It has pale yellow flowers about 5 mm across in October / January. The green fruits are about the size and shape of a hen's egg. The yellow pulp around a hard stone is reminiscent of an avocado.

Ocotea gabonensis is generally a shrub, sometimes growing to be a small to medium sized tree, up to about 12 m and 30 cm diameter. It has alternate leaves (10 x 4 cm) resembling European bay leaves. The small white flowers are about 5 mm across and develop into shiny black fruits about 1 cm long. These sit in a small cup shaped base which gives them the appearance of small acorns. *Ocotea gabonensis* is a species which, like *Pentadesma grandifolia* (P. 124) tends to occur at high altitude. The presence of these montane species enables us to reconstruct part of the vegetation history of the Lopé (see p. 212).

Hypodaphnis zenkeri

LEGUMINOSAE; SUBFAMILY: CAESALPINIOIDEAE

Legiminosae, the 'legumes', is the dominant family in most tropical rain forests. Taxonomists split it into three 'tribes', or subfamilies: Caesalpinioideae, Mimosoideae and Papilionoideae. This latter subfamily, in particular, is familiar to most people because it includes cultivated beans, peas and peanuts.

Detarium macrocarpum (Alen) is a large tree which can exceed 60 m high and 2 m diameter. It is relatively common in galleries, as well as in the main forest block. In Lopé it often stands like a natural obelisk at the junction of many large elephant trails, which radiate out from its prominent trunk. The base of the trunk can be swollen to enormous dimensions, by years of elephant damage. The elephants use their tusks to lever off the bark, which they chew and suck dry, before spitting it out in fibrous bundles. However, the tree has adapted a means to combat the elephants. Its bark is composed of many short, tough fibres. When these are prised away from the trunk they break apart, preventing the elephants from removing large slabs of bark. Many tree species which are fed on by elephants have bark with this structure and develop similar bulbous, swollen, bases in response to the elephants persistent efforts.

The trunk narrows 3 m or more above the base. Here the bark is silvery - grey, with dark vertical cracks which become wider as the tree grows. The compound leaves are arranged alternately on the branchlets. There are 8-20 alternate, asymmetrical, leaflets (6 x 4 cm). They have a fine network of curved, parallel secondary veins, connecting to a marginal nerve. The underside appears stippled with translucent dots when viewed close up. The whitish flowers are about 0.5 cm across, arranged on slender panicles which grow from the leaf axils. These develop into a striking fruit with the form of a flattened mango. When ripe they are about 7-8 cm diameter, with a leathery, olive-green, skin. The pale green flesh is soft and oily, with a powerful yeasty smell. The seed is a thick, woody stone which, when cleaned of persistent fibres, has a characteristic wrinkled shell (p. 214). Unusually, the fruits ripen in the long dry season and so are particularly important for many of the frugivorous mammals. Elephants, the only seed disperser, are particularly fond of *Detarium* fruits, hence the large paths which lead to their bases. Only gorillas, pigs and mandrills have jaws powerful enough to break through the tough nut to eat the large seed, although in west Africa chimpanzees use sticks and stones to break into the nuts.

Hylodendron gabunense (Mvana) is a tall, elegant tree, easily identified by its smooth, cream-coloured bark and numerous, high, narrow buttresses. It is common in galleries and bosquets, as well as areas where the soil is thin. Here, its buttresses probably act as stabilisers, enabling it to grow higher than most of its neighbours, reaching over 50m. The buttresses have thin fibrous bark which is particularly difficult to remove, so it is rarely stripped by elephants. In fact, development of high, thin, buttresses may well be a different adaptation to reduce damage from bark feeding by elephants in some cases, since the bark is difficult to strip and they prevent close access to the main trunk. However, if elephants do manage to get a grip and they often tear off long strips of bark, sometimes eventually killing the tree.

The young, pinkish leaves are sheathed in a leathery stipule about 5 cm long, which persists at the base of the compound leaf. There are 8-15 alternate leaflets, 9 x 3 cm) with form and veination similar to those of *Detarium macrocarpum*. It fruits between December and February, producing papery, leaf-like pods, each containing one or, rarely, several seeds. These drift away from the parent tree twisting in the wind, sometimes travelling 200m or more. During the fruiting season seeds carpet the ground for several weeks, providing food for the many forest rodents. In years when fruit is scarce these become an important food source for gorillas, who spend hours searching through dense leaf litter for the seeds. Not all the seeds are eaten however. The characteristic seedlings of *Hylodendron gabunense* are amongst the commonest young plants in the forest. They are particularly striking when they have newly emerged, vivid pink, leaves. As is often the case for plants at Lopé, the leaves of the seedling are very different in appearance to those on the adult.

The name «*Dialium*» comes from the Greek word meaning «destroyed», refering to the fact that the petals fall almost as soon as the flowers open. As its name suggests, ***Dialium lopense*** was discovered in the Lopé. In fact, it was only named for the first time in 1994, from a specimen collected close to the forest edge, by researchers at the Station d'Etudes des Gorilles et Chimpanzés. It is most abundant in galleries and on the forest edge, but also occurs both within Marantaceae and Mature forest. It is a species with a very limited distribution and is only known to occur within an area of radius about 75 km centred on the Lopé Hotel.

***Hylodendron gabunense* seedling**

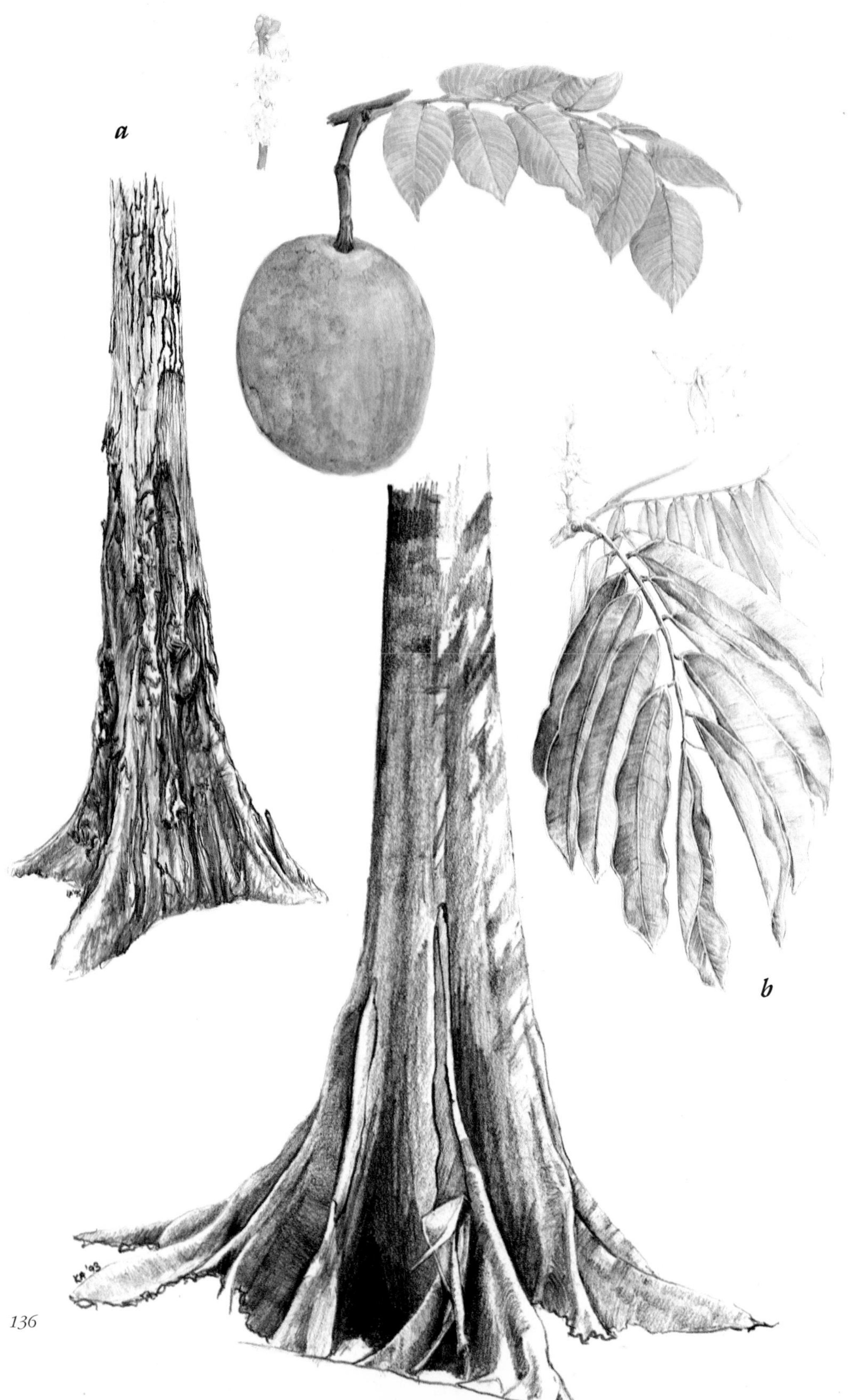
a
b
KA'93

Dialium lopense is quite an easy species to recognise. The trunk is a mottled, russet colour and the bark flakes off in small,roughly circular, patches. It is often somewhat twisted. The foliage is dense. As with many species of Caesalpiniaceae, *D. lopense* has compound leaves. There are generally four or five dark green leaflets. These are tough and leathery, with prominent veination, although, when young, they are pale and limp and are eaten by several species of mammal. As they age, the leaflets turn yellow and fall to the ground, adding some colour to the forest floor, until they finally brown and blend in with the other leaf litter. *Dialium lopense* produces small yellow-green flowers in December / January. The sugary fruit is enclosed in a black-brown, velvety capsule which stands erect on the outside of the canopy and ripens from April onwards, with some persisting into early July. If you are lucky enough to find fresh fruits pop open the capsule and suck the dry, sherbet around the seed.

Dialium fruits and seeds are eaten by animal species. They are particularly appreciated by gorillas, who climb up into the canopy, bend a few branches to make a platform, or day nest, and then gradually proceed to dismantle the tree. They pull large branches in towards their perch, where they sit carefully popping open every capsule with their teeth and swallowing the seed and flesh within. If you listen carefully you can hear the 'pop pop pop' at a distance of 30 or 40m, as they eat up to 30 fruits a minute. They sometimes eat several thousand in a day. By the time a group of gorillas have finished feeding in a tree with a good fruit crop, up to half of its canopy can be broken - it has been 'aped'.

Two other species of *Dialium* are relatively common in the Mature Forest. ***Dialium dinklagei*** is a tall, elegant tree with smooth, pale bark and slight buttresses when large. Each leaf has about eight pairs of relatively small leaflets (generally less than 5 cm long) with short, velvety hairs on their underside. Its fruits are not flattened, like those of most *Dialium* species, but are spherical, and persist on the ground for a long time after fruiting has finished. ***Dialium soyauxii*** is relatively common in Mature forest, but has no particular features to aid identification. Although it does grow to be a large tree, these are relatively rare and most individuals are small or medium sized. Its leaf generally has 9 or 10 alternate leaflets which are, in fact, more typical of the genus as a whole, which includes a further five species in Gabon, some of which are found in the southern half of the Lopé Reserve. The leaves are similar to those of *Augouardia letestui* (p. 173) but the two trees are only confused when the latter lacks multiple trunks.

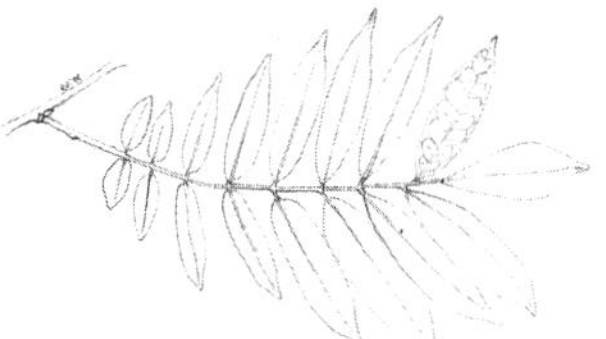

Dialium dinklagei

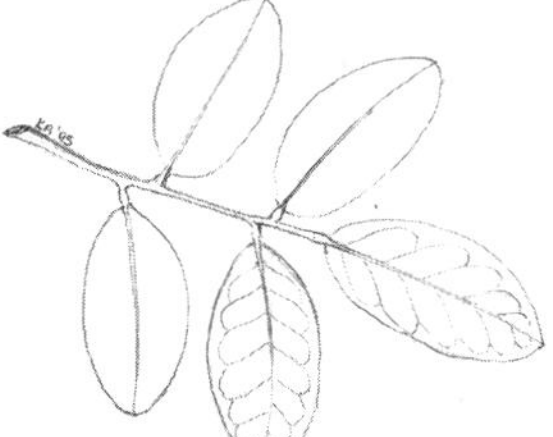

Dialium lopense

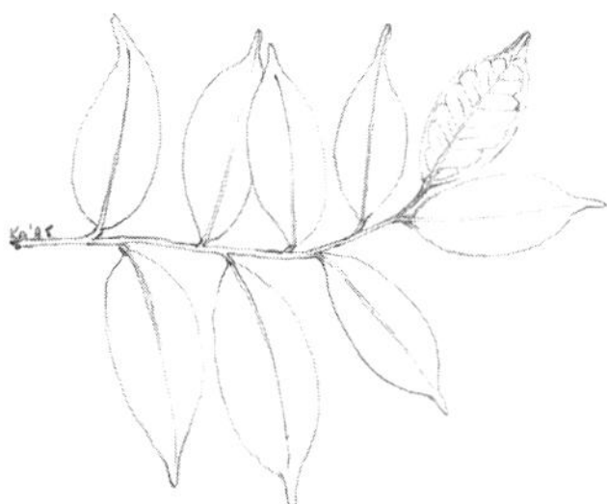

Dialium soyauxii

***Dialium dinklagei* fruits**

LEGUMINOSAE; SUBFAMILY: MIMOSOIDEAE

Pentaclethra macrophylla (Mubala) is common in galleries and bosquets as well as in Marantaceae forest, but is less frequent in Mature forest. It is a medium to large tree, generally 20 - 30 m tall. The bark on older trees is dark and flakey, except at the base, where there is generally extensive elephant damage. On young trees or smaller branches the bark is smooth and greyish, resembling that of *Pentaclathra eetveldeana*. It has large, bipinnate compound leaves, like many Mimosoideae. The leaf has up to 16 pairs of opposite pinnae, each with about 10 pairs of opposite leaflets, up to about 2 cm in length. The young leaves have a rich coppery hue, making *P. macrophylla* particularly striking when covered in flush.

Left:

a) Detarium macrocarpum
b) Hylodendron gabunense

KA '94

Left:

Dialium lopense

The flowers are large, eye catching bundles of red spikes which abound around Easter. These produce copious amounts of sugary nectar which attract primates, as well as insects and birds. Chimpanzees in particular are fond of licking these flowers, like children with an ice cream. The fruit is a spectacular velvety black-brown pod up to about 65 cm long by 10 cm wide, resembling an enormous bean, hanging down amongst the foliage. It contains several large, shiny brown seeds, up to 7 x 4 cm. The pods are woody and extremely tough, effectively protecting the seeds from most predators. However, adult grey-cheeked mangabeys, black-colobus monkeys and mandrills are able to break into them with their strong teeth and eat large numbers of unripe seeds. When the fruits mature, after the long dry season, they gradually dry out until the two valves explode apart with a loud crack, throwing seeds up to about 30 m. These seeds have large, starchy cotyledons, which can be boiled and ground into an edible flour. They may have been an important food for Stone Age and Iron Age peoples living in the region, which would explain their abundance in bosquets, which are generally too far away from the forest to be colonised naturally by *Pentaclethra macrophylla*. The freshly fallen orange-brown pods are often found on the ground under the tree, gradually dulling to brown. These make excellent barometers, curling up or opening out as air humidity changes.

Pentaclethra eetveldeana (Engona) has similar distribution and phenology to its close relative *P. macrophylla*. However, they are quite easily distinguished, particularly by their leaflets, which are a different size and shape. *P. eetveldeana* has smooth, pale bark and the trunk tends to be somewhat irregular. It is almost always severely deformed at its base by elephant feeding, and quite often becomes rotten as a result of the repeated damage. The leaves are bipinnate with up to 16 opposite pairs of pinnae, each with 15-30 pairs of small leaflets (1cm x 2mm) ending in a point, resembling curved swords. The fruits are smaller than those of *P. macrophylla* and are held erect, above the canopy. They have smooth, shiny, black valves up to 20 x 4 cm, with 3-8 shiny brown, flattened oblong seeds about 3 x 2 cm (p. 214).

Cathormion altissimum is common in galleries where it can be confused with *Pentaclethra eetveldeana*. It is a medium to large tree, rarely exceeding 20 m but occasionally over 1 m diameter. The bipinnate leaves have up to 9 pairs of opposite pinnae each with up to 20 pairs of opposite leaflets each about 1 cm x 3 mm, rounded at their tips. The flowers are small white balls. The characteristic coiled, segmented, pods allow easy identification when present.

Piptadeniastrum africanum (Dabéma) is a particularly striking tree which is common along the forest edge and within both Marantaceae and Mature Forest. It is a large tree which can become extremely tall, emerging above surrounding canopies to dominate the horizon. Exceptional individuals can exceed 65 m. When viewed from afar its vast, flattened crown and dark green foliage are easily recognised. When flowering, the top of the canopy appears cream or gold.

The pale grey bark is smooth, with many horizontal ridges. The trunk is typically tall and straight, without branches until quite high up. It has numerous, high, thin, spreading buttresses, which often divide repeatedly and may extend several metres from the base of the tree. These usually show some signs of elephant damage. The leaves are bipinnate, with 10-12 alternate pairs of pinnae, which have up to 60 pairs of tiny leaflets (5 x 1 mm). The flowers are thin white or yellowish spikes. The fruit is a thin pod about 20-30 cm long. They ripen in March / May, opening down one side to release flattened seeds surrounded by a papery wing. The seeds are attached to the pod by a thin stalk resembling an umbilical cord at the centre of the seed.

Newtonia leucocarpa (Ossimiale) is easily confused with *P. africanum*. The form is very similar, although the buttresses are less numerous and do not branch. Its leaves resemble those of *P. africanum*, but on close inspection can easily be distinguished. They are bipinnate, with 10-12 pairs of opposite pinnae. There is a small gland on the rachis between each pair. Each pinna has up to 40 pairs of tiny leaflets (7 x 1.5 mm). Flowers are produced at the beginning of the long dry season and fruits ripen in September. When flowering the top of the canopy is initially golden but then darkens to brown. The pod is similar to that of *P. africanum*, but the winged seed is easily distinguished by its size and its attachment. These seeds are an important food for grey-cheeked mangabeys, *Cercopithecus albigena*, in the long dry season.

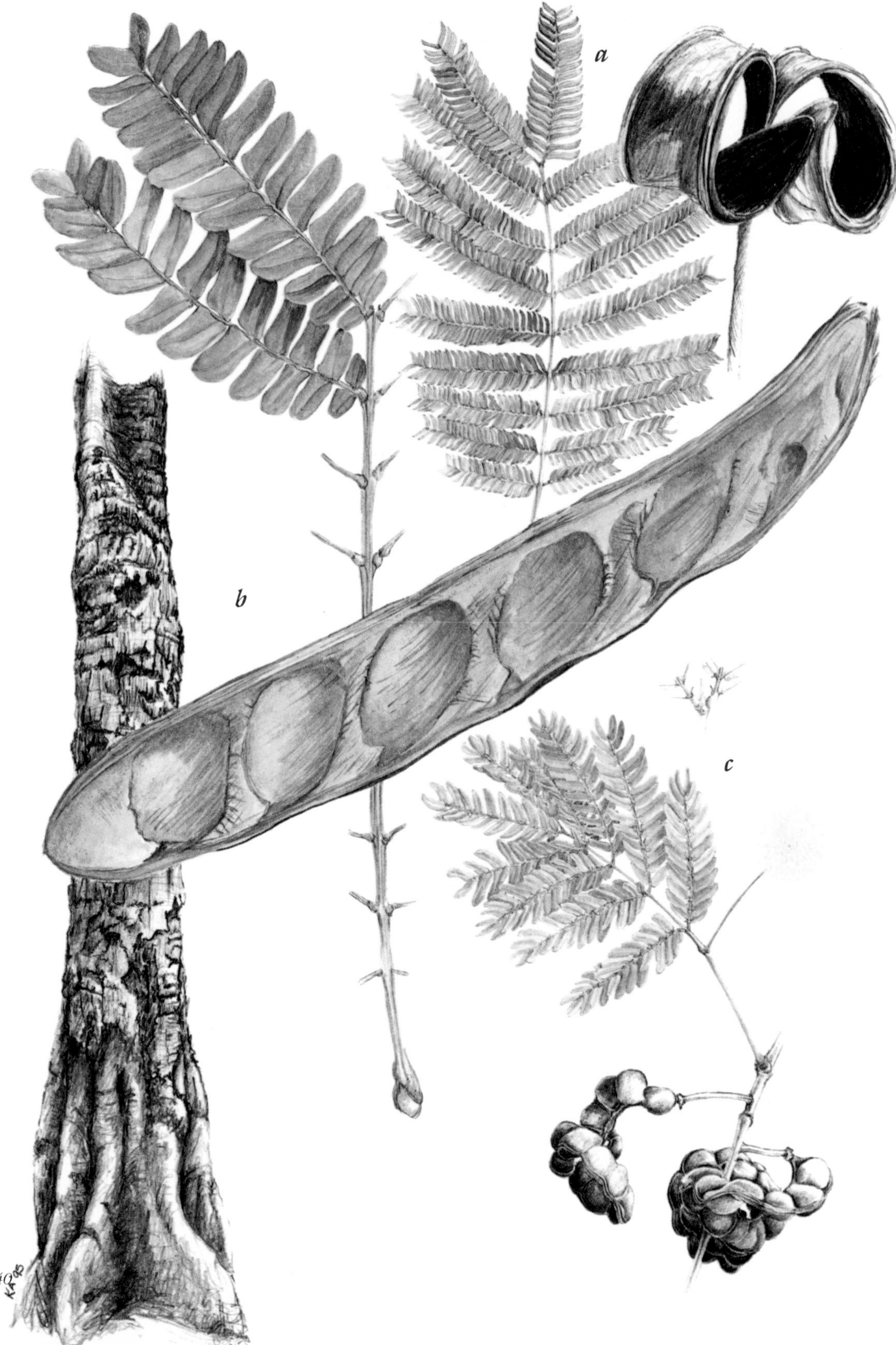
a
b
c

There are two species of *Parkia* in Lopé, ***Parkia bicolor*** and ***Parkia filicoidea***, both known by the forestry name 'Essang'. Both have thin buttresses which are often damaged by elephants, with orange-brown bark, which flakes off in small, round patches. Both species have bipinnate leaves but can be distinguished on the basis of their leaflets. *P. bicolor* has 12-22 opposite pairs of pinnae each with up to 32 small leaflets (7 x 2 mm). *P. filicoidea* has 7-12 opposite pairs of pinnae each with up to 31 leaflets (1.5 cm x 4 mm). They flower from November / February. The blooms are large red-pink balls with an orange collar of infertile flowers at their base. They hang down on stalks, or peduncles, up to 30 cm long. At night the infertile flowers produce copious ammounts of sweet nectar, which attracts bats. Pollen accumulates on their chest hairs and they pollinate as they move around feeding on the nectar. The fruits are fleshy pods up to about 40 cm long for *P. bicolor* and 65 cm for *P. filicoidea*, which hang in bunches attached to the swollen tip of the peduncle. They ripen from March / May. Fruit of *P. bicolor* is wine red and that of *P. filicoidea* is dark green. The green seeds, rather like broad beans, are enclosed in a white protective skin and embedded in a bright yellow (*P. bicolor*) or orange (*P. filicoidea*) powdery pulp. These are eaten by many of the primates, including chimpanzees and gorillas.

Samanea leptophylla is quite a rare species restricted to Mature Forest in Lopé, which grows to over 45 m tall and 120 cm diameter. It has never before been recorded in Gabon, but this is partly because it is often mistaken for *Parkia bicolor* by logging company prospectors. It has rounded buttresses which tend to be fattened by elephant damage. The bark is orange-brown and flakes off in roughly circular patches. The leaf is bipinnate, with 12-34 pairs of pinnae each with up to about 40 tiny leaflets (3 x 0.5 mm). The flowers are small, white balls about 1.5 cm diameter. The fruit is a dry, indehiscent, segmented pod. The mechanism of seed dispersal remains a mystery. A close relative, *Samanea saman*, the South American "rain-tree", has attractive pink flowers and is planted as an ornamental tree.

Left:

a) Pentaclethra eetveldeana
b) Pentaclethra macrophylla
c) Cathormion altissimum

Parkia bicolor

Parkia filicoidea

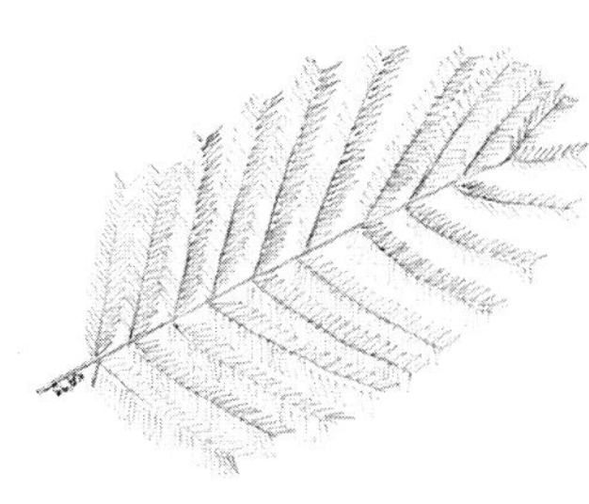

Samanea leptophylla

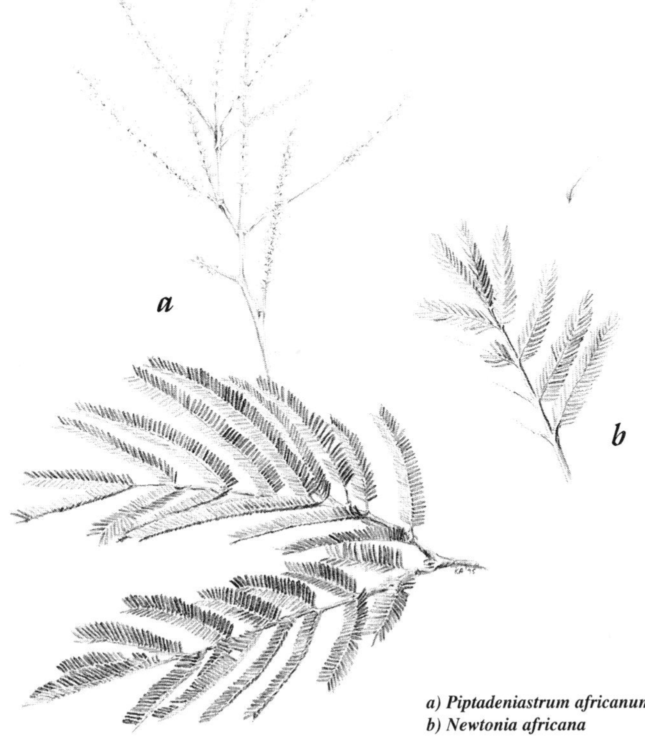

a) Piptadeniastrum africanum
b) Newtonia africana

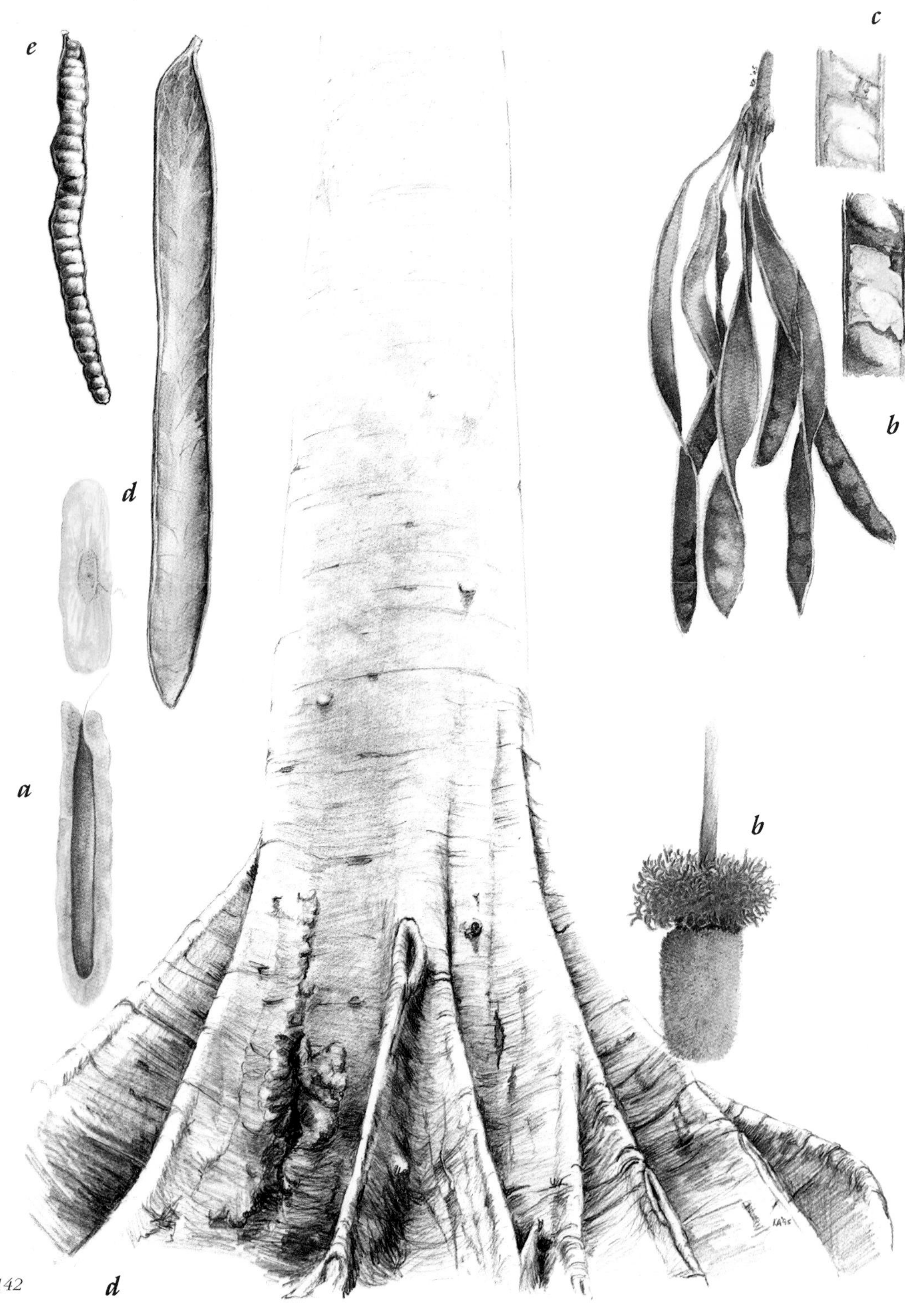
e
d
a
c
b
b
d

LEGUMINOSAE; SUBFAMILY: PAPILIONOIDEAE.

Baphia leptobotrys is rare in Lopé, but is particularly attractive when flowering. A small pocket occurs on the trail 'Grand Circuit' and they are easily identified by their white flowers and pointed, dehiscent pods (see p. 173).

Craibia laurentii is a medium sized tree found in galleries, bosquets and Marantaceae forest. It grows to about 15 m tall and 30 cm diameter. Large individuals stand out when growing on the savanna edge because of their thick, arching, branches, radiating from the trunk. The bark is smooth and pale. The compound leaves have 5-7 alternate leaflets (14 x 6 cm). In December, *Craibia laurentii* is covered by numerous pure white flowers. These are arranged in large bunches on the ends of the twiglets, creating vivid splashes of white along the forest edge. Each flower is about 1.5 cm long and a hundred or more bloom in each bunch at any one time. The fruits are flattened fleshy pods about 4 x 2.5 cm.

Millettia laurentii (Wengué or grey ebony) is a large forest tree reaching about 45 m high and 1 m diameter. The trunk is pale grey, with numerous lenticels grouped in vertical strips. The base has slight, rounded, buttresses. The leaves have 4-9 pairs of opposite and one terminal leaflet (10 x 3 cm). The flowers are in erect bunches held above the canopy and fall to the ground in December, forming an attractive lilac carpet. The fruit is a dehiscent pod (15-25 x 3-5 cm) with 2-4 seeds. The dense, hard, heartwood is dark brown, with an attractive black grain and is used in furniture making and for carving.

Pterocarpus soyauxii (Padouk) is a large tree found in all forest types. It can exceed 50 m tall and 2 m diameter. The trunk is straight and cylindrical with high, sharp buttresses at the base. The bark is grey-brown and flakes off in long, thin, rectangular scales. It has large, spreading branches and a thin, domed canopy, which gives the impression of a cathedral roof when viewed from below. The compound leaf has 11-17 alternate leaflets (6 x 2.5 cm) with 15 or more pairs of indistinct lateral nerves. These are dark green, except when the crown is flushing after losing all its leaves, when they are emerald. Leaf loss is more common in December / February, but may occur at other times of the year. In December / February *Pterocarpus* bursts into bright yellow flowers. At this time the canopy stands out from afar. These flowers are an important food for all of the primates, including gorillas and chimpanzees, who drop many twigs and small branches on the ground. In Greek, "pteron" means 'wing' and "carpon" means 'fruit'. Hence, *Pterocarpus* signifies "winged fruit". Each seed is enclosed in a papery wing 5-6 cm across. When young these are covered in dense, velvety hairs, which become more sparse and fine as they ripen in January / April. Like the flowers, the seeds are eaten by many animals, but they are produced in such quantities that many thousands survive to be carried away on the wind.

The wood, and particularly the roots, of Padouk are used to make a bright red powder, widely employed as a body paint in traditional ceremonies in much of Africa. In fact, "red wood", or Padouk, was Gabon's first timber export for this reason. Today it remains amongst the 10 most important species for export.

The following three legumes have been grouped together because they all have pods which contain succulent flesh, which encourages animals to swallow and disperse their seeds.

Swartzia fistuloides (Pau Rosa; sub-family: Caesalpinioideae) is one of the most valuable timber species found in Gabon and is much sought after by foresters. It is a medium to large tree, rarely exceeding 80 cm diameter and 40 m in height. The bark is yellowish and quite flakey, similar to that of *Dacryodes buettneri* (p. 116). They are always swollen at the base by elephant damage and this quite often results in infection which allows rot to set in. The trunk is often crooked, with low branches, which reduces its commercial value. The compound leaves are about 25 cm long, with 9-13 leaflets (8 x 3 cm). When leaflets fall to the ground they develop a characteristic golden edge as they brown. Flowering and fruiting are asynchronous throughout the year. The flowers are often first noticed on the ground below the tree. They have one large white petal with yellow markings and are strongly perfumed. The fruit is a dark brown pod up to about 30 cm long, with circular cross section. It has a strong, yeasty smell which attracts elephants, the main seed disperser. There are numerous seeds within the pod, each enclosed in a hard protective shell, which prevents damage by elephant teeth. The easily recognised seedlings (see p. 4) are common in elephant dung throughout the year.

Cassia mannii (sub-family: Caesalpinioideae) is less common than *Swartzia fistuloides* and is restricted to galleries and Marantaceae forest. From a distance its compound leaves appear similar to those of *Swartzia*, but a closer inspection will reveal only 7 - 10 pairs of opposite leaflets, each with close, parallel veins.

Left:

a) Newtonia leucocarpa
b) Parkia bicolor
c) Parkia filicoidea
d) Piptadeniastrum africanum
e) Samanea leptophylla

Page 144:

a) Craibia laurentii
b) Pterocarpus soyauxii
i) unripe fruit
ii) ripe fruit

Page 145:

a) Cassia mannii
b) Swartzia fistuloides
c) Tetrapleura tetraptera

Millettia laurentii

Swartzia fistuloides

a
ii
i
b
b
KA'95

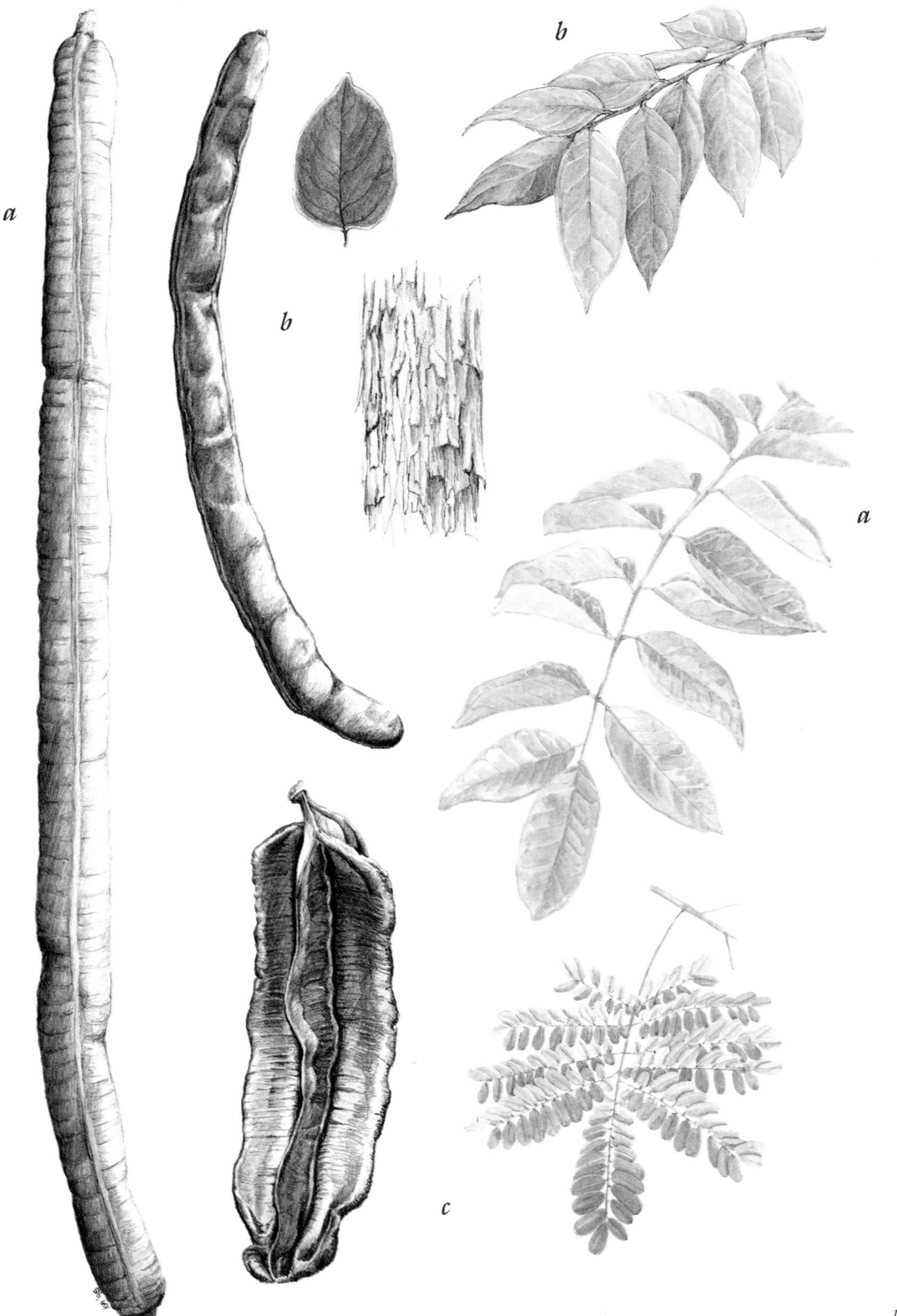
a
b
b
a
c

Right:

a) Carapa procera
b) Entandrophragma candollei
c) Trichilia prieureana

Cassia mannii produces showy bunches of pink flowers in September which have a strong scent, similar to that of a rose, attracting large numbers of bees. The black pod can be up up to 90 cm long, with a circular cross section of about 3 cm diameter. It contains many small seeds, each enclosed within a neat compartment, which can be distinguished as ripples on the surface of the pod. When dry the pods make perfect rattles, which traditionally served as musical instruments for peoples in the region.

Tetrapleura tetraptera (subfamily: Mimosoideae; Nkouarsa) is found in most forest types. It has bipinnate leaves with 5-13 pairs of opposite pinnae, each with up to 24 small, rounded leaflets (10 x 5mm) with distinct veination. Flowering is throughout the wet season. The flowers are arranged in erect spikes on the outer edge of the canopy and range in colour from yellow to orange to pink. The distinctive fruit is up to 25 cm long with four sections in the form of a crucifix. The lateral sections are hard and probably provide mechanical protection for the flattened, circular seeds. The seeds are arranged vertically in the centre of the fruit, enclosed in jelly-like flesh, with a strong, chocolatey odour, a little like the drink 'Bailey's Irish Cream'. In Lopé only elephants seem to disperse the seeds, but gorillas in some places are also known to eat the fruit. In parts of Africa the flesh is used to flavour soups and sauces and fruits are collected and transported in large numbers for sale in the markets of towns and cities far from the forest. In Lopé the pods are boiled up as an alternative to coffee.

MELIACEAE

This is the Mahogany family, which yields many top quality red woods, such as *Khaya ivorensis*, the African red mahogany, which are exploited by foresters wherever they are found. Some of these large timber species occur in Lopé, but they are rare and the common Meliaceae here are all small to medium sized trees. In Central and South America several mahogany species have been exploited for timber for long periods and there are almost no trees of good form remaining, except in very remote areas. It is thought that the constant removal of tall, straight trees has resulted in genetic changes, similar to those induced by humans breeding races of domestic dogs. Care needs to be taken to ensure that similar changes are not induced in Gabon's forest, particularly for species like Okoumé (p. 78).

E. candollei

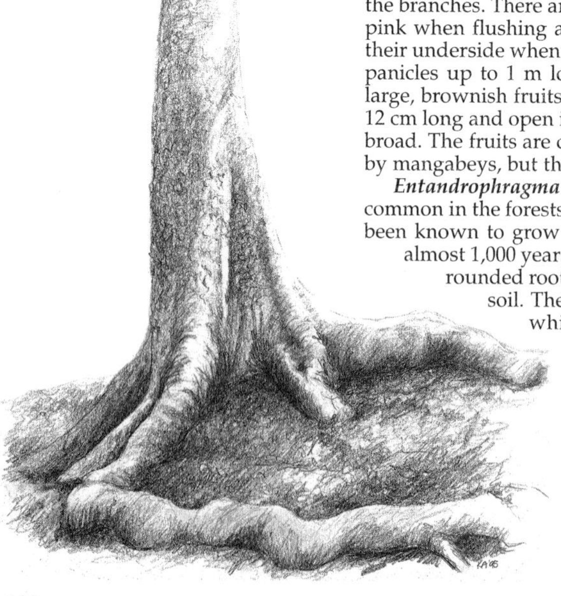

Carapa procera (African Crabwood) is a small to medium sized tree found most often in mature forest in Lopé. It takes its forestry name from its close relative *Carapa guianensis*, a large tree found in South America which produces excellent timber. *Carapa procera* rarely exceeds 15 m tall and 20 cm diameter, although larger individuals are reported from some places. The bark is pale brown, with regular fissures about 1 cm across. The general appearance of the tree is similar to *Trichoscypha abut* (p. 114). It has wide, arching branches in larger individuals, which are absent in young trees. The compound leaves are up to 2m long, with thick, woody petioles and are borne in a few large tufts on the tips of the branches. There are about 12 alternate leaflets (24 x 9 cm). Leaflets are bright pink when flushing and have characteristic pale yellow-brown colouration on their underside when mature. The small white flowers, about 1 cm across, are in panicles up to 1 m long, standing erect above the leaves. These develop into large, brownish fruits with 5 distinct, knobbly, lobes. When ripe they are about 12 cm long and open into 5 capsules, releasing 15-20 angular seeds about 2.5 cm broad. The fruits are cryptic and are rarely seen on the tree. The seeds are eaten by mangabeys, but the mechanism of seed dispersal is a mystery.

Entandrophragma candollei (Kosipo) is rare in Lopé, but becomes more common in the forests of north eastern Gabon. It is an impressive tree which has been known to grow to 70 m tall and 3 m diameter. Individuals this size are almost 1,000 years old. The base has several thick buttresses, ending in large rounded roots, which snake away from the tree along the surface of the soil. The rough, greyish, bark flakes off in small, irregular, scales, which leave pinkish patches where they detach. The compound leaves are about 25 cm long, arranged in star-like bunches. There are 5-10 pairs of leaflets (6 x 3 cm) with strong veination, giving a corrugated effect. Leaf arrangement and veination are similar to those of *Canarium schweinfurthii* (p. 118). The green-yellow flowers resemble those of *Trichilia prieureana*. The fruit is a black-brown, elongated capsule about 20 cm long, like a fat cigar. It splits at its tip into 5 curved segments, releasing wind dispersed seeds about 2 cm across, each with a single wing about 8 cm long.

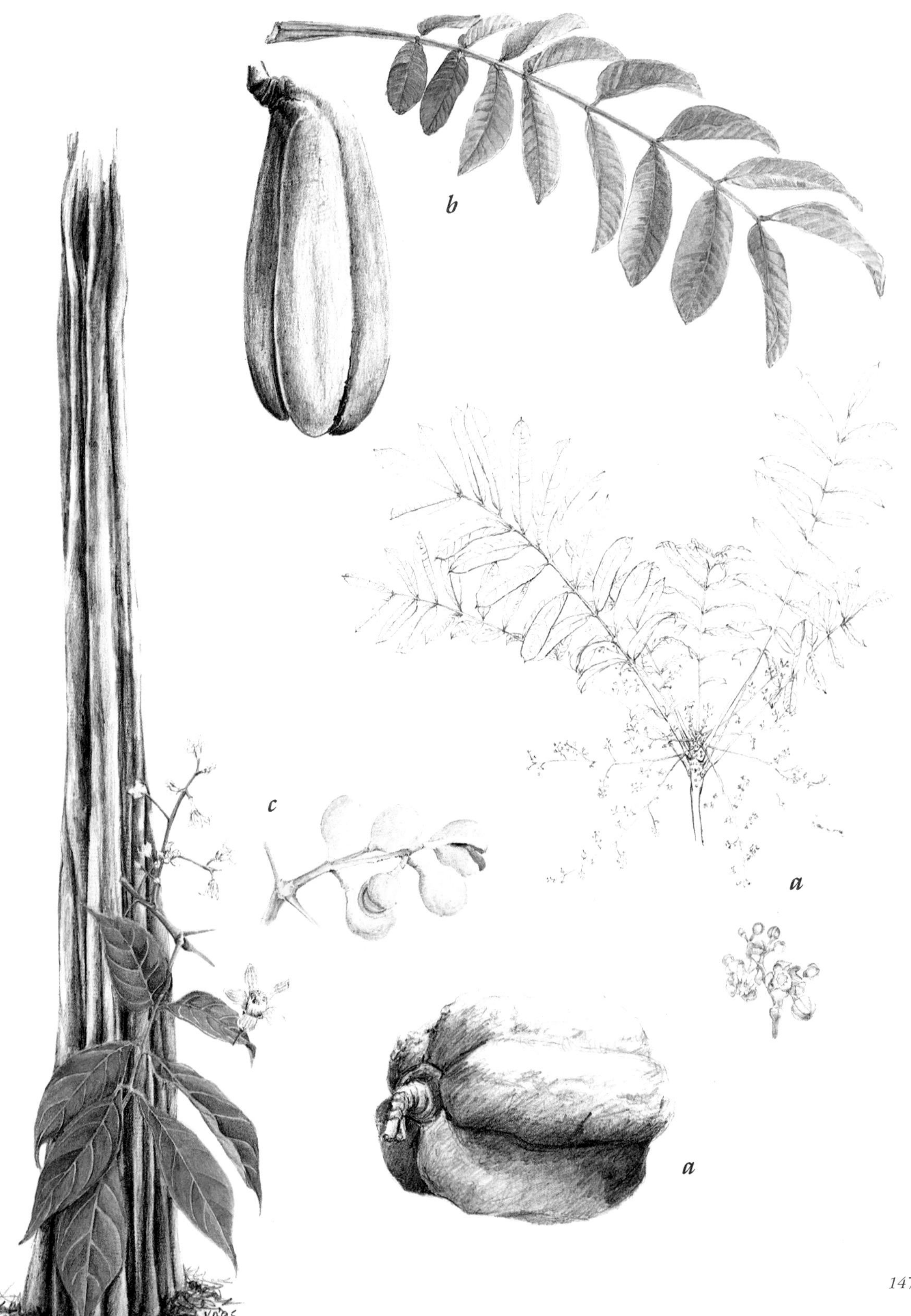
b
c
a
a
KA'95

Trichilia prieureana is a medium sized tree (up to 20 m tall and 40 cm diameter) found in all forest types. The irregular, fluted trunk resembles ***Duboscia marcocarpa*** (p. 158), but the grey-brown bark is darker, with broader flakes. It is easily distinguished from *Duboscia* by its compound leaves, with 2-3 pairs and a terminal leaflet (13 x 5 cm). The pale green flowers are in short panicles. The pale pink fruits are about 2 cm long when ripe and split to reveal 2-4 shiny black seeds each with a startling orange aril, which is an important food for monkeys, hornbills and blue turacos early in the long dry season.

Heisteria parvifolia **(see p. 180)**

PANDACEAE

Before people living in the central Africa adopted agriculture as a means of producing a reliable, year-round food source, they lived as hunter-gatherers; opportunists, who took advantage of different foods as they became available in the forest. At this time, nuts were particularly important, partly because they are an excellent food source, but also because they can be stored for use at a later date. The importance of seeds in the diet of Stone Age and Iron Age peoples in Lopé is attested to by numerous smooth, rounded depressions about the size of a nut, found in rocks around old village sites. It was here people cracked open nuts collected in the forest, to obtain the precious kernels, rich in oil and protein. A number of species found in Lopé have edible nuts (see also pp. 66, 122, 130, 182). Two of the more important nuts come from, *Panda oleosa* and *Poga oleosa*:

Panda oleosa (Afane) is a medium sized tree of the forest under-storey, rarely exceeding 20 m in height. The greenish-brown bark is smooth above the base, which is invariably swollen and pitted as a result of elephant damage. The trunk is irregular. It has alternate, large, leathery, asymetrical leaves (up to 18 x 9 cm) with well defined toothed edges. The young leaves are vivid red-pink and seem to glow in the shadows of the forest under-storey. The flowers are on stems which hang in bunches from the upper trunk and main branches. They have five red petals. *Panda oleosa* is a dioecious species. That is, individual trees are either male or female. Close inspection will reveal that all flowers fallen under any tree are either male, with 10 stamens, or female, with three or four stigmas. The female flowers develop into large, spherical green fruits about 7 cm diameter. These have a thick flesh within which there is a hard, bony nut. Its shell is traversed by cavities, which give the outer surface a characteristic pitted appearance.

The only seed dispersers are elephants, which swallow the fruit whole and digest the flesh, passing the cleaned nut out in their dung. It requires quite an effort to break open a *Panda* nut. In Gabon, only humans know how to crack the hard shell, but in parts of west Africa, chimpanzees have learnt to use stones to extract the three or four boat-shaped seeds. At times of the year when *Panda oleosa* is fruiting, these chimpanzees spend long hours cracking the nuts. Youngsters peer over their mothers' shoulders and learn how to manipulate the stone tools. It remains a mystery why chimpanzees in central Africa have not developed this skill, since they make a variety of tools for other purposes, such as to extract honey from bees' hives. Humans pound the seeds and add them to sauces in the same way that they use the kernels of *Irvingia gabonensis* (p.132).

Canthium **sp.**

RHIZOPHORACEAE

Poga oleosa (Afo) is a large tree growing to almost 150 cm diameter and over 40 m. It has smooth, dark grey bark, which is often marked by numerous horizontal and vertical cracks, and fat, rounded buttresses. The alternate, leathery leaves are up to 15 x 7 cm, with a characteristic rolled margin. They turn yellow as they age. It has tiny white flowers arranged on spikes which resemble catkins. The fruit is very similar to that of *Panda oleosa*, but has a rounder stone, the surface of which is rippled like a human brain. It contains four seeds which are esteemed for their valuable oil. Again, elephants are the only seed dispersers.

RUBIACEAE

The Rubiaceae contains the greatest number of species of shrubs and small trees of all the Families found in Lopé. They all have simple, opposite leaves with stipules. The family includes the cultivated coffee shrubs of the genus *Coffea*, which are grown in parts of Gabon, and the quinine producing plants of the genus *Cinchona*, introduced to Africa from South America.

Canthium sp. is characteristic of the savanna edge and disturbed areas, growing to about 15 m tall. It is easily recognised by the 'herring-bone' arrangement of its branchlets, particularly when this is emphasised by the bunches of white flowers, which stand erect above the leaves (8 x 2.5 cm).

Right:

a) Panda oleosa
b) Poga oleosa

b
a
KA 95

Right:

a) Corynanthe mayumbensis
b) Massularia acuminata
c) Pausinystalia johimbe
d) Psychotria venosa
e) Tricalysa anomala
f) Vangueriopsis rubiginosa

Pauridiantha efferata

Corynanthe mayumbensis is found in all forest types in Lopé, growing to about 15 m tall and 20 cm diameter, although usually smaller. It has smooth pale bark. The leaves (11 x 5 cm) turn bright, almost fluo pink, as they die. *Corynanthe* is particularly attractive when it has white clusters of flowers or red young fruits. The fruits dry black and open to release small seeds, with a long membraneous tail at each end, which are dispersed by the wind.

Heinsia crinita is found throughout the main forest block, generally quite close to water (see p. 197). Its leaves (11 x 4.5 cm) are paler on the underside, with obvious lateral and secondary nerves. The attractive white flowers are about 4 cm across. The fruit is yellow-orange when ripe, about 2 cm long, with persistent sepals. It is sugary and quite pleasant to taste, and contains numerous small, pitted seeds.

Massularia acuminata is found in all forest types, but is most common in Marantaceae Forest. It grows to about 5 m tall and occasionally exceeds 10 cm diameter. The bark is smooth and pale and the leaves are typically about 25 x 8 cm, with 10-15 pairs of obvious lateral nerves. The flower is about 2 cm long, with dark red petals. Its ridged fruits are found at most times of the year. They are generally about 10 cm long, with a cream coloured, waxy skin. Elephants eat the fruit, dispersing the many small seeds within, and also eat the leaves. The tough wood is ideal for making axe handles.

Pauridiantha efferata is common in young vetetation types and in Marantaceae Forest. It grows to about 10 m tall and 15 cm diameter. The yellow-brown bark is fissured and flakes off in papery scales. There are relatively few, long, parallel branches, which can be mistaken for large compound leaves. The leaves (20 x 7 cm) have 18-21 well defined lateral nerves. The smaller branches and underside of the leaves are covered in pale hairs. Flowers and fruits are in small bunches, growing from the leaf axils. Leaves are often eaten by elephants, which frequently break much of the tree whilst feeding. ***Pauridiantha floribunda*** closely resembles *P. efferata* in form and habitat, but is also occasionally found in mature forest and can exceptionally grow to about 20 m tall and 20 cm diameter. The leaves (20 x 6 cm) have 14-19 obvious lateral nerves. The underside of the leaf and the nerves usually have a pink sheen. Flowers are borne in the same way as for *P. efferata*. This species is also frequently broken by elephants.

Pausinystalia johimbe (Yohimbé), grows in all forest types in Lopé and can become a medium sized tree, up to 30 m tall and 30-50 cm diameter. The smooth bark is beige-green and often has large vertical cracks, which have healed leaving scars. The large, leathery leaves (up to 40 x 15 cm) are arranged in dense whorls, in groups of 3. Its perfumed balls of white flowers, its fruits and its seeds all resemble those of *Coryanthe mayumbensis*. The bark of *Pausinystalia johimbe* contains an alkaloid called yohimbine, which is a powerful stimulant and aphrodisiac, and is harvested on a commercial basis in parts of Cameroun. It is said to stimulate the release of testosterone, improving male sexual performance and increasing musculation. A second species, ***Pausinystalia macroceras*** is easily mistaken for *Corynanthe mayumbensis*, but has fissured yellow-brown bark and grows to about 30 m tall and 50 cm diameter.

Psychotria venosa occurs in all forest types, but is most common along the forest edge. It grows to about 25 m tall with a diameter up to 40 cm. The leaves (12 x 5 cm) have a stalk of about 2 cm. They are particularly noticeable in March / April, when covered in white flowers.

Tricalysia anomala grows to about 15 m tall and 10 cm diameter. The smaller branches and leaves (8 x 3 cm) are covered in pale hairs. Its characteristic fruits (1.5 cm) with feathery persistent sepals are often found on the ground in April / June. Like several other Rubiaceae, *Tricalysia anomala* is often found broken along elephant feeding trails.

Vangueriopsis rubiginosa occurs in mature forest in Lopé, growing to about 25m tall and 40 cm diameter. It has bright ginger, flakey bark and drops characteristic white flowers in April/May.

SAPINDACEAE

This family is represented by about 60 species in Gabon, mostly small-medium sized trees. All of the species found to date in Lopé have compound leaves.

Allophylus africana is a shrub or small tree, reaching about 15 m tall and 25 cm diameter. It is easily recognisable by its tri-foliolate leaves, with three serrated leaflets each about 10 x 5 cm, dark green above, with paler undersides. The tiny white flowers are arranged on prominent spikes, which catch the eye in December / January and attract many small flies with their perfume. The flowers develop into clusters of small yellow-orange fruits about 5 mm diameter, which are dispersed predominantly by birds.

c
e
b
d
a
f

Aporrhiza paniculata

Until found in Lopé ***Aporrhiza paniculata*** had only previously been recorded from Zaire. It is a shrub or small tree, reaching about 10 m tall and 15 cm diameter. It is easy to confuse with *Eriocoelum macrocarpum* (see below) except when in fruit in November and December. The branchlets, rachis and lateral veins are slightly hairy, unlike *Eriocoelum macrocarpum*. There are generally around 6 pairs of leaflets (12 x 4.5 cm). The fruit is a pale velvety capsule which opens to reveal vivid pink-red inner walls and 2 shiny brown seeds with bright orange arils, eaten by birds and monkeys.

Blighia welwitschii is a medium-large tree up to about 45 m tall and 1 m diameter. It has smooth grey bark and is often lightly fluted with ill defined buttresses when large. The leaf has 3-4 pairs of leaflets (10 x 6 cm) with 10-14 pairs of prominent lateral nerves. Its small, perfumed flowers are cream coloured. The startling fruit (8 x 5 cm) is triangular in cross-section, with three smooth valves. These tend to ripen in December / February, but may also be found at the end of the long dry season. They are bright red and contain three shiny purple-black seeds with bright yellow arils. The aril is eaten by many animals and is a particular favourite of the African grey parrot. It is also edible for humans, but less appreciated than that of a close relative, *Blighia sapida*, the 'Akee Apple'. This was named after Captain Bligh, the 18th century British navigator, best remembered because of the mutiny on the Bounty, who gave its fruits to sailors aboard his ships to prevent scurvy. This species occurs in Gabon and has been introduced to India and America, but is not found in Lopé.

Chytranthus talbotii grows in all forest types in Lopé. It is a shrub or small tree up to 10m tall, which can be mistaken for *Trichoscypha acuminata* (p. 114), because of its form and long, compound leaves. The leaves are up to 1 m long, with 8-11 pairs of stiff, papery leaflets (20 x 5 cm). These are dark green, glossy above and paler below. Stalks bearing many flowers emerge from slight swellings, close to the base of the trunk, in October and November. The flowers have off-white petals and pale pink stamens. The fruits are spindle shaped, about 12 cm long, with 6-8 distinct lobes, becoming yellow-orange when ripe. A second, rarer, species, ***Chytranthus macrophyllus***, is found in the understorey of Mature forest. Its leaves have only 4-6 pairs of leaflets and unlike *C. talbotii*, the end of the branches and the rachis are covered in pale brown hairs. The white flowers have a red calyx, giving them a pink appearance.

Eriocoelum macrocarpum is a medium sized tree, up to 35 m tall and 60 cm diameter, with smooth, grey, bark. It is found in all forest types in Lopé, but is most abundant close to the savanna edge. The leaves have 2-3 pairs of leaflets, (15 x 5 cm) with about 14 pairs of prominent lateral nerves. It has tiny, white flowers in the long dry season, arranged on panicles, which develop into characteristic fruits. These have 3 smooth, woody valves, which become orange when ripe, splitting to display 3 shiny black seeds, each about 1.5 cm long, with red arils (see p. 92). These sit in conspicuous tufts of hairs growing from the base of each capsule, which give the genus its name, *Eriocoelum* meaning 'woolly hollow' in Greek. The seeds are eaten in large quantities by colobus and mangabeys, but are probably principally dispersed by birds, which are attracted by the bright, nutritious aril and swallow the seeds intact. A second species, ***Eriocoelum oblongum***, closely resembles *E. macrocarpum*, but the underside of the leaflets are covered in dense, pale brown hairs. The ripe orange fruit is also hairy and the shiny seeds have an orange, not red, aril.

Ganophyllum giganteum is a large tree reaching about 40 m tall and over 1m diameter. The trunk is often crooked and is sometimes rotten, where large branches have broken. It has small or medium sized buttresses. The flakey bark is brown-red and easily mistaken for that of Okoumé (p. 80). Some trees have particularly flakey bark with long, persistent, up-curving scales, giving a shaggy appearance to the trunk. The crown is often irregular. The leaves have about 11 assymmetrical leaflets (10 x 4 cm). New leaves are covered in resin, secreted from special cells, which gives the foliage a shiny appearence, hence the generic name, from the Greek "ganos" = shiny, and "phyllum" = leaf. *Ganophyllum* trees seem particularly susceptible to insect damage and sometimes lose much of their foliage, particularly in December / February. They produce tiny white flowers in November, which develop into sugary, yellow-orange fruits, about 2 cm long. These ripen in a two week period in mid-late January, or early February, when they are the centre of attention for many frugivores. One group of gorillas was observed to visit areas of the forest where *Ganophyllum* was common, about 2 weeks before the fruit ripened. They were tracked as they visited all of the *Ganophyllum* trees and then left the area, only to reappear 2 weeks later, just as the fruits ripened, to feast on their sweet flesh. It seems that they not only knew where all of the trees were, but were also able to predict accurately when the fruit would be ripe.

Right:

a) Allophylus africana
b) Blighia welwitschii
c) Chytranthus talbotii
d) Ganophyllum giganteum

d
a
b
d
c
KA '95

Ganophyllum giganteum is one of a number of tree species in Lopé known to depend upon low dry season temperatures in July / August to trigger flowering. The dry season is the gloomy time of the year, when dense, low clouds block out the sun, and the night time temperature falls below 20 °C. To stimulate flowering in *Ganophyllum* the temperature must fall to 19°C or below. In years when this does not happen, *Ganophyllum*, and other species like it, such as *Dialium lopense, Cola lizae, Diospyros polystemon* and *Irvingia gabonensis*, fail to flower and set fruit. In these years the frugivorous animals go hungry. Because of pollution caused by modern industry, the earth is currently experiencing the most rapid climate change of the last 10,000 years. It is generally accepted that global temperatures are rising, because increased concentrations of carbon dioxide in the atmosphere trap heat, rather like a greenhouse. If the 'greenhouse effect' results in a rise in temperatures of even just 1 or 2°C, this could mean that dry season temperatures will no longer fall to 19°C and all of the plant species dependent on this cue will stop flowering. This obviously has serious implications for many plant species but the consequent decrease in availability of fruits may also cause great hardship for many birds and mammals. It is sinister to think that modern pollution could have such far reaching effects, but unless we come to terms with it soon, it may be too late.

SAPOTACEAE

Omphalocarpum procerum (Mebimengone - the Fang which means «breasts of a young girl») is a medium sized tree (20m tall and 40cm diameter) found principally in Marantaceae forest. The grey bark is slightly flakey, sometimes with a faint orange hue. The base of its trunk tends to be scarred and swollen, where elephants have fed upon the bark over many years. If an elephant has fed recently you will see sticky white sap, characteristic of all plants in the Sapotaceae family, oozing out to seal the wound and protect it from infection. Like most of the Sapotaceae family, *Omphalocarpum* trees have large leaves arranged in distinctive whorls. This tree is generally easy to recognise because of the large brown fruit (20 cm diameter) which they bear through much of the year. The fruit resemble round loaves of bread and are about the size of a human head when ripe. They grow out of slight swellings on the trunk and larger branches. Formation of fruit on the trunk is relatively common for tree species growing in the tropical rain forest and is known as 'cauliflory'. It is thought to be an adaptation to favour pollination of the flowers by insects, such as the ants that can be seen marching up and down almost every trunk in the forest. It is the remarkable appearance of the fruit which gives the tree its local Makina name, «Mebeli me Nkouendi», which, if translated literally, means "the moon's breasts". If you come across a tree laden with fruit don't spend too long directly underneath, for they weigh about 2 kg when ripe and fall to the ground with a resounding thump. Each fruit contains about 30 - 40 large, shiny brown seeds (see page 215).

Like 70% of plant species found in the Lopé, *Omphalocarpum* trees rely upon animals to disperse their seeds. However, only elephants have jaws strong enough to crack open the hard, thick shell which protects the succulent white flesh around the seeds. The smell of garlic attracts elephants to the tree, and they wrap their trunks around any fallen fruit and lift them to their mouths. With an explosive crack they crunch into the shell, just as you might bite into a crusty loaf of garlic bread. There are hard nodules on the inner side of the shell which appear to be specially designed to stop the elephants grinding their teeth together and damaging the seeds. They swallow the seeds along with the pulp, without harming them. The fruit are full of sticky sap, which people used to collect and paste onto branches to trap birds. This can soon be seen oozing out of the elephants mouth in long strands if they find several fruits at once.

After passing through the elephant's gut, the seeds are deposited in a rich pile of natural compost. When they germinate, a few weeks later, this gives them a head-start in the race to grow up into the canopy, where they can get enough light to flower and fruit themselves.

In parts of Africa where poaching has eliminated the elephants, *Omphalocarpum* fruits rot on the ground, their seeds wasted and the trees are unable to reproduce. No species of animal or plant can survive alone. They are all part of an ecosystem within which a complex web of interactions exists. If any strand of that web is broken it will result in distortions which are difficult to predict and which may be impossible to repair.

Right:

Omphalocarpum procerum

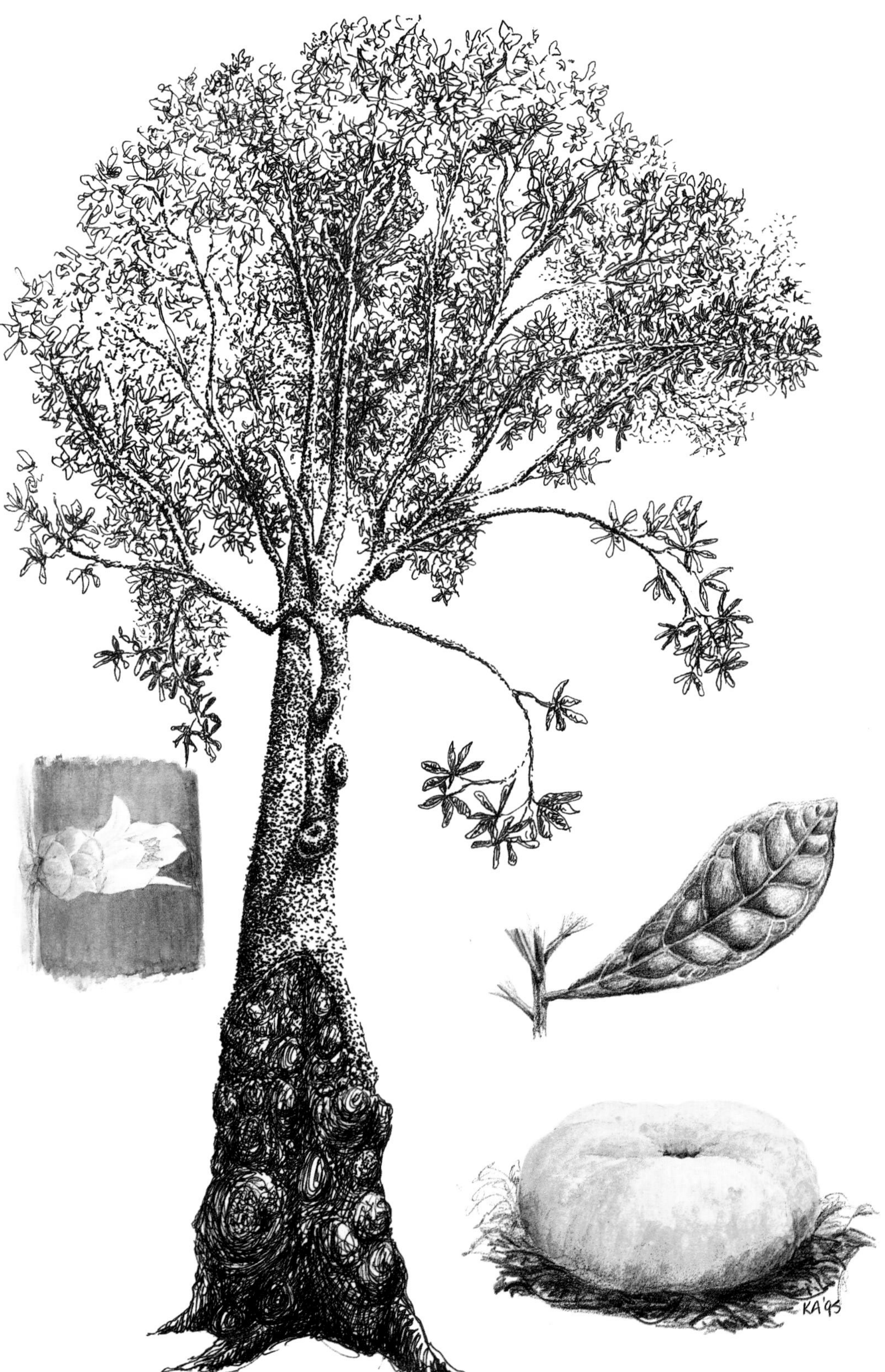
KA'95

STERCULIACEAE

The Sterculiaceae take their name from the Latin 'stercus', meaning 'dung', because of the evil smelling flowers of certain species in the genus *Sterculia*. The family is best known for the genus *Cola*, which contains almost 100 species, some of which produce 'cola nuts'; seeds rich in caffeine, which are chewed as a stimulant and which lend their name to the drink Coca Cola (see also p.207). The seeds of another Sterculiaceae, *Theobroma cacao*, yield cocoa, from which chocolate is made.

Cola lizae is one of the prominent tree species in the Lopé Reserve, because of its abundance and its striking appearance. It is the commonest tree species within Marantaceae Forest, occurring at densities of over 6,000 trees per square kilometre. You can imagine the surprise of researchers at the 'Station d'Etudes des Gorilles et Chimpanzés' therefore, when they discovered that it was a species unknown to science. It was named in 1987 by an expert at the Natural History Museum, Paris, after Liz Williamson, who was studying gorillas in Lopé, and collected some of the first specimens of its flowers and fruits.

Cola lizae trees are generally of medium height. They are easily recognised by their huge leaves. These are typically 40 or 50 cm across but, particularly in young trees, can reach 100 cm long by 120 cm wide. They have long, woody petioles and make perfect umbrellas if you are caught out in the rain. The leaves resemble the large freshwater ray, *Dasyatis ukpam*, which is occasionally caught by fishermen in the Ogooué, and the local Sakai name for the tree is that of the fish: «Poukoupoukoué». Where *Cola lizae* is abundant the ground is covered by its large leaves. In the dry season these crackle underfoot, making it impossible to move quietly through the forest. It is like trying to walk on crispy papadoms!

Its small, red flowers are produced from September to November when they carpet the forest floor in many places. The unripe green fruits are difficult to see amongst the large leaves, but as they ripen in January / March they become bright crimson and catch the eye both in the tree and on the ground. The fruits are thick, rubbery pods, each containing five to eight large seeds bathed in a clear liquid. Each seed has two pink cotyledons surrounded by a succulent yellow flesh, the mesocarp, and protected by a transparent skin.

Many of the Lopé primates eat the fruits of *Cola lizae*. It is interesting to watch them process the fruit. They bite into the pod and carefully drain off the liquid within, before eating the sugary flesh around the seeds. Similar liquid in other *Cola* species contains chemicals which act as growth inhibitors. It could be that this chemical protection is designed to prevent animals like elephants, which are unable to process the fruit in this way, from consuming them whole, since they would probably damage the otherwise unprotected seeds.

Most primates eat the mesocarp and then spit the seeds out quite close to the parent tree. These seeds tend not to grow well. Only gorillas swallow the seeds in large quantities. Seeds can take anything from one to several days to pass through a gorilla's digestive system. They are then deposited, intact, in the dung. In Marantaceae Forest in Lopé, gorillas tend to nest in clearings where there is a dense growth of herbaceous vegetation. They leave much of their dung in or close to the nest site. *Cola lizae* seedlings thrive in the light conditions in these sites and by folding vegetation down to make nests, the gorillas make it easier for seedlings to grow above the dense ground cover. Hence there is a very close relationship between gorillas and *Cola lizae*. The tree provides food for gorillas, who may eat more than 150 fruits a day, and they in turn are the only seed disperser of note. Such relationships are termed co-evolution.

Cola lizae has a very restricted range, almost exclusively within the Lopé Reserve. It seems specially adapted to grow in Marantaceae Forest. Its enormous leaves enable it to shade out the abundant wild gingers and arrow roots found in this habitat and therefore to escape their smothering fronds. It is one of a number of species which seem to have evolved in the dynamic forest-savanna mosaic of the Lopé Reserve, and emphasises the importance of the Reserve for plant as well as for animal conservation.

Nesogordonia papaverifera (Kotibé) is a large tree growing to over 40 m tall and 1 m diameter. It is found throughout the main forest block in Lopé, but is rare. The trunk is usually long and straight, with thin buttresses. It has grey bark with shallow, vertical fissures, which flakes off to expose dark brown patches. It is easily identified by its fallen leaves (10 x 5 cm) which have stalks about 2 cm long, and 6-10 prominent lateral nerves. The underside is sparsely covered in short, stellate hairs. The fragrant flowers are yellowish-white with 5 petals, each just over 1 cm long. The woody, bell-shaped fruits are about 2.5 cm long, covered in rusty-brown stellate hairs. They are in 5 sections and split when ripe to release 10 winged seeds. The strong, dark red, wood has many uses, particularly in heavy duty construction and as tool handles.

Right:

Cola lizae

KA'94
KA'95

Right:

a) Nesogordonia papavifera
b) Pterygota bequaertii
c) Scaphopetalum blackii
d) Sterculia tragacantha

Pterygota bequaertii is a large tree growing to over 40 m tall and up to 80 cm diameter. It is rare and found only in mature forest. It has smooth grey-brown bark and quite high, thin, buttresses. The branchlets and young foliage are densely covered in woolly, brown stellate hairs. *Pterygota bequaertii* has a rounded leaf (13 x 9 cm), with a stalk about 5 cm long. The strong veination is characteristic, with 5 nerves leaving at the base. The flowers are in short panicles, with a cream calyx about 1 cm long and ginger hairs on both the outside and the inside. The centre of the flower is crimson-red. The easily recognised pod is about 11 cm long, held on a long stalk and persists on the ground for several months, after falling from the tree. It opens to release numerous winged seeds each about 7 x 2.5 cm. These seeds give the genus its name, derived from the Greek for 'winged'.

Scaphopetalum blackii is a small tree growing up to about 6 m, which becomes common in the understorey on the higher ridges in mature forest. It has a twisted trunk up to 20 cm diameter, similar to that of *Ouratea flava* (p. 191). The large leaves (20-25 x 8 cm) have strong, characteristic nervation and a rough underside. The small yellow and purple flowers, like miniature ball gowns, are unmistakable. The pink-purple fruit, about 4 cm long, is made up of 5 valves. These split to reveal 2-4 seeds, each about 1 cm long, covered in an irregularly toothed aril. A second species, *Scaphopetalum thonneri* is rare in the northern half of the Lopé Reserve. It can be distinguished from *S. blackii* by a remarkable hollow pocket-like swelling close to the base of the leaf, in which ants of the genus *Engramma* nest. In return for shelter these ants afford protection, like those found in *Barteria fistulosa* (p. 90) and *Nauclea vanderguchtii* (p. 204).

Sterculia tragacantha is a medium sized tree which rarely exceeds 25 m or 75 cm diameter. It is generally found quite close to rock outcrops in Marantaceae Forest in Lopé. The bark is silvery-grey and flakes off in irregular scales. Buttresses are sometimes present, becoming thick roots which snake away from the trunk for up to 40 m or more along the ground. These roots anchor *Sterculia tragacantha* trees into the thin soils around rock outcrops, enabling them to grow taller than surrounding vegetation. The rounded leaves (12 x 8 cm) have 3-5 nerves starting from the base. The underside of the leaves is covered by stellate hairs, giving them a rough texture. Leaves yellow and fall in July / October, leaving the canopy bare. In this state *Sterculia tragacantha* can easily be mistaken for *Lannea welwitschii* (p. 112). The reddish-pink flowers are densely covered in brown stellate hairs. The fruits are composed of 4-5 boat shaped segments, each about 6 cm long. Young fruits are green, covered in coarse velvet, which becomes bright red as they ripen. The fruits are prominently displayed when the leaves are lost and open to reveal 5-6 shiny black seeds, eaten by hornbills.

TILIACEAE

Duboscia macrocarpa (Akak) is one of the most distinctive trees in the Lopé. Its trunk is irregularly fluted with a twisted, tortured form, rising to 35 m tall. It has slightly flakey, pale bark. The alternate leaves (10 x 5 cm) are asymmetric at the base and have distinctive veination. There are hairs on both surfaces, but particularly on the underside which has the texture of fine sand paper. The slight serrations on the leaves of adult trees are much more distinct in seedlings and saplings, which are common in the under-storey (see p. 2). The flowers are borne on short stalks opposite the leaves. Between 3-6 pale bracts enclose 2-3 flowers, each with 4 hairy, pink sepals, small white petals and numerous anthers which are red at the base and white above. The fruits are up to 5 cm long with 5-8 angular ribs. They are hard and fibrous and covered in a pelt of short hairs, which, if viewed with a hand lens, appear star shaped (stellate hairs). They have a strong odour like that of an apple pie cooking in the oven. There are numerous, small, triangular seeds embedded in the fibrous flesh.

Duboscia macrocarpa is a good example of a species with asynchronous flowering and fruiting. Each individual has a well established rhythm, flowering every 17 months immediately after changing its leaves. However, different trees do not flower in synchrony and fruits ripen in a staggered fashion over several months. During a study of the ecology of forest elephants, undertaken in the Lopé Reserve, seeds of *Duboscia macrocarpa* were found in their dung in all 12 months of the year. The fruits are eaten by many animal species. Parrots spend long hours in fruiting *Duboscia* trees, systematically extracting and chewing the seeds. This is of no benefit to the tree, since the parrot is acting as a seed predator (it is destroying the seeds), not a seed disperser. When finished they drop the frayed core of the fruit to the ground.

Desplatsia dewevrei **(Tiliaceae)**
A small-medium sized tree which is rare in Lopé but common in many central African forests. The leaves are similar to those of *Grewia*. The fruits are elephants' equivalent of chewing gum. They contain numerous small seeds which are swallowed before the husk is spat out.

c
a
b
d
d
KA'95

Both mandrills and grey-cheeked mangabeys feed on the seeds in the same way. Gorillas and chimpanzees eat the fruit rather as we would an apple, discarding the woody core. Because of our similar digestive systems it is safe to assume that we humans can eat anything that these close relatives consume. However, you will probably agree that eating the fruits of *Duboscia macrocarpa* would be akin to chewing on a scrubbing brush. It is difficult to know what chimps and gorillas see in this fruit, but because *Duboscia* exhibits asynchronous fruiting it is available during the long dry season when there is little else to eat, and in such circumstances perhaps is not so bad. Elephants also eat large quantities of fallen *Duboscia* fruit. The tough, fibrous flesh which surrounds the small seeds protects them from being damaged by the elephants large molars and they are swallowed down intact. For some seeds passage through an elephant's gut improves the chances of germination. It is not known if this is the case for those of *Duboscia macrocarpa*, but they certainly germinate well in elephant dung. One rarely finds an old pile of elephant dung without at least a few *Duboscia* seedlings sprouting up from the fibrous mass.

Grewia coriacea, another tree species in the Tiliaceae, also occurs in the Lopé. It is rare in the northern half of the Reserve, although its spongy, pear shaped seeds, each about 1.5 cm long, are occasionally found in gorilla and chimpanzee dung around December. It is a small tree growing to about 15 m tall, which tends to grow in moist areas. It has large, smooth, symmetrical leaves (17 x 8 cm) with characteristic veination similar to that of *Duboscia*.

Syzygium cf. staudtii

The final three species in this section are grouped at the end because they all have similar, small, sugary fruits eaten by animals:

MYRTACEAE

Syzygium cf. staudtii (Etom) is restricted to high altitude forest in Lopé. It is a large tree which grows to about 40 m tall and over 1.5 m diameter. The shaggy, dark brown trunk has numerous irregular cracks and fissures, creating a tortured effect (see p. 213). The trunk is usually crooked and the base is fluted in larger trees. The opposite leaves (5.5 x 2.5 cm) have numerous, parallel lateral nerves. The flowers have numerous white anthers about 1 cm long. The round, purple fruits are about 1 cm diameter, ripening late in the long dry season. A second species, perhaps ***Syzygium guineense***, occurs in low altitude forest in Lopé. Its trunk is paler but equally fissured and it is very difficult to distinguish the two species.

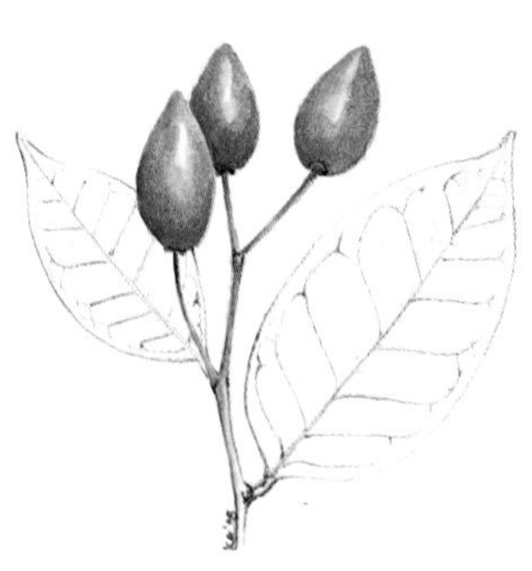

Scytopetalum sp.

SCYTOPETALACEAE

Scytopetalum sp. is a medium sized tree, up to about 20 m tall and 40 cm diameter, found throughout the forest in Lopé, which has yet to be identified to species level. It has a rough, grey-brown trunk. The alternate leaves (6 x 3cm) have about 10 indistinct lateral nerves. The small, white flowers are about 4 mm across. Its red fruits, about 2 cm long, have a thin, sugary flesh, when ripe from April to August. They are one of a very limited number of succulent fruits which are available in the long dry season, and are eaten by many animal species. The characteristic seeds have 7-9 ridges (p. 215).

ULMACEAE

Celtis tessmannii (Diania) is a large tree found throughout the forest in Lopé. The trunk is straight and cylindrical and the base often has thick, rounded buttresses, although sometimes it is simply somewhat swollen. The grey bark appears smooth from a distance, with numerous horizontal ridges, but is in fact covered in narrow, vertical fissures, giving an appearance like elephant skin. The wavy branches are similar to those of *Irvingia gabonensis*, although they are more angular. The large canopy appears grey-green, almost metallic, except in December / April when leaves are lost and pale young foliage appears. Small green flowers grow in November. The purple fruits, about 1.5 cm long, ripen in February / March. They have a thin, sweet, succulent flesh which is highly favoured by many of the animals. Gorillas and chimpanzees eat large quantities of fruit and elephants arrive in numbers to feed on those which fall to the ground. Elephants go to the extreme of eating the gorilla and chimpanzee dung, which is full of *Celtis tessmannii* seeds, apparently crunching up the seeds.

Right:

Duboscia macrocarpa
i) leaf of young plant

i

Celtis tessmannii is quite a common tree which would provide an important food source if it fruited every year. However, despite the fact that flowering is annual, it only seems to produce fruit once every 3-4 years, probably because flowers or young fruits are often destroyed by insects. This illustrates the unpredictable nature of food availability for frugivorous animals, which must remain extremely flexible and adaptable if they are to find sufficient food to survive. It was perhaps this need for flexibility that honed the intelligence of our forest dwelling ancestors, setting in motion the process that lead to the emergence of modern man.

6/ MATURE FOREST

In the half of the Reserve that has experienced great vegetation change in the last millenium or so, Marantaceae forests are gradually developing into more mature forest. The remainder of the Lopé Reserve has been relatively stable and is dominated by mature forest, which has existed for many thousands of years. Mature forest can be identified by the presence of more classic rain forest vegetation. There are many large and medium sized trees, creating a complex structure. The canopy cover is almost complete and conditions near the ground are cool and shady. The under-storey vegetation is sparse and consists mostly of shrubs and lianes, which are specially adapted to life in the dim under-storey. Occasional huge lianes snake up from the ground high into the canopy.

Some trees are enormous, occasionally exceeding 65 m tall. These emerge out of the closed canopy into the bright sunshine. Their wide trunks and spreading buttresses attest to their great age. The trunks of some species grow at a rate of only 1 or 2 mm per year, and some large individuals can be almost a thousand years old. These living monuments become mini-ecosystems in themselves. Their trunks and branches are shrouded in epiphytes, small 'hitch hikers' which take advantage of other plants to grow high in the canopy. Their crevices provide ideal nesting sites for hornbills, palm civets and arboreal pangolins, whilst a multitude of invertebrates live concealed under their bark or in their foliage. Scientists working in South America recently found many thousands of species of beetles living in the canopy of a single large rain forest tree, many of which were new to science. The canopy of the rain forest, like the depths of the oceans, is one of the last great unexplored realms on Earth. Unfortunately it is fast disappearing and many of its secrets will soon be lost for all time.

When one of the giant forest trees dies it creates a gap in the canopy which lets light into the forest below. If they die standing, gradually disappearing as branches rot and drop to the ground, the resulting gap is small. However, if they

Baillonella toxisperma ○;
Diospyros dendo ●, Unknown species ○; Coula edulis ●, Polyalthia suaveolens ●,
Diospyros boala ○, Dialium species ●; Garcinia afzelii ○, Dacryodes buettneri ○,
Unknown liane ○; Penthaclethra macrophylla ●; Mareyopsis longifolia ○;
Santina trimera ●; Ongokea gore ●, Ptychopetalum petiolatum ●,
Sinderopsis letestui ●, Carapa procera ●, Phyllanthus acidus ●.

Right:

a) Helictonema velutinum
b) Hippocratea myrioneura
c) Salacia callensii
d) Salacia cornifolia
e) Salacia cf. elegans
f) Salacia cf. mayumbensis
g) Salacia whytei

Pavetta hispida (Rubiaceae)
(see p. 110)

Lavigeria macrocarpa (Icacinaceae) is a liane found in mature forest which has a large underground tuber, like those of wild yams. Its edible fruit is used as an aphrodisiac.

Ground vegetation in gaps soon becomes lush and dense as new herbaceous plants establish and a race begins. The race, between young individuals of species which grow to be tall forest trees, is to be the first to reach the hole high above in the canopy. The winner will eventually spread its branches to fill the gap, and throw all the plants below it into shade. Gaps allow many light loving plant species to establish and grow. These provide important food for elephants and gorillas, whose tracks are often evident in forest gaps. In fact, they are the favourite nesting place of gorillas, who fold the dense ground vegetation into thick, springy mattresses to ease their night's sleep. Elsewhere in Africa, the Okapi, a rain forest version of the giraffe, relies almost exclusively on the leaves of shrubs and small trees which grow in light gaps.

The mature forest in Lopé is very diverse. There may be over 150 species of tree in just one hectare, more than four times as many as occur in the whole of Great Britain. It is teaming with life from the ground to the tip of the highest branch. When you go into the forest take time to sit quietly in a concealed spot and watch the activity all around. If you eat a sandwich, within minutes you will notice ants busily carrying away the crumbs. Butterflies and bees will arrive to sip your perspiration. Birds are on the move all around. Leaves fall from above into the thick layer of leaf litter, where insects and mushrooms will gradually break down their structure and recycle the nutrients they contain.

Soils in Lopé are very poor. They contain few nutrients and are extremely acid. Most of the available minerals are stored above ground in the vegetation itself. The layer of leaf litter that crunches underfoot is a vital component for the functioning of the forest, a factory which recycles the nutrients that fall from above, making them available to support further plant growth. If you come across a fallen tree with its roots wrenched out of the ground, you may be surprised by their shallow penetration. One would expect a large tree to have a deep root system to hold it upright, but instead the rain forest tree's roots spread out in a dense network close to the surface of the soil, where the few nutrients are stored.

Lianes

CELASTRACEAE

Helictonema velutinum is a liane which climbs to 25-30 m, found principally in galleries and Marantaceae Forest. It tends only to be noticed when dropping its peculiar flowers to the ground in the dry season, or when fruiting. The fruit is a pod with three, finger-like, sections. These are covered in dense brown velvety hairs and split to release small winged seeds which twirl to the ground.

Hippocratea myrioneura is a liane which climbs to 30 m or more. It has opposite leaves which, if torn, remain joined by fine fibres. Some *Salacia* species also have this character. Its large bunches of white flowers are particularly prominent in galleries at the beginning of the long dry season. These develop into silvery-green capsules, which dry out and darken to brown as they ripen. They split, releasing seeds similar to those of *Helictonema velutinum*.

Gabon's forests are very rich in plant species, containing a greater diversity of plants than the whole of West Africa. The genus *Salacia* is a good example of this - the forests of Gabon and Cameroon contain at least 60 species and are the richest area in the World for this genus. We have only found 11 species to date in Lopé, but unless fruiting they tend to be rather cryptic and there are probably many more left to discover. They are shrubs and lianes found mostly in mature forest, although some occur in galleries. They all have opposite, or near opposite, serrated leaves, although these vary in size and shape. The flowers are small, generally a few mm across, and usually pale yellow. It is easy to see that the fruits are animal dispersed; they all have waxy fruits with bright eye catching orange skins and have sugary flesh. The species most often seen are drawn on the plate and can be distinguished on the basis of leaf and fruit form.

Herbs

The mature forest in Lopé is more diverse than other vegetation types. Currently 1,530 plant species have been recorded in the Lopé Reserve, although it is thought that there are actually at least 3,000 - 4,000 species in all. It is not possible to describe all species in the Reserve in this guide, but to demonstrate the variety of small flowering plants in the mature forest we will illustrate a few of the epiphytic orchids that occur here (see pages 166 & 167).

e
d
f
c
g
a
b

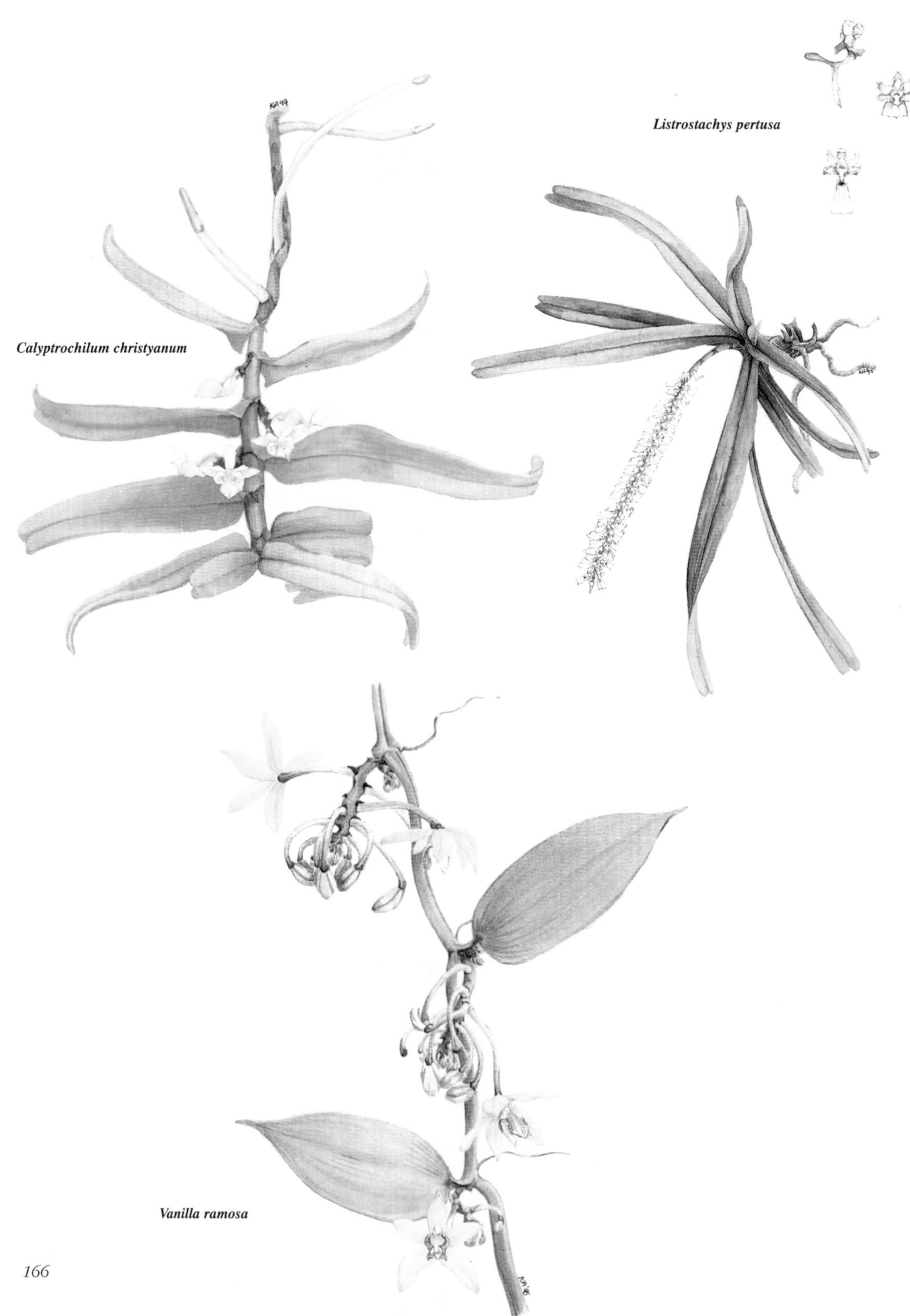
Listrostachys pertusa
Calyptrochilum christyanum
Vanilla ramosa

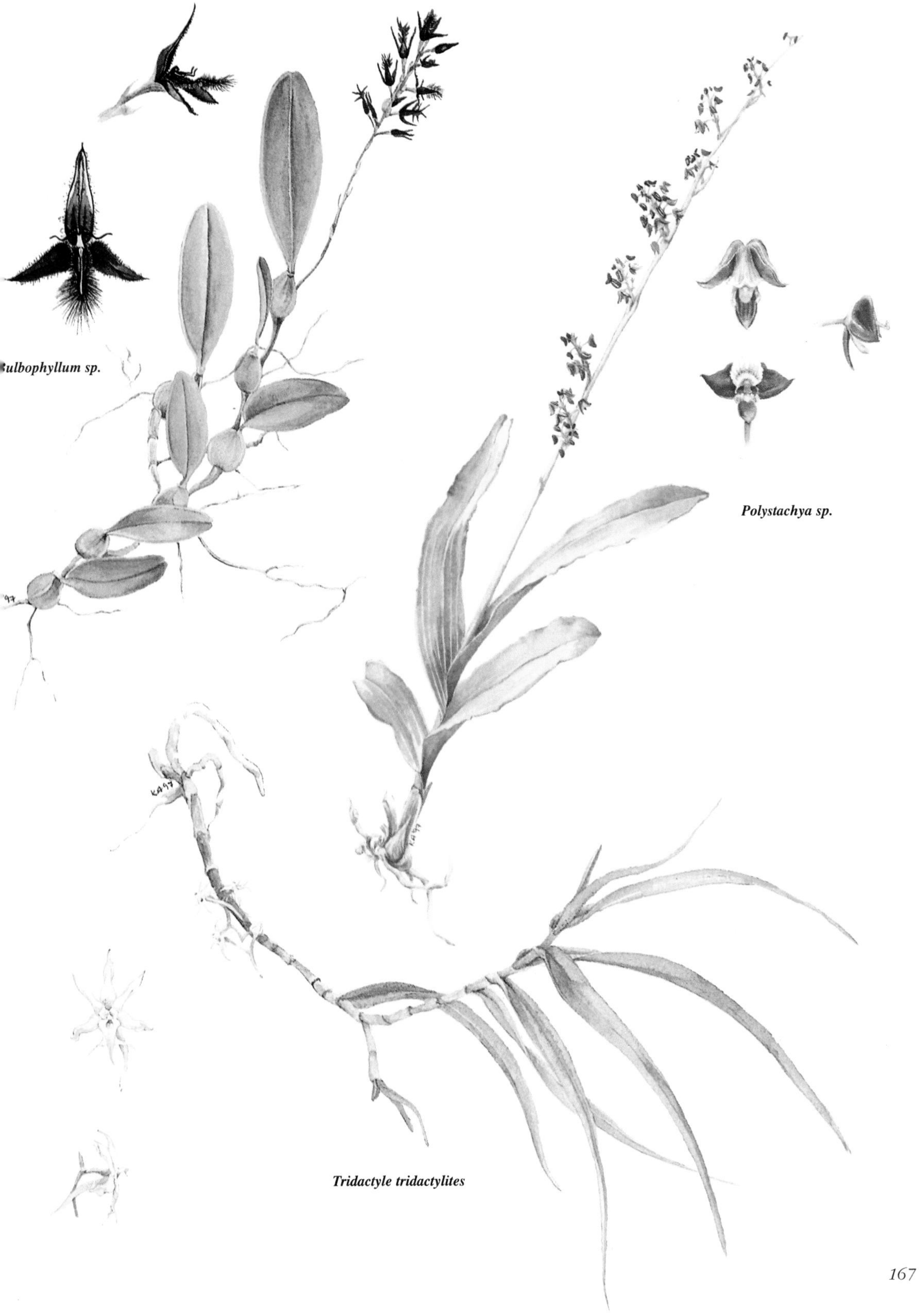

Bulbophyllum sp.

Polystachya sp.

Tridactyle tridactylites

Right:

Huaceae
a) Afrostyrax lepidophyllus
Icaciniaceae
b) Lasianthera africana
Olacaceae
c) Ptychopetalum petiolatum
Pandaceae
d) Centroplacus glaucinus
Violaceae
e) Rinorea ilicifolia
f) Rinorea cf. parviflora

Rourea solanderi
(Connaraceae - see p. 52)

Jollydora duparquetiana
(Connaraceae - see p. 52)

Under-storey trees

HUACEAE (previously STYRACACEAE)

Afrostyrax lepidophyllus or "wild garlic", is restricted to mature forest in Lopé, growing to about 15 m tall and 25 cm diameter. It has smooth yellow-brown bark with lenticels, which flakes off in patches. *Afrostyrax* can be identified by its characteristic, alternate leaves (17 x 6 cm) which are pale golden brown on the underside, with about 7 pairs of upcurving lateral nerves. If cut, the bark smells strongly of garlic, and is often harvested, like that of *Scorodophloeus zenkeri* (p. 176), to flavour sauces. Young leaves are also used in this way. The fruits are grey-shelled, spherical nuts about 2 cm diameter which fall to the ground in December / January. The seeds have a strong garlicy flavour and are used in cooking, but their odour exudes from the skin for much of the following day.

ICACINACEAE

Lasianthera africana is found in all forest types in Lopé, occasionally becoming quite common. It rarely reaches 10 m tall and is usually less than 10 cm diameter. It has smooth, pale bark and often has several trunks. The leaf (11 x 4 cm) has characteristic shape and veination. It has delicate balls of fluffy, white flowers, throughout much of the year. The leaves are eaten by gorillas and elephants and the wood is used to make axe handles and cross-bows.

OLACACEAE

Ptychopetalum petiolatum is rare and is restricted to mature forest in Lopé. It grows up to about 10 m tall and 15 cm diameter. The leaves resemble those of *Lasianthera africana*, but are leathery and have more compact and well defined veination, which is unusually clear on the upper-side of the leaf. It has a small, knobbled red fruit which dangles on a stalk like a cherry. The fruits ripen in January / February, are sweet to taste and are eaten by apes.

PANDACEAE

Centroplacus glaucinus is a common tree in the under-storey of mature forest in Lopé, growing to about 15 m tall and 20 cm diameter. The bark is dark brown with numerous narrow vertical fissures and the branches begin parallel to the ground but curve down, like those of *Scottellia coriacea* (p. 130). The leaves, (12 x 4 cm) are pale grey-green on their underside, with about 5 pairs of obvious, upcurving lateral veins. The small white flowers bloom in December and are particularly eye catching when caught by beams of early morning sun penetrating the forest understory. Small pink fruits, about 6 mm long, ripen in January / March, opening to reveal an orange aril around the seed.

VIOLACEAE

The genus *Rinorea* contains many species of shrub and small tree found in the forest understorey, particularly close to water. Except for those with characteristic leaves, the different *Rinorea* species can only be distinguished by microscopic examination of the flowers by an expert.

Rinorea ilicifolia is a shrub or small tree up to about 5 m tall, found occasionally in small stands in all forest types in Lopé. It has a smooth twisted trunk and is easily identified by its remarkable leaves (20 x 9 cm), which are tough and leathery, with pronounced spiny teeth all around their margins. The yellow flowers and pink-fawn fruits, which split into 3 sections when ripe, throwing seeds a few metres, are typical of all *Rinorea* species. ***Rinorea cf. parviflora*** occurs along the banks of rivers and streams in Marantaceae forest. The serrated leaves (13 x 5 cm) are more typical of the genus as a whole. The flowers and fruits are similar to those of *R. ilicifolia*.

Medium and large trees

CLUSIACEAE

Garcinia afzelii is a small-medium sized tree growing to about 20 m tall and 25 cm diameter. It has smooth, pale brown bark and angular branches, with a rounded, bushy crown. The opposite leaves (12 x 5 cm) have a tight network of parallel lateral veins like many of the Clusiaceae. However, they can easily be distinguished by their numerous visible, thin, wavy, resin canals or 'false veins', which run through the leaves, roughly parallel to the midrib. Flowers are male or female, forming in October / November. They are cream in colour, about 1.5 cm across and female flowers posess a sticky disc formed by the stigmas. The fruits are green-yellow, about 1 cm across, containing 1-2 seeds. They ripen in December / February and are eaten by many of the frugivores.

f
b
e
c
a
d

Right:

a) Garcinia afzelii
b) Mammea africana
c) Symphonia globulifera

Xylopia staudtii
(Annonaceae - see p. 74)

Like many of the *Garcinia* species found in African rain forests, the cream-yellow sap of *G. afzelii* contains an anti-bacterial agent and the wood can be used as a 'tooth-brush'. The wood is softened by chewing and the frayed end then used to rub the teeth and gums. Other *Garcinia* species occur in galleries in savanna and along the Ogooué (p.19). The bark of ***Garcinia kola***, the «Bois amer» (bitter wood), which is rare in Lopé, is commonly used in Gabon to flavour palm wine. It is said to preserve the wine, improve its flavour and increase its intoxicating effects. Another species, *Garcinia mangostana*, the mangosteen, said to have one of the world's most delicious fruits, is sometimes cultivated in Africa.

Mammea africana (Oboto) is a large tree which grows to about 40 m tall and 1 m diameter. The base is usually swollen by elephant feeding, but larger individuals may have thick, rounded buttresses. The scaly bark is yellowish-grey. The larger branches are wavy, growing perpendicular to the trunk and the dense canopy is dark green. The opposite leaves (12 x 4 cm) are thick and leathery, with a dense network of parallel lateral nerves and many conspicuous translucent dots. The spherical flower buds are pink and about 7 mm across. The flowers open in October / November. They are about 3-4 cm across with white petals and red sepals. The round fruits are up to about 10 cm diameter. They have a pale, warty skin and contain about 3 very hard seeds, in a yellowish pulp which is excellent to eat when ripe. The fruits are eaten by most frugivores, but their seeds are only dispersed by elephants. Obotos are considered to have excellent wood, but are rarely cut in Gabon.

Symphonia globulifera is a medium sized tree found most often on ridges in mature forest in Lopé. Interestingly, elsewhere it is most often found beside water or in swamps. It occurs across tropical Africa, and the same species is also found in tropical America, dating back to the period when the two continents were closer together. The base is without buttresses and sometimes suffers quite serious damage by elephants, exuding large quantities of bright yellow sap. The smooth bark is chocolate coloured, but tends to be marked by many pale patches of lichen, producing an intricate pattern. The branches are short and thin, arranged in horizontal tiers at the top of the tree in a small, rounded canopy. They grow perpendicular to the trunk, but curve down towards their tips. The branchlets and leaves are in opposite pairs. The leaves (8 x 3 cm) have narrow, parallel veination. Flowering trees are particularly conspicuous. The flowers crowd along the length of the branches like bright red berries. Flowers produce nutritious nectar which attracts sun birds. A single tree can contain many territories, defended by aggressive males, who spend most of their day fighting rather than feeding. The fruits are about 3 cm long when ripe, with a pale-brown, warted skin, crowned by the persistent stigmas.

LECYTHIDACEAE

This family is best known for the South American species *Bartholletia excelsa*, the Brazil nut. Several species occur in the mature forest in Lopé.

Napoleonaea vogelii is a small to medium sized tree growing to about 10 m and 20 cm diameter in mature forest. It was named in honour of the Emperor Napoleon I. The trunk has pale bark and appears rough and gnarled. The branches are twisted, giving the impression of a tree growing on an exposed hillside, battered by countless strong winds. The alternate, leaves (12 x 4 cm) are caudate. Its intricate flowers grow amongst the leaves, as well as on the larger branches and the trunk. They have a delicate cream and red corolla about 3 cm across. The woody fruit are brownish to reddish, with a pitted skin and persistent sepals. They are about 5 cm across and contain several large seeds covered in sweet, succulent flesh. A second species, ***Napoleonaea egertonii***, is rare. Its large spiny fruit (14-16 cm diameter) contains several triangular seeds rather like huge *Cola* nuts and can be mistaken for *Treculia obovoidea*.

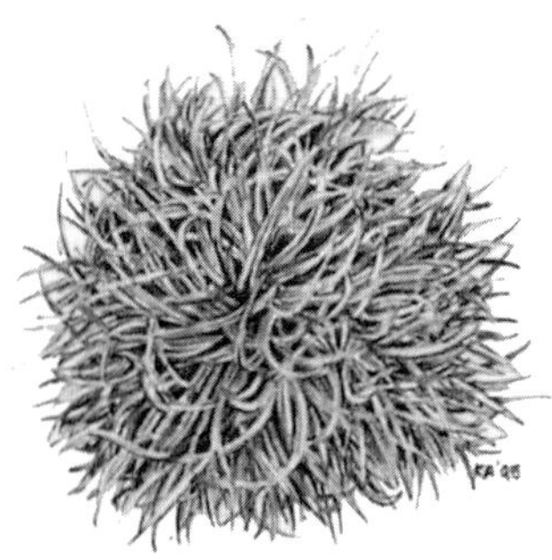

Treculia obovoidea **(Moraceae) is a medium sixed tree found on ridges in Lopé. Its spiny fruits resemble those of European chestnuts. They contain numerous edible seeds which even taste like chestnuts and which can be used to make flour in the same way as those of *T. africana*.**

Petersianthus macrocarpus (Essia) grows to 40 m or more in height, with a diameter over 1 m. All trees have swollen bases because elephants regularly remove large patches of bark. Close inspection of wood exposed by old injuries will reveal an unusual adaptation to the regular removal of bark. As well as regenerating from the edge of the injury, as do most trees, *Petersianthus* bark also grows from pores in the wood itself. There are often many patches of regenerating bark on exposed wood, growing steadily outwards towards each other, greatly speeding the recovery and therefore reducing the chances of infection setting in. Above the distorted base the bark is brown and deeply marked by many interlocking vertical fissures. The alternate leaves (15 x 7 cm) are slightly toothed and turn bright red as they age. The presence of these eye-catching fallen leaves is often the first sign of a nearby tree. The small white flowers are generally only noticed when falling to the ground in December. They develop into a large wind dispersed fruit about 4 cm long, with 4 papery, semi-circular wings at right angles to one another. These resemble the fruits of *Combretum* (p. 48) and indeed *Petersianthus* was once known by the scientific name *Combretodendron*, which in Greek means a «Combretum-like tree».

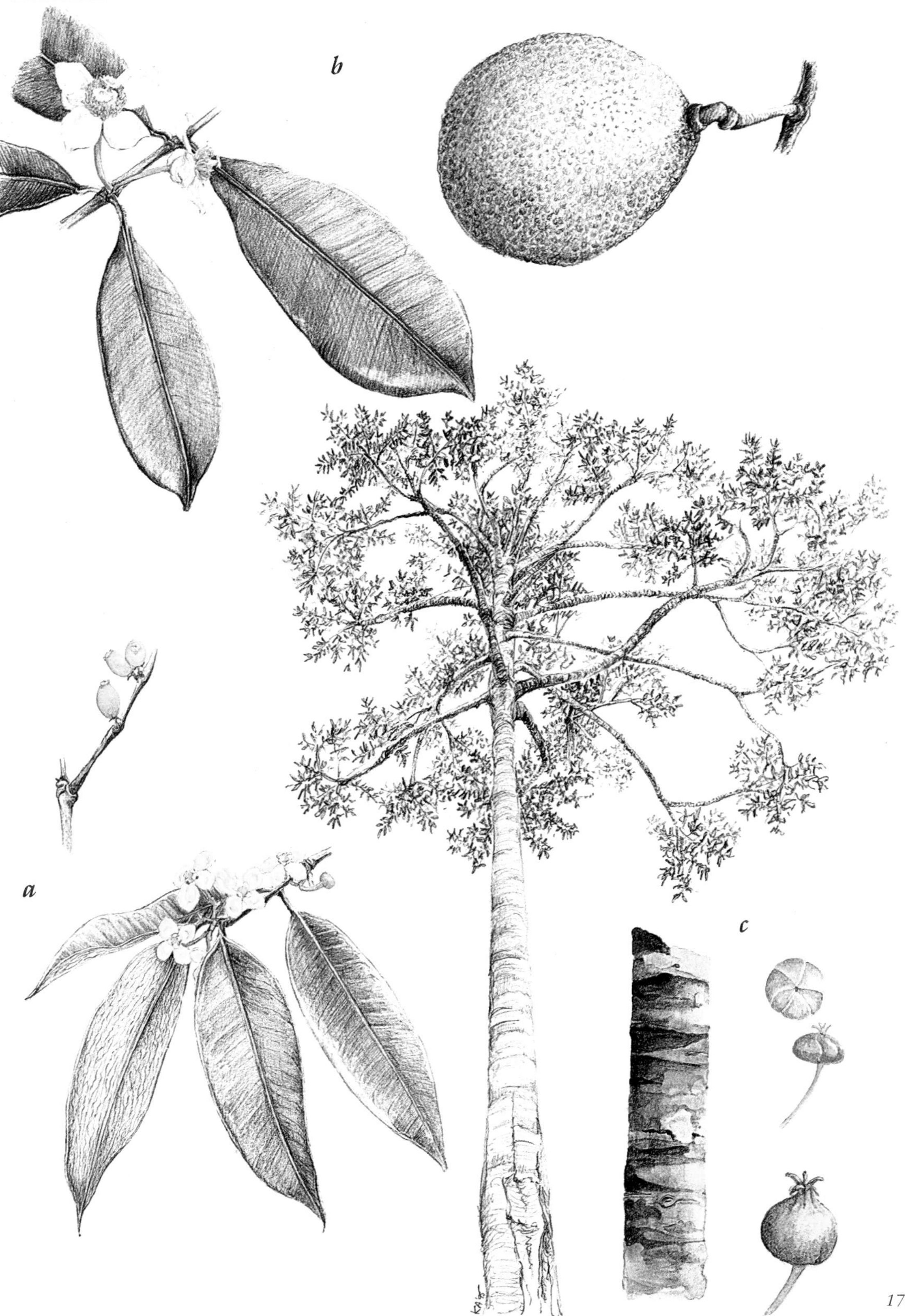
b
a
c

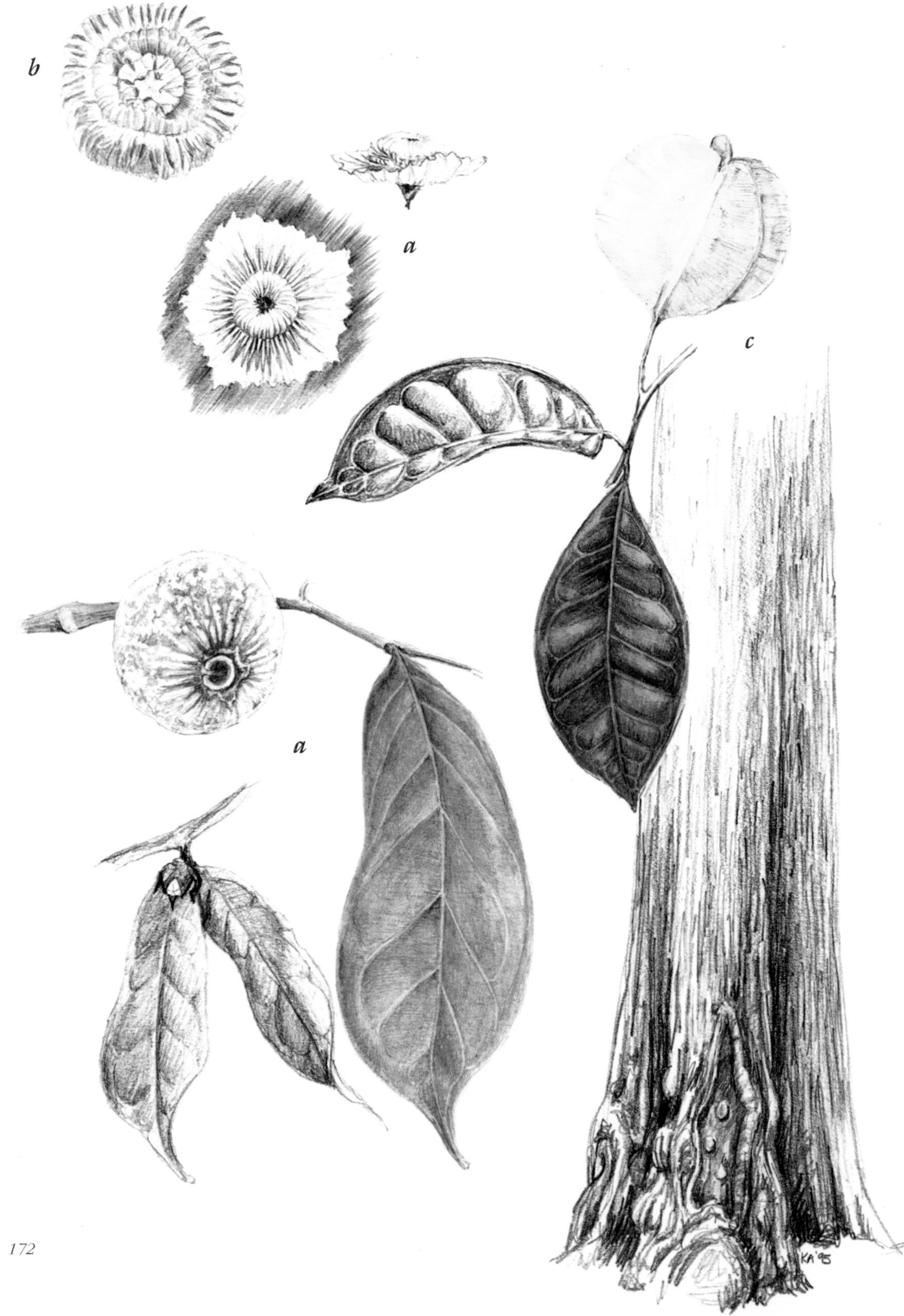
b
a
c
a
KA'95

LEGUMINOSAE; SUBFAMILY: CAESALPINIOIDEAE

At times in the past when Africa's climate became drier, forest species retreated into a few, isolated refuges. When conditions became moister the forest could once again expand. However, certain plant species were better able to take advantage of this opportunity. Species able to grow out in the open were favoured over those adapted to the cool shaded conditions of the forest. In addition, species whose seeds are dispersed long distances by animals could spread faster than those whose pods split, throwing seeds 10 or 20 m. Hence, plants of the Caesalpinioideae, which is dominated by species with dehiscent pods, tended to expand slowly and today can be used to map older forest types. When you find that you are surrounded by members of this family you can be sure that the forest you are walking through is several thousand years old.

Augouardia letestui is endemic to Gabon and the Mayombé in Congo. It is a common, medium-sized tree in much of the Lopé, growing to about 20 m tall. It has multiple trunks, giving it a superficial resemblance to a coppiced tree in a managed European wood. Its grey-brown bark is smooth, with numerous fine vertical cracks. The compound leaves generally have 5 pairs of leaflets (10 x 4cm) with indistinct lateral nerves. The leaves are easily confused with those of *Dialium soyauxii* (p. 138). It produces large panicles with numerous small white flowers about 5 mm across. When research began in Lopé, *Augouardia* remained unidentified for a long time and it was thought to be a new species. Researchers monitored trees over a large part of the Reserve, waiting for them to flower. Finally, in October 1989, all of the monitored trees produced short-lived flowers in the same week. It is a mystery how thousands of trees, up to 50 km apart, are synchronised, but it is a very good adaptation to ensure successful pollination. The fruit is a pod about 14 x 5 cm which ripens and splits in January / March.

Neochevalierodendron stephanii tends to occur in pockets in which it becomes common. Like *Augouardia letestui* it often has multiple trunks. The bark is smooth and pale grey. It is easily recognised by its characteristic compound leaf which has 4 asymmetric leaflets. The lower pair (9 x 5 cm) are alternate and the upper pair (12 x 6 cm) are opposite in the form a lobster claw. It flowers in October and November. The buds are enclosed in green, petal-like bracteoles which become partly pink as the buds mature. The flowers have three white-pink petals about 1.5 cm long. The pods are about 20 x 7 cm and around February their split valves carpet the ground where *Neochevalierodendron* is common, twisting into coils as they dry.

Pellegriniodendron diphyllum occurs in dense pockets within mature forest, often in moist gullys or along small streams. It can de identified from its compound leaf, with a single pair of asymmetrical leaflets (14 x 4.5 cm) New young leaves are limp and bright pink. There are a pair of small stipules at the base of the leaf and a stipel at the base of each leaflet. The flowers have one large white petal (15 x 5 mm) and three red anthers. The pod (10 x 5 cm) has 1-3 seeds and the valves twist around one another after it has split.

Copaifera mildbraedii (Anzem-éviné) is an uncommon tree in Lopé and is restricted to mature forest. In Latin 'copaifera' means 'copal bearing', referring to the fact that some species of this genus produce the gum copal. It can grow up to 65 m tall. The bark is grey, with fine vertical fissures similar to *Sindoropsis letestui*. In large individuals the base of the trunk is slightly swollen and fluted, but there are no distinct buttresses. It has alternate, compound leaves about 15 cm long, with 10-20 small, characteristic leaflets (2.5 x 1 cm). The leaflets are asymmetrical, indented at their tip and covered in numerous translucent dots on the underside. They have one distinct marginal and numerous lateral nerves. The tiny white flowers are borne on spikes, which branch off panicles about as long as the leaves. The fruit is a fleshy, green-purple, pod which blackens when ripe in July/August. It splits to reveal a single black seed about 2 cm across, with a thin orange aril. These fruits are quite resinous and burn with a noisy, aromatic flame, even when green.

Daniellia klainei (Faro) is a large tree found only in mature forest. It has smooth, pale bark, with numerous, small, horizontal ridges. Even large trees have little or no thickening at the base of the trunk. The compound leaves have 4-6 pairs of large leaflets (12-30 x 4-10 cm). Fallen leaflets resemble the leaves of *Klainedoxa gabonensis* (p. 84). The flowers and young pods are red-pink and are particularly eye catching when they fall to the ground at the end of the dry season. The fruit ripens in January. The pod is about 12 x 4.5 cm with a single wine coloured seed about 5 x 2 cm.

Left:

a) Napoleonaea vogelii
b) Napoleonaea egertonii
c) Petersianthus macrocarpus

Baphia leptobotrys
(Leguminosae, Papilionoideae), a tree found in mature forest (see p. 143).

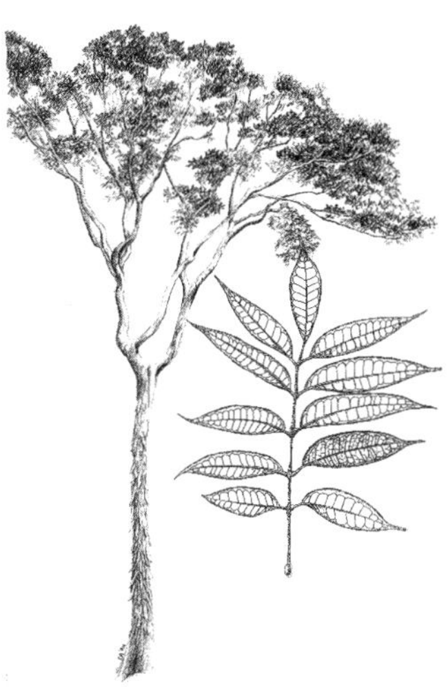

Dacryodes buettneri
(Burseraceae - see p. 116)

Page 174

a) Augouardia letestui
b) Neochevalierodendron stephanii
c) Pellegriniodendron diphyllum

Page 175

a) Copaifera mildbraedii
b) Daniellia klainei
c) Guibourtia tessmannii
d) Sindoropsis letestui

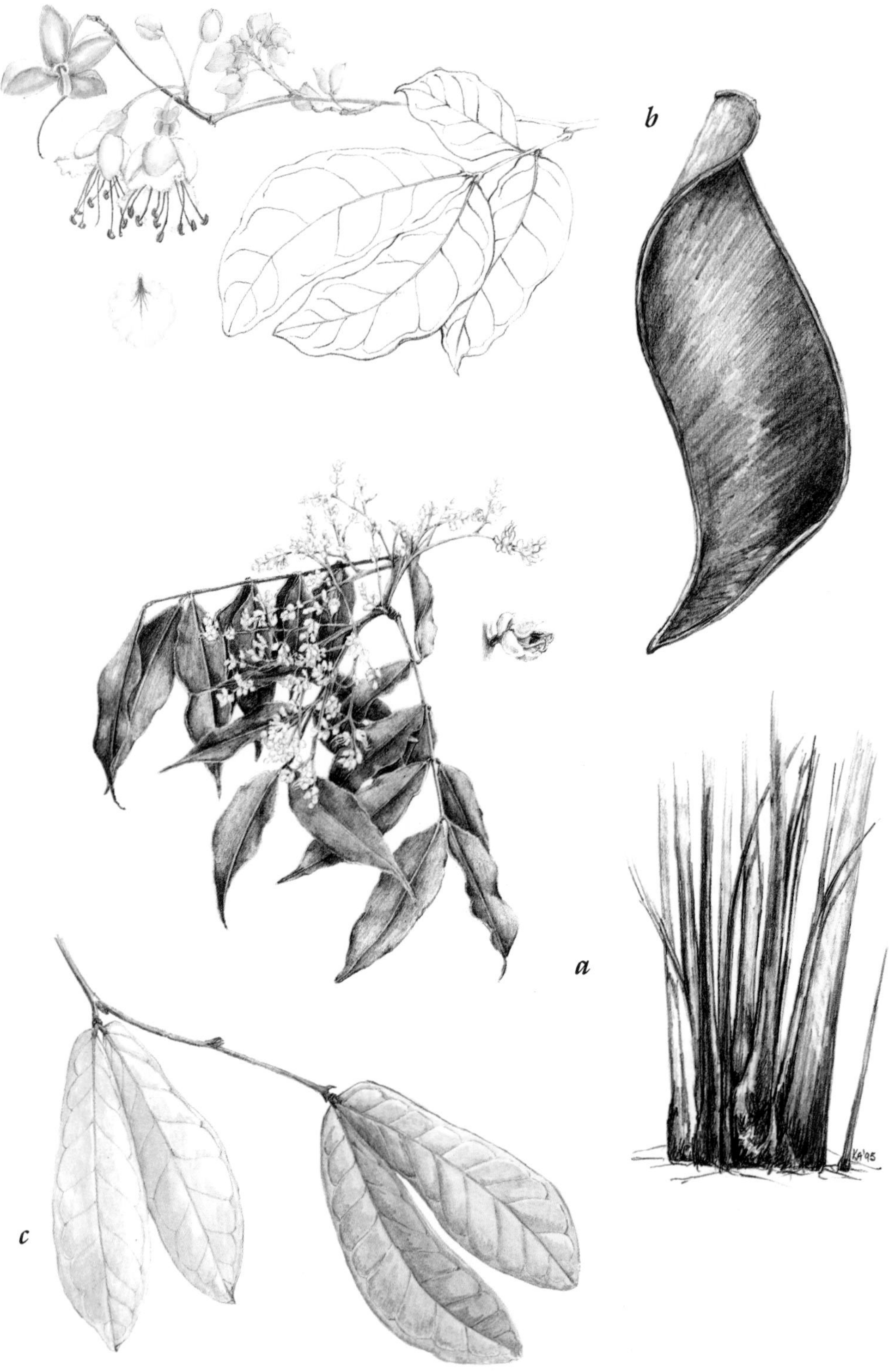
b
a
c
KA'95

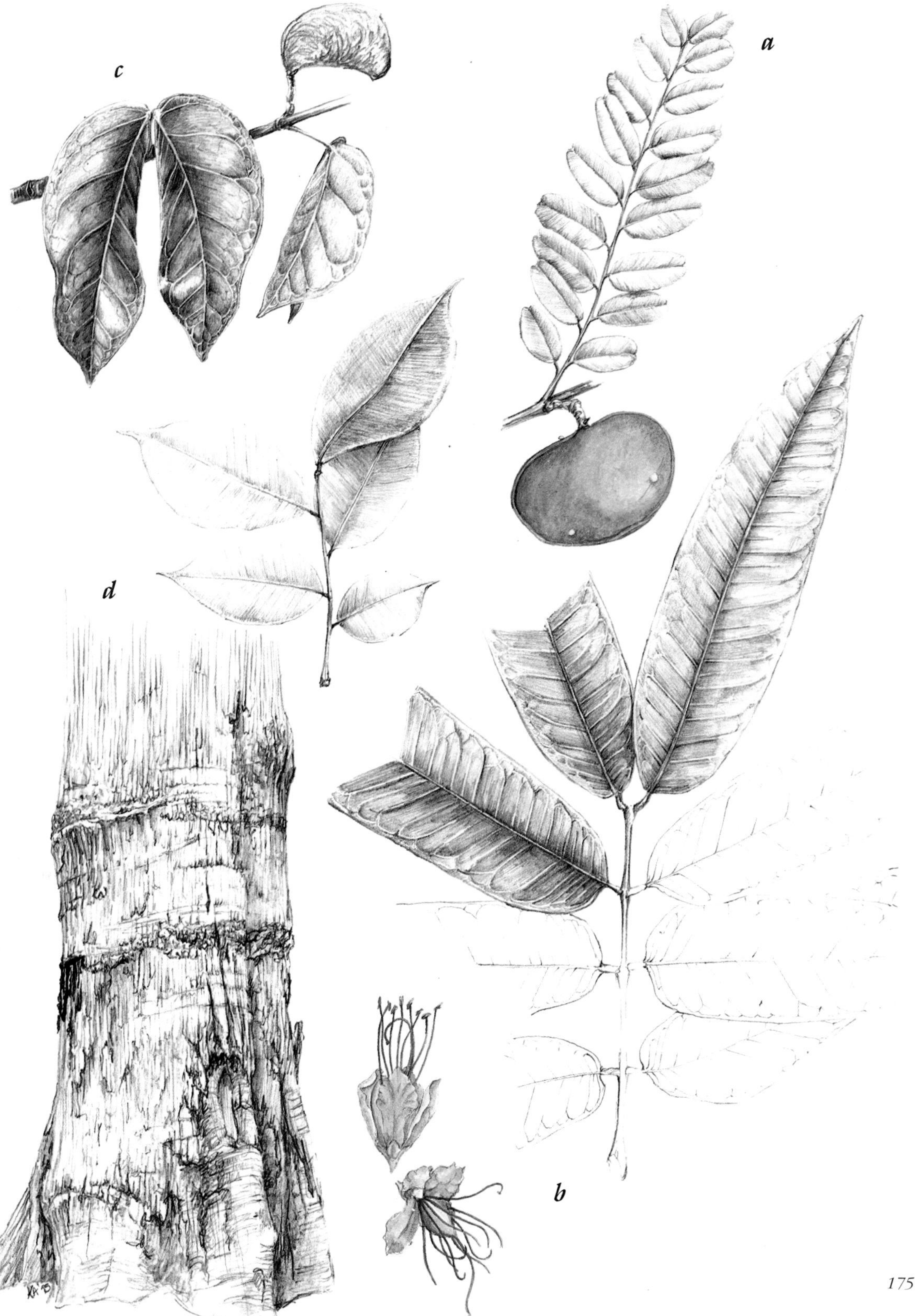
a
b
c
d

Guibourtia tessmannii

Guibourtia tessmannii (Kévazingo) is found in both Marantaceae and mature forest. It can become particularly large, exceeding 2 m diameter. It has large, thin buttresses which can rise quite high up the trunk. The red-brown bark is rough and covered in orange, circular, depressions, where scales have flaked off. Some rare individuals have yellowish bark with dark circular patches. The distinctive, compound, leaves have a single pair of asymmetrical leaflets (10 x 5 cm) in the form of a crab's claw. The flowers are held above the canopy on thick stems, but are difficult to see except when fallen to the ground below. They are about 5 mm across, with 4 small, white, petals. The fruit is a leathery, dark copper-brown pod (3 x 2 cm). These pods split to reveal a single seed with a red-orange aril. The inner wall of the ripe pod is dark blue-black. The seed are eaten by monkeys, chimpanzees and hornbills.

Kévazingo is cut by foresters and one often sees their striking trunks, with cream sap wood surrounding dark brown heart wood, loaded on trains heading for the port in Libreville. Some of them are destined to become long clubs used by American policemen. An infusion made from the bark is particularly good for back ache!

Paraberlinia bifoliolata (Béli) is a large tree which becomes common in mature forest in parts of the Lopé. It has smooth reddish bark with some small scales and narrow buttresses. A characteristic of this species, and of *Julbernardia brieyi* (p. 202), is that it almost always shows signs of bark feeding by flying squirrels. They gnaw at the bark, producing roughened, orange-brown, patches. One can sometimes see the squirrels aerial flight-paths leading to and from these trees. The squirrels can chew through quite thick branches and by doing so they clear away obstacles allowing them to glide freely to and from their food trees.

The compound leaves of *Paraberlinia bifoliolata* have a pair of opposite leaflets (11 x 3 cm) which resemble those of *Pellegriniodendron diphyllum* in form. It flowers at the end of the dry season. The flowers have tiny petals which barely emerge from the pale brown sepals. The fruit is a pod (13 x 4 cm) containing 2-3 seeds, which ripens in February, splitting to throw the seeds up to about 20 m. Béli has attractive pale yellowish wood with a dark grain and is cut by loggers.

Scorodophloeus zenkeri (Divida or «wild onion») is a medium to large tree, growing to about 80 cm diameter. The pale yellow-grey bark is smooth in young trees, but becomes somewhat flakey in older individuals, which often also develop a slightly fluted base. If you make a small cut in the bark you will detect a strong smell of onions. The compound leaves are alternate, with 5-10 pairs of asymmetrical leaflets (2-2.5 x 0.8 cm). The white flowers form a tight bunch and develop into a relatively small, pale green pod, about 8 x 3.5 cm, in August/September. The bark and seeds are harvested for use as a seasoning in sauces. The bark also has medicinal properties. An infusion made from the bark alleviates constipation and powdered bark is taken to cure headaches.

Sindoropsis letestui

Sindoropsis letestui (Ghéombi) is a common and striking tree in mature forest in Lopé. It can exceed 60 m in height and 2 m diameter. The bark is dark grey, but often has paler patches of lichen and moss, which give it a mottled appearance. It has a dense network of shallow, vertical fissures. The base of larger trees has a number of regular, thick, rounded buttresses. These tend to contain deep cracks, where it seems as if the trunk grew faster than the bark, causing it to split. The trunk is generally tall and straight, but often has deep horizontal cracks, from which a thick, dark green, resin oozes. This is a type of copal. The compound leaves have 6-11 alternate leaflets (6 x 3 cm). These have a fine network of lateral nerves extending to the margin. The small white flowers, which bloom at the end of the dry season, develop into unmistakable pointed pods. These are 7-10 x 2.5-4 cm, containing 1-2 attractive, hard, black seeds, which are dispersed a short distance when the pods split in January.

Tetraberlinia bifoliolata (Ekop) is a large tree which can grow to a diameter of 1 m. It is often slightly swollen at the base, sometimes with slight, rounded buttresses, which fuse with the roots. The smooth grey bark has numerous lenticels. The compound leaf has a pair of opposite leaflets and closely resembles that of *Paraberlinia bifoliolata*. The flowers have one long petal about 14 mm long, and four more which are barely developed. The characteristic pod is easily identified. It is about 11 x 6 cm and when young has two distinct ridges on each valve. As it matures in September / October one ridge becomes somewhat wavy and broken, but the second continues to link the base of each valve to its tip.

Right:

a) Paraberlinia bifoliolata
b) Scorodophloeus zenkeri
c) Tetraberlinia bifoliolata

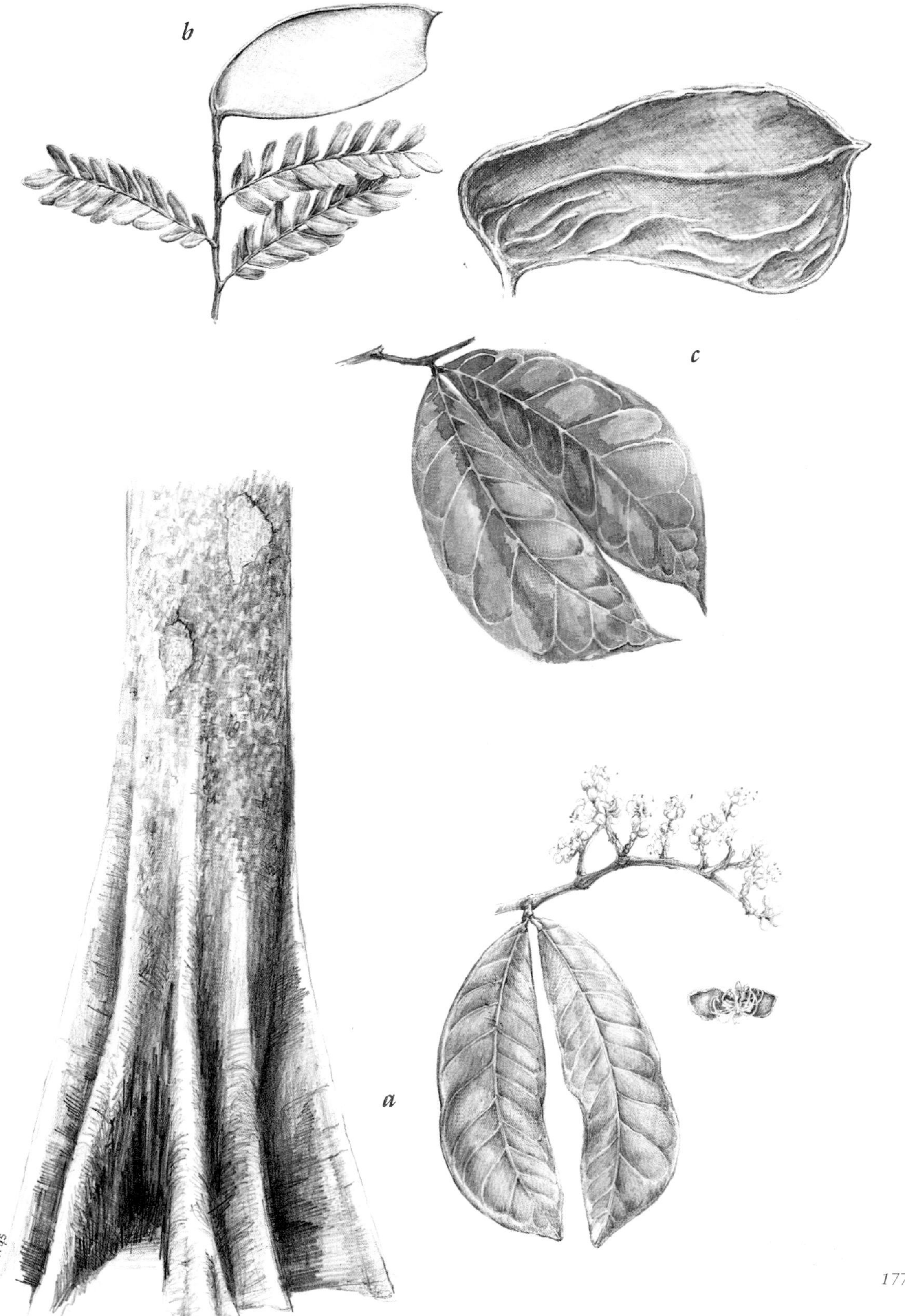
b
c
a
KA'95

LEGUMINOSAE; SUBFAMILY: MIMOSOIDEAE

Filaeopsis discophora (Nieuk) is a large tree which can reach over 40 m, with a diameter of 70 cm or more. Close to the tree there is often a distinctive smell, somewhat like that of rotten garlic. In Lopé its base is always swollen by elephant damage. The bark of young trees is smooth and pale, but covered with a network of deep pits. In older individuals the bark is ochre and flakey and the base appears lightly fluted. The bipinnate leaf generally has two pairs of opposite pinnae, each with 4-8 alternate leaflets (5 x 3 cm). The white flowers are spikes which are rarely seen, except when fallen to the ground. The fruit is a large, papery pod, covered with a network of shallow veins which connect the thickened margins. The young pods are bright green, but dry as they mature to the texture of leathery parchment. Each pod contains about 6 large, winged seeds, about 12 x 4 cm, with a central attachment. The seeds are a favourite food of black colobus monkeys.

Cylicodiscus gabunensis (Okan) is an impressive large tree found in Mature forest in Lopé. It can reach a height of about 60 m and a diameter of 170 cm. It has thick, spreading buttresses and in older individuals these appear gnarled and contorted from repeated bark feeding by elephants. The bark is dark brown and flakes off in thick, more or less rectangular scales. Young trees are covered in spines which gradually disappear as they mature. It has bipinnate leaves with one or two pairs of opposite pinnae. There are 5-10 alternate leaflets (7.5 x 4 cm) which are difficult to distinguish from those of *Filaeopsis discophora*. The flowers are cream spikes which appear in March and April. The fruits are long, leathery pods which reach almost a meter in length by 5 cm wide, which open on one side to release numerous winged seeds resembling those of *Piptadeniastrum africanum*, but with the attachment at the top. These are eaten by several species of primate.

The leaves of Okan are chewed to relieve migraines and a lotion made from the bark is said to soothe rheumatism. The bark can also be used as an alternative to soap to wash clothing. Some pygmy peoples consider this tree to be magical. If the powdered bark is rubbed into small incisions made on the ankle it supposedly makes the limbs supple.

Cylicodiscus gabunensis

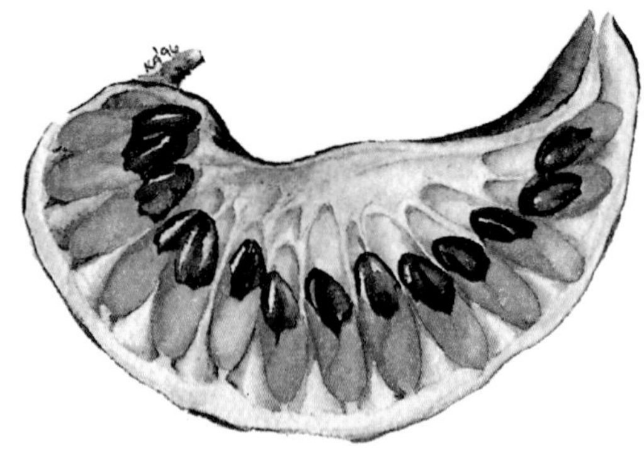

Afzelia bella
(Leguminosae - Caesalpinioideae) is quite rare in Lopé. It has a striking orange-brown trunk with concentric scales rather like an oyster shell and slight buttresses. The pod (up to 20 x 10cm) opens to reveal about 15 shiny black seeds with striking orange arils.

Right:

a) Filaeopsis discophora
b) Cylicodiscus gabunensis

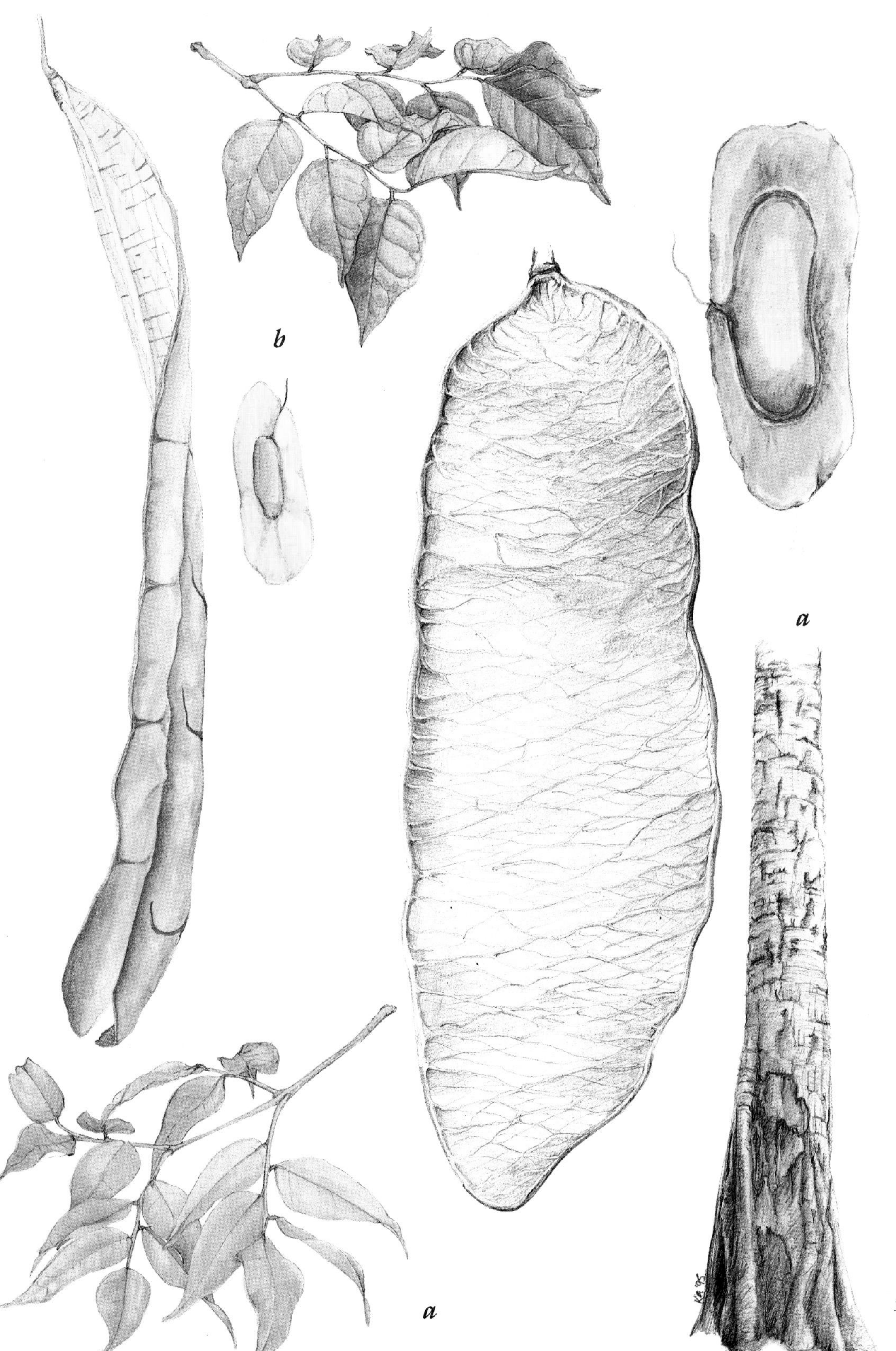
b
a
a

MYRISTICACEAE

This family takes its name from *Myristica fragrans*, the nutmeg tree, named after the greek word 'myristikos', which means 'a perfumed ointment'. Plants in this family play a crucial role in many forests. They have fruits with thin, oil-rich arils which are eaten by many animal species. These are often produced during periods of the year when overall fruit availability is low, such as the long dry season in Lopé. In this way they support much of the frugivore community during periods of scarcity. Plants which fulfill this role are termed 'keystone resources'. In Lopé several large forest trees belong to the Myristicaceae.

Coelocaryon preussi (Ekoune) is a large tree found in mature forest, growing to about 40 m and up to 90 cm diameter. Buttresses are small or absent. The bark is rusty coloured and flakes off in numerous thin scales leaving yellowish patches. The alternate, leathery, leaves (18 x 5 cm) have a stalk about 2 cm long, which is deeply channelled on the upper side. Fallen leaves take on a yellow-orange colouration. The overall appearance is similar to many *Beilschmiedia* species (p. 134). The flowers are either male or female. They are yellow, about 6 mm long, in upright panicles amongst the leaves. The yellow fruits ripen in July/August. They are about 2.5 x 1.5 cm, with 2 fleshy valves which open to reveal shiny black seeds with a startling pink aril. The seeds are the source of an edible oil.

Staudtia gabonensis

Pycnanthus angolensis (Illomba) is a large tree found throughout the forest in Lopé. It has fissured, grey-brown bark, dappled with silvery lichens. The buttresses, when present, are small, regular and rounded. The angular branches are arranged in whorls at the top of the trunk and give the canopy a layered effect. The alternate leaves (20 x 5 cm) are tightly arranged on smaller branches giving the effect of long, compound leaves. They are caudate at the base, with 20-60 pairs of well defined lateral nerves. The underside is covered by a rust-coloured felt of short hairs which tends to wear off with age. Leaves usually show signs of insect damage. The flowers are in dense clusters amongst the leaves and are obvious between December / March. They develop into large bunches of fruit (4 x 2 cm), with 2 dull green valves which open when ripe to reveal a yellow inner wall and intricate pink aril around a shiny black ridged seed. When ripe from August / November these attract large numbers of hornbills, monkeys and chimpanzees, which disperse the seeds (see p. 215).

Scyphocephalium ochocoa (Sorro) is a large tree which is common in mature forest. It can grow to have a large diameter, occasionally exceeding 2 m, but is rarely above 35 m tall. The high buttresses rise and merge into the fluted trunk, giving it a crooked, twisted appearance. The bark is dark red but is mottled with pale lichens. It flakes off in irregular scales, leaving brick-red patches with many lenticels. The canopy and leaf arrangement greatly resemble *Pycnanthus*. The leaves (20 x 4 cm) have 15-20 pairs of prominent lateral nerves. The flowers, which develop in October / December, are arranged on 1-3 small spherical heads, off a common stalk arising amongst the leaves. Each inflorescence has 50-100 small flowers, covered in a felt of brown hairs. They develop into large yellow fruits, about 6 cm across, densely covered in short, soft, rusty-brown hairs, which ripen in January / April. The thick, resinous flesh encloses a single large, flattened seed about 3 cm across. If cut in half this resembles a walnut. The white seed is aromatic and used to be used as a spice to flavour sauces. It is occasionally eaten by gorillas.

Pycnanthus angolensis

Staudtia gabonensis (Niové) is a medium-large tree which rarely exceeds 40m tall or 1 m diameter. There are no buttresses, but the base tends to be lightly fluted in larger individuals. The bark is yellowish, with numerous orange or pale brown depressions where thin, circular scales have flaked off. If you make a small cut in the bark a red exudate flows freely, like blood from a deep wound. The canopy is small with dense, wavy branches. The alternate leaves (10 x 3 cm) are dark green above and paler below. The flowers are small and form dense clusters close to the branches in October / January. The fruits are about 3 x 2 cm with two fleshy valves densely covered in brown hairs, which gradually rub off as they ripen in August / October. The outer valves become yellow, opening to reveal orangey-red inner walls and a single, large, seed covered in a juicy, scarlet aril. The aril is consumed by many species of animal.

Niové is occasionally cut to make bridges in Gabon and in other parts of Africa is quite heavily exploited for timber. The sap slows the flow of blood and speeds recovery if rubbed into a wound and is rubbed into the gums of young children to sooth teething pains. The seeds yield a yellow, aromatic oil which can be used for body massage.

Right:

a) Coelocaryon preussi
b) Pycnanthus angolensis
c) Scyphocephalium ochocoa
d) Staudtia gabonensis

b
d
a
c

Right:

a) Coula edulis
b) Diogoa zenkeri
c) Ongokea gore
d) Strombosia zenkeri
e) Strombosiopsis tetrandra

OLACACEAE

Coula edulis (African walnut) is a medium-large tree restricted to mature forest in Lopé. It can reach about 30 m tall and a diameter of over 1 m. When young, the grey-brown bark is fissured, but older individuals have flakey bark detaching in thick, roughly rectangular scales. There are no buttresses, but large trees are often fluted at the base. They tend to branch low and the trunk is usually crooked and irregular. The canopy is dense and leafy. The alternate leaves are large (up to 30 x 10 cm) and have up to 14 pairs of parallel lateral nerves extending to the leaf edge, which are highly visible when looking up into the canopy. They have small white flowers, about 4 mm across, around March / April. The fruits ripen between December and March. They are spherical, about 4 cm diameter, with a white and pink skin which stands out against dark leaf litter. Each fruit contains a large nut with a thick, woody shell. The kernel within is excellent to eat. The shell can be broken with a stone or knife, but it is best to leave the nuts to dry for a few days in the sun, after which they split into three parts, surrendering the kernel. The nuts are eaten by many species. Elephants crunch them between large teeth with a sharp crack. Herds of wild pigs can be heard from far away, cracking the nuts in their jaws during the fruiting season. In addition, fragments of the shell of *Coula edulis* have been found during excavations of Iron Age village sites in Lopé dated to about 150 AD.

Diogoa zenkeri (Ekoba) grows to about 25 m tall and 50 cm diameter. The bark is grey-brown, with slight longitudinal and transverse fissures. The canopy is dense and bushy. The alternate leaves (20 x 6 cm) are deep green and glossy above, with stalks 3 cm long and 5-7 pairs of prominent, upcurving, lateral nerves. *Diogoa* is most easily identified from its fruit which ripens in January / March. It is about 5 cm long, in the form of a spinning top. It contains a nut about 3 cm across in a hard, ridged, shell. The seeds are often found washed up on sand banks along the Ogooué.

Heisteria parvifolia grows to about the same size as *Diogoa*. It has slight buttresses and a pale, flakey bark. It tends to branch low, into a dense, bushy, trailing canopy. The alternate leaves (15 x 5 cm) have indistinct veination. The terminal branchlets are rarely without a few limp, pink, new leaves and there are generally also a few yellow senescing leaves about to fall. The tiny flowers develop in September / November and have a persistent green calyx, which grows to enclose the developing fruits. As the fruits ripen in February / March the calyx, now about 3 cm long, turns red, resembling that of *Diospyros dendo* (p. 193). It opens to reveal a pearly white fruit about 1 cm long, with a thin, edible, sugary flesh. The fruits are eaten and dispersed by many species of animal.

Duboscia macrocarpa **(see p. 160)**

Ongokea gore (Angeuk) is the largest of the Olacaceae found in the north of the Lopé Reserve, occasionally reaching about 50 m high and just over 1 m diameter. It has a long, straight trunk without buttresses. The bark is grey and resembles lizard skin, with a fine pattern of irregular fissures and some small scales, which flake off in patches. The leaves (6 x 3 c), have a characteristic pale underside and fine veination. The tiny green-white flowers are in eye-catching clusters visible from January / June. The fruit is about 3 cm diameter and is completely enclosed in the persistent green calyx as it develops. On ripening, between August / November, the calyx splits into 2 or 3 valves revealing the yellow flesh of the fruit. The immature fruit are eaten by several species of monkeys, particularly black colobus, in the long dry season. When ripe it is occasionally swallowed by elephants, but the major seed dispersers are duikers, who swallow the fruits and later regurgitate the seeds, once they have digested the flesh. They leave small piles of characteristic spherical seeds about 2 cm diameter with a hard shell (p. 215).

Strombosia zenkeri is a medium sized tree, up to about 35 m tall and 70 cm diameter, with irregular buttresses and a crooked trunk. Its grey bark is easily recognised because numerous thin scales flake off, leaving pale patches with many lenticels. These gradually darken giving the trunk a mottled appearance. The leaves are variable in size (4-15 x 2-6.5 cm) with 5-7 thin, curved, lateral nerves. The small greenish white flowers develop into thin green fruits, about 2 x 1 cm, on a stout stalk about 2 cm long, each with a small disk at its tip. The ripe fruit is purple and contains a single seed with a hard, pitted shell.

Strombosiopsis tetrandra grows to about 25 m tall and 50 cm diameter. It has smooth, grey-green bark, which tends to be marked with pale lichens. In larger individuals the trunk is slightly fluted. The large leaves (20 x 9 cm) are similar to those of *Diogoa zenkeri*, with 6-10 pairs of prominent upcurving lateral veins. It has small, cryptic white flowers, which develop into pear shaped fruits about 4 cm long. These turn pink when ripe, in July / September or January / March. The seed has a thin, hard shell, resembling the seeds of *Diogoa zenkeri*, *Ongokea gore* and *Strombosia zenkeri* and persists on the ground for a long time.

d
b
e
c
a

Right :

Baillonella toxisperma

SAPOTACEAE

This varied family contains several commercially valuable trees and many species with succulent fruits, important for animals and sometimes for humans. They all have simple, alternate leaves and exude white sap if wounded. The seeds have hard, shiny brown skin, or tegument, with obvious attachment scars.

Baillonella toxisperma (Moabi) is one of Africa's most spectacular and beautiful trees. It can grow to be over 70 m tall, with a trunk over 3 m in diameter. The base of the trunk is free of buttresses, but is invariably swollen by elephant damage. White sap can often be seen oozing out of recent wounds in its thick bark. The dark reddish brown bark on the trunk and branches is deeply fissured. The trunk tends to be straight and cylindrical and does not branch until it is high above the crowns of most surrounding trees. The crown is relatively shallow, with wide radiating branches, which gives the impression of a huge umbrella if the tree is viewed in profile. The large leaves (30 x 10 cm), covered in red-brown hairs on their underside, have about 25 pairs of prominent, parallel secondary veins. They are arranged in distinctive whorls at the end of stout twigs. The flowers are on stalks about 2-3 cm long, clustered in amongst the leaves. The fruits (6-8 cm diameter) are yellow-green when ripe. They have sweet, yellowish flesh, similar in consistency to that of an avocado, with a strong, yeasty smell. They contain one or two large seeds, about 4 x 2.5 cm, with tough, shiny brown skin and a large attachment scar (p. 215).

The fruit are eaten by many animal species, but only elephants swallow and disperse the seeds. When a large tree is fruiting the strong odour of the fruit can be detected from far away, guiding animals to the rich food source. It is also possible that the sound of falling fruit attracts animals. Imagine the loud thud of a fruit, weighing about 250 g, falling from 60 m. Elephants use low frequency calls, which are not attenuated by vegetation, to communicate over distances of up to 5 km in the forest. Perhaps they are also able to detect these low frequency vibrations, resulting from the impact of a Moabi fruit, far from the tree. They could then use the odour of the fruit to find it as they moved closer.

Humans also eat the flesh of the fruit, but the seeds are far more valuable. These are a source of a much appreciated oil, used for cooking. In some places people move into temporary camps in the forest when *Baillonella* is fruiting in January / February, in order to collect the seeds. The oil is a valuable source of income for these people, as well as being highly nutritious. To make the oil the seeds are heated and compressed.

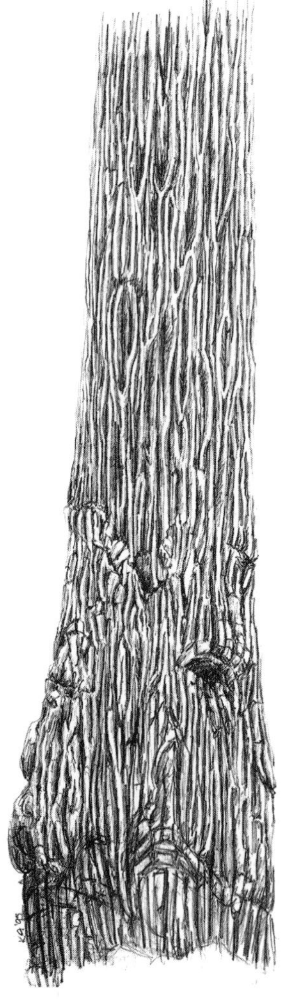

Baillonella toxisperma

In recent years the valuable brown-pink wood of *Baillonella toxisperma* has become much sought after by foresters. It is exploited everywhere it is found. If you look closely at a train passing the Lopé station, you will see many trunks with deeply fissured brown bark from which white sap is oozing, as well as the numerous pink Okoumés. So, Moabis are becoming rarer and many young children have never tasted its oil. In addition, the loggers open the forest up to poachers, who often target elephants for their valuable ivory. Hence, not only is *Baillonella toxisperma* being killed in large numbers, but at the same time its only seed disperser has become much rarer throughout large tracts of the forests of Central Africa. We canot say for sure what the result will be for *Baillonella toxisperma*. But it seems likely that one of Africa's most spectacular natural wonders will decline, or even disappear, except in areas where it and the elephants are protected.

Donella pruniformis (Oyiop) is a rare tree found in mature forest, growing to 30 m tall and up to about 60 cm diameter. The base is always scarred by elephant damage. It is easily recognised by its characteristic leaves (5 x 2 cm), with numerous fine lateral nerves and a long thin apex and indented tip. The pale yellow fruits and the seeds resemble those of *Donella ogoouensis*, found on the Ogooué (p. 23) but are extremely bitter and not at all good to eat.

Gambeya africana (Longhi) is a large tree, reaching over 50 m tall and 1.5 m diameter, found mostly in mature forest. The trunk is straight and cylindrical, with several high, thin buttresses. The bark is grey-brown with quite deep, regular fissures. The broad spreading canopy has a golden brown hue, rather like *Dacryodes buettneri* (p. 116). The characteristic, large leaves (30 x 12 cm) are dark green above and golden brown below, with 15-30 pairs of obvious lateral nerves. Its small cryptic flowers develop into large, rounded fruits. The fruits ripen in October / November, turning yellow-orange. They are about 4-6 cm diameter, with 2-5 immediately recognisable seeds (p. 215). Branches bearing fruits tend to lose their leaves as they ripen, producing a bright yellow beacon for birds and arboreal mammals. When ripe, the juicy flesh around the seeds is sweet and is eaten by many animals, including gorillas, elephants and man. A second species, *Gambeya lacourtiana*, which occurs in northern Gabon, has similar fruits which are red and are often sold in markets.

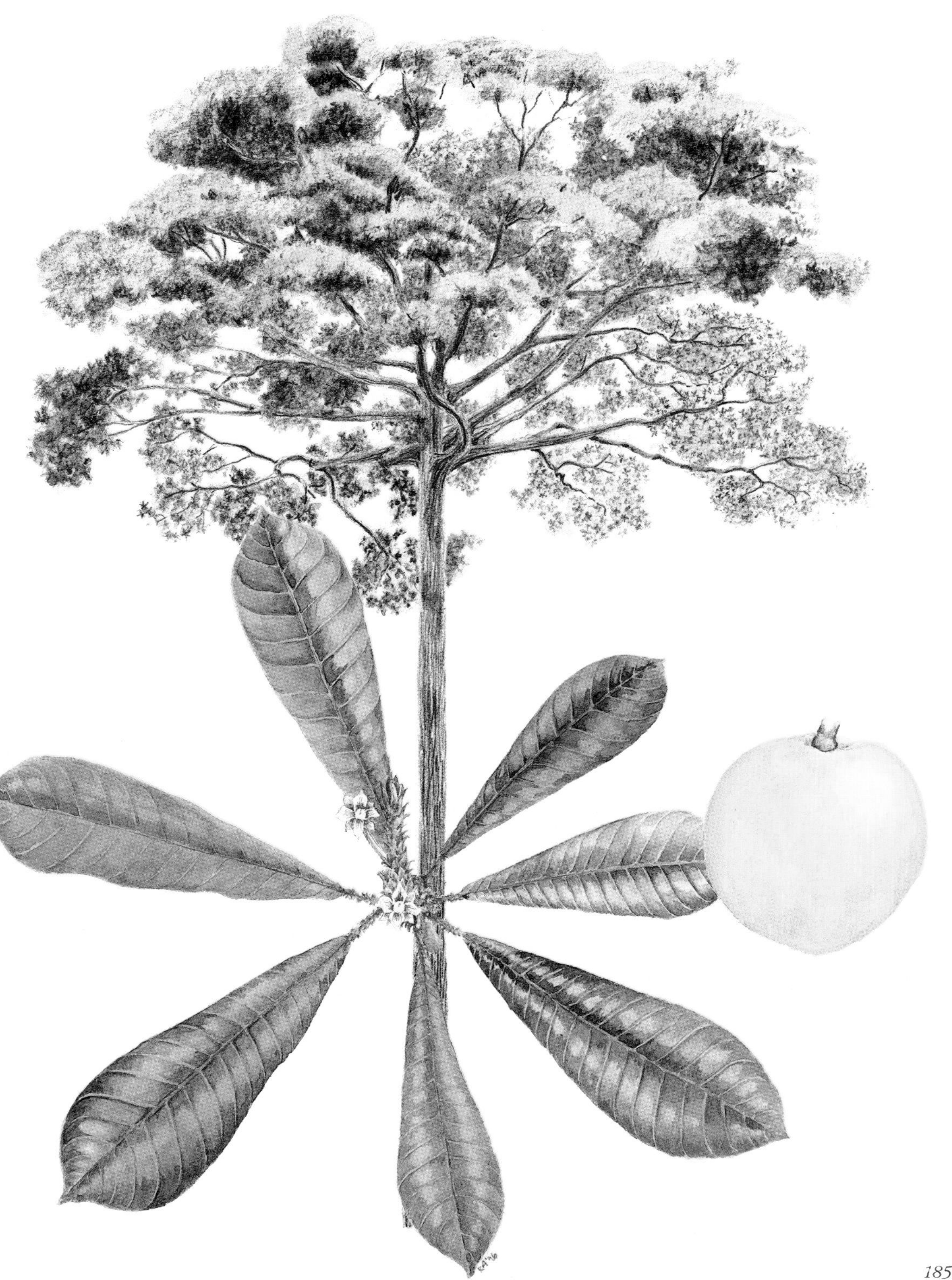

Right:

a) Donella pruniformis
b) Gambeya africana
c) Gambeya subnuda
d) Manilkara fouilloyara

Gambeya subnuda (Mbébame) is a medium-large tree up to about 30 m tall and 50 cm diameter. The trunk resembles *Gambeya africana*. It has smaller leaves (15 x 6 cm) which are green, not golden, on the underside, with 8-10 lateral nerves. The small white flowers open in September / October and the green-yellow fruits ripen from January / March. The fruits are about 3cm diameter, with 5 seeds (p. 215). The seeds are eaten by black colobus. The fruits are sweet, with a flavour very like that of lychees, but the white sap they contain is very sticky. They are eaten by many animals and elephants, in particular, migrate into parts of the forest where *Gambeya subnuda* is common, when it is fruiting.

Letestua durissima (Kong afane) is an impressive large tree which can be confused with *Baillonella toxisperma*. It grows to over 50 m high and 120 cm diameter. The straight, cylindrical trunk is swollen at the base. The rough bark is dark brown, flaking off in rectangular scales, separated by vertical fissures. The leaves (20 x 6 cm) have 12-16 pairs of lateral nerves and are arranged in bunches at the ends of the branchlets. Small white flowers grow amongst the leaves in October / November, developing into fruits about 4 cm long, containing a single characteristic seed which is sharply pointed at both ends.

Manilkara fouilloyara is a large tree reaching about 40 m and up to 80 cm diameter, found in mature forest, particularly on high ridges. It has smooth, fissured, greyish bark. Its leathery, heart-shaped leaves, which are dark green above and pale, sometimes silvery, below, are easily recognised. The fruits are about 2 cm long and ripen in January / February. Unripe fruits, whose seeds have been eaten, are often found on the ground under the tree, generally eaten by black colobus.

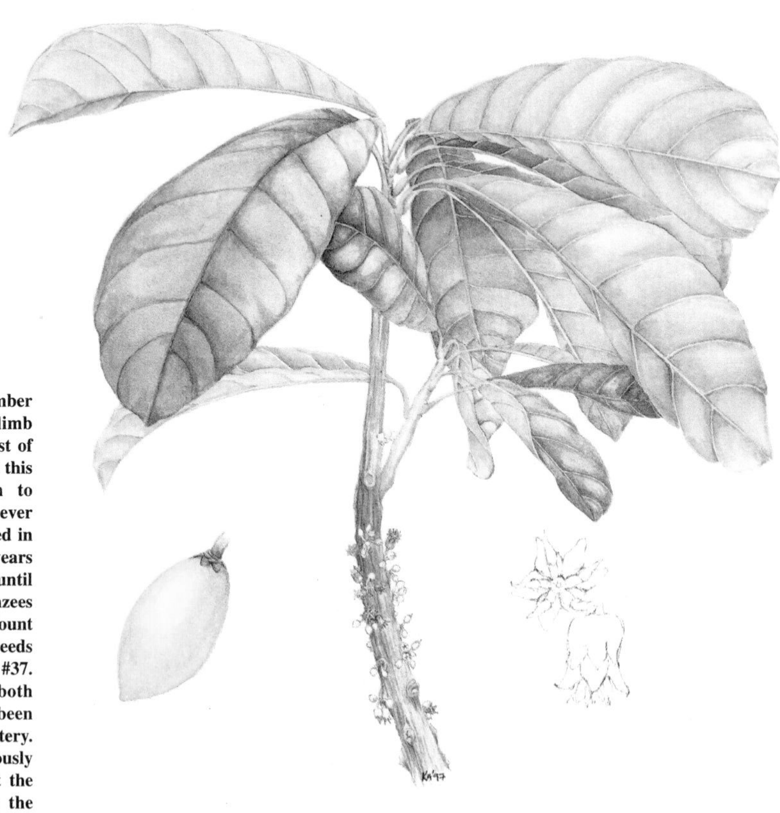

Each year in November / December gorillas and chimpanzees climb Mount Yindo, located to the west of SEGC, to feast on the fruits of this mystery Sapotaceae - known to researchers as «Sapotaceae #37» ever since its seeds were first observed in gorilla dung in 1984. For many years only the seeds were known, until 1990, when a group of chimpanzees were seen feeding high on Mount Yindo in an unknown tree - the seeds on the ground below belonged to #37. Botanical specimens with both flowers and fruit have now been collected, but #37 remains a mystery. It is probably a species, previously called *Gambeya nyangensis*, but the Lopé collections suggest that the species actually belongs in the genus *Synsepalum*.

a
b
c
d
KA'95

7/ ROCKY AREAS

As you drive around in the savanna you will notice many large, exposed outcrops of granite boulders, where the soil was eroded away long ago, at a time when the climate was more humid and rainfall higher. Today many of these outcrops have stunted palm trees or other plants growing in crevices that the savanna fires never touch.

Similar «inselbergs» occur within the forest. These too were once in the savanna, but they have been trapped by the advance of the forest. Today they form «island» ecosystems, isolated in a sea of forest. On the exposed rock faces conditions are tough. Plants growing here are exposed to the full force of the sun's rays and have little or no soil moisture to sustain them between rain storms. However, soil and organic matter such as leaves and branches gradually accumulates in crevices, allowing savanna grasses and herbs, including some specialised orchids, to establish. The forest gradually phagocytoses the outcrop.

Around the outcrop soils are generally thin. There is little opportunity for trees to develop root systems which provide sufficient anchorage to resist strong winds, which swirl around any break in the continuous forest canopy when storms pass. The thin soils store little moisture, so trees growing here are prone to water-stress. Moving away from the outcrop the vegetation changes progressively. Around the edge of the outcrop small shrubs scratch out a living on shallow soils. A little further away, where the soil is perhaps 10 or 20 cm deep, there are small trees. Most of these are ebonies, which are slow growing and rarely exceed 15m in height. They grow in tightly packed stands which form a continuous, even canopy. Ground vegetation is sparse, consisting mostly of small shrubs, giving the appearance of open woodland. As soil depth continues to increase new species establish which are able to grow taller. To be able to survive in shallow soils and to grow above the low canopy of the other trees, where they are exposed to the strong winds that precede most heavy rain storms, these species have to be specially adapted. They spread thick roots up to 40m in all directions, to anchor them solidly in the ground. Further away still, the effect of the rocks becomes more subtle and is difficult to distinguish from surrounding forest types. It is in these areas that one has the best chance to glimpse the rare bare-headed rock fowl, *Picathartes oreas,* a colourful forest bird which builds its nest on steep rock faces with mud carried from nearby streams.

Orchids

Several species of terrestrial orchid are restricted to the rocky outcrops in the forest. ***Eulophia gracilis*** (see p. 17) is common in the ebony forest around rock outcrops, as well as in the gallery of the Ogooué. ***Habenaria sp.*** which has intricate white flowers around Christmas, grows in moist cracks and depressions in rock faces. ***Oecoclade maculata*** lives in the leaf litter under shrubs fringing rock outcrops. It has variegated leaves rather like a *Sanseviera* (see p. 107) and flowers in November / December.

Ferns

Some ferns are found most often on rock outcrops within the forest. Some are specially adapted to exposed savanna-like conditions on large rock outcrops, whilst others only grow in places shaded by other vegetation.

Arthropteris orientalis is common in shaded areas. Its leaves are up to about 60 cm long, but may be fertile when as small as 8 cm.

Asplenium africanum is common on rock outcrops and grows in even quite exposed conditions. This genus has many species some of which have a quite different form, such as ***Asplenium jaundeense***, also found on rocks. ***Pellaea holstii*** is a small leathery fern, up to about 30 cm high, found in exposed crevices on large rock faces.

Phymatosorus scolopendria has a characteristic leaf up to about 80 cm high, and large spots of orange-brown sporangia. It is found in shaded parts of rock outcrops within the forest, and also as an epiphyte on trees.

Pitryogramma calomelanos grows up to about 40 cm high and has unmistakeable silver sporangia which cover the underside of the leaves. It is found on rocks both in the forest and in the savanna.

Psilotum nudum is an unusual fern found growing out of vertical rock faces within the forest, or as an epiphyte in the Ogooué gallery.

Habenaria sp.

Oecoclade maculata

e
d
b
a
c
g
f

Shrubs

OCHNACEAE

Several species of Ochnaceae shrubs become common in the under-storey, mostly in areas with thin soils. They also occur as scattered individuals which are particularly eye catching when in flower.

Campylospermum elongatum grows to about 5 m tall, sometimes forming quite dense populations. At first glance they resemble young *Lophira alata* trees (p. 88), since their leaves are similarly bunched along the main stem. The leaves can quite easily be distinguished from those of *Lophira* by their serrated edge and curved lateral nerves. The leaves are often 50 cm or more long. The bright yellow flowers hang down on a long stalk. The green sepals persist on the fruit, turning red as it matures along with the fleshy receptacle of the flower, in which up to five black seeds are displayed. These are eaten by birds.

Ouratea flava is a shrub or small tree up to about 8 m tall and 12 cm diameter. It has small serrated leaves (12 x 4 cm) with similar curved nervation to *Campylospermum elongatum*. It has eye catching delicate yellow flowers about 1.5 cm across, which hang down on a branched stalk. Like *C. elongatum*, these develop into fruits with persistent sepals and a fleshy receptacle, which turn orange and then red, with up to five red fruits, also becoming black when ripe.

Ouratea cf. myrioneura is a closely related species, but differs from *Ouratea flava* because of its fine, parallel lateral nerves, similar to those of *Lophira alata* and its flowers and fruit which are on erect stalks. As the flowers develop into fruits the petals fall and the sepals become orange, then wine red and finally red-black. Along with the leaves, these form a classic red-green Christmas display, along the savanna edge, from December to February.

Trees

ANNONACEAE

Monodora angolensis is a small tree which only occasionally exceeds 10 m. It is only found close to rock outcrops in Lopé, where it occasionally forms small stands. The bark is smooth and grey. The leathery leaves (10 x 4 cm) are bright pink when new. The intricate flowers bloom in October and are pink-peach at first, darkening to purple. The characteristic green fruits blacken on the ground, persisting quite a long time under the tree. They are about 10 cm long and contain numerous pale brown seeds (12 x 9 mm). These seeds are collected and made into necklaces which are said to protect babies from illness. The fruits are eaten by gorillas and chimpanzees. Two Annonaceae shrubs, *Monanthotaxis congolensis* and *Uvaria versicolor* (p. 105) are also often found in rocky areas.

CELASTRACEAE

Euonymus congolensis is a small tree up to about 10 m tall and 15 cm diameter, found almost exclusively close to rock outcrops and in areas with shallow soil. It is easily recognised by its mustard coloured bark, with obvious, narrow vertical fissures and its long, narrow, serrated opposite leaves (9 x 2 cm). It has small, white flowers. The fruits are green capsules about 7 mm long, containing small, arillate seeds.

DICHAPETALACEAE

Dichapetalum barteri is a small tree rarely exceeding 15 m and 20 cm diameter. In Lopé it is found almost exclusively on thin soils around rock outcrops, where it is common. The bark is smooth and grey and the crown dense and bushy. The alternate leaves (15 x 9 cm) have two small glands either side of the midrib at their base. They have a characteristic wavy margin and 4-6 pairs of prominent, upcurving lateral nerves. Senescing yellow leaves are often evident on the tree, or on the ground below. Clusters of small, cream coloured flowers form at the ends of inflorescences growing from the leaf axils. The wrinkled fruits, about 2.5 cm long, turn yellow when ripe. They are eaten by gorillas, chimpanzees and many of the monkeys and their smooth, pale seeds litter the ground in rocky areas when the fruits ripen in November / January.
Dichapetalum gabonense is a lianescent shrub or liane, up to about 10 m long, found throughout young vegetation types and Marantaceae forest, but more common close to rock outcrops. Its leaves are similar to those of *D. barteri*, but tend to be smaller (11 x 5 cm) and lack glands. The fruits are orange when ripe, about 3 cm long, with sweet flesh around a single seed.

Left:

a) Arthropteris orientalis
b) Asplenium africanum
c) Asplenium jaundeense
d) Pellaea holstii
e) Phymatosorus scolopendria
f) Pitryogramma calomelanos
g) Psilotum nudum

Monodora angolensis

a
b
c
KA'94
KA'95

IXONANTHACEAE

Ochthocosmus congolensis is found in gallery forests in the savanna and along the Ogooué and close to rock outcrops. It rarely exceeds 10 m tall or 20 cm diameter. It has smooth, silvery bark and a twisted, low-branching trunk. It has alternate leaves (10 x 3.5 cm). Young leaves are startling purple. It is most often noticed when covered in small, bright white flowers. The fruits are small capsules (5 mm long) containing 1-3 seeds, with tiny orange arils, eaten by birds.

RHIZOPHORACEAE

Cassipourea congoensis which rarely exceeds 15 m tall or 15 cm diameter, is found around rock outcrops and in rocky parts of the Ogooué gallery. It has smooth, brown, marbled bark. It can be recognised by its toothed, opposite leaves. The small, greenish-yellow flowers are about 6 mm across. The fruits are capsules with 3 valves, which open when ripe to reveal 1-3 shiny brown seeds, about 4 mm long, with yellow-orange arils.

SAPINDACEAE

Lecaniodiscus cupanoides grows up to about 15 m tall and 30 cm diameter, generally around rock outcrops or in gallery forest along rocky rivers. The compound leaf has 4-6 pairs of leaflets (12 x 5 cm) with 8-12 pairs of bold lateral nerves. The small, fragrant flowers are greenish-yellow. Male flowers have prominent stamen and females have a conspicuous 3-lobed style. The fruits have a yellow, velvety skin when ripe. They are about 1.5 cm long and contain a single characteristic seed (p. 215) within a sweet, succulent pulp.

EBENACEAE

The family Ebenaceae, the ebonies, is represented by one genus, *Diospyros*, with over 400 species world wide. There are at least 32 species in Gabon, of which 18 have been found in the Lopé to date. They are mostly shrubs and small trees found in rain forest. The true ebony-tree, ***Diospyros crassiflora***, can grow to be about 25 m tall and may reach a diameter of 120 cm, although it is generally smaller. It has precious, hard, black heartwood and has disappeared from much of central Africa due to over-exploitation.

Many of the species found in Lopé are most common on the thin soils around rocky areas, where they are the dominant component of a distinct plant community. They produce fruits which are eaten by all of the frugivorous primates, so rocky areas become a centre of activity at times in the year when *Diospyros* are fruiting. In addition, their immature seeds are eaten by gorillas and chimpanzees in poor fruit years. The majority flower after the major dry season and their fruits ripen around Easter. Most species that occur in the Reserve can be distinguished on the basis of bark and leaf characters, but they also have distinctive fruits, which aid identification when present, and which also provide a tasty snack in some cases.

Diospyros abyssinica is a fairly large tree, with diameter up to 40 cm, reaching 30m in height. Until found in the Lopé it had not been recorded in Gabon. It tends to be found in dry forests outside the rain forest belt. In Lopé it only occurs on thin soils close to rocks. It has a rough, fissured trunk, small, thin leaves and small fruits (1 x 5 mm) which are red when ripe.

Diospyros dendo is a medium-sized tree growing to about 15 m tall. It is most abundant in rocky areas, but occurs in most forest types. The bark is silvery with black patches and flakes away from the trunk in papery strips. The small red fruit are borne on the major branches (a variation on cauliflory, known as ramiflory) enclosed in a red-green calyx which opens as they ripen. As for all *Diospyros* the thin, white flesh around the seed is very difficult to remove. This is an adaptation to encourage animals, particularly primates, to swallow the seed. If you take the time to process the fruit as a monkey might, the seeds are like small, sugary «pear drop» sweets when sucked.

Diospyros mannii is generally rare, but is more common on shallow soils. It is a medium sized tree with a smooth trunk. The leaves have distinctive veination and their underside is pale and hairy. Its white flowers are typical of many *Diospyros* species although they bloom in July / August. Its apple sized fruits form on the trunk and larger branches, ripening in January / February and are covered in short, brown, irritant hairs. Unusually for *Diospyros* it is adapted to elephant dispersal, with strong odour, large seeds and abscision on ripening. If you have the patience to scrape off the protective hairs it is one of the most delicious fruits in the forest.

Diospyros piscatoria has smooth, brown bark, but otherwise closely resembles *D. abyssinica*, although the long drip tip on its leaf and its more spherical fruit can be used to separate them.

Left:

a) Campylospermum elongatum
b) Ouratea flava
c) Ouratea cf. myrioneura

Newbouldia laevis
(Bignoniaceae - see p.78)

Paropsia grewioides
(Passifloraceae), a small tree found in rocky areas and along the forest edge.

f
e
d
c
a
b

Diospyros polystemon is relatively common around rocky areas and in Marantaceae forest, although not previously known from Gabon. It can become quite a large tree, occasionally exceeding 70 cm diameter and 40 m in height. The bark is silvery black with distinct vertical fissures, although in older individuals it becomes quite flakey near the base. It has large cream flowers like *D. mannii* and its medium sized fruits turn pinky-red when ripe.

Diospyros suaveolens is difficult to distinguish from *D. mannii*. If you look closely you will notice that the trunk is flakey; the leaf is hairy and of similar colour, but has different veination; and the fruits are about half the size.

Diospyros viridicans bark and trunk are similar to *D. abyssinica*, but it has distinct leaves which are larger and velvety on the underside. The young leaves are eaten by chimpanzees.

Diospyros zenkeri is rarely found far from rocks. It is a medium sized tree, rarely exceeding 20 cm diameter. The bark is smooth and pale. Its young leaves are vivid purple and the fallen leaves turn black-blue on the ground. Its medium sized fruits grow out of the trunk and branches, turning yellow when ripe. The flowers are strongly scented and bloom in October / November. If you cut one open the pale flesh becomes blue-black within a minute or so. It is sweet, but has a slight garlicy after taste. *D. zenkeri* grows very slowly, averaging 0.5 mm per year, so even quite small individuals can be unexpectedly old.

Several species of *Diospyros* occur in habitats away from rock outcrops.

Diospyros boala is a medium sized tree up to about 15 m tall, found principally in Mature forest. The trunk is fissured vertically like *D. polystemon*, but it has a larger leaf (12 x 5 cm) and its round, yellow fruits, which are about 2 cm diameter, have a large red calyx similar to that of *D. dendo*.

Diospyros crassiflora, the true ebony, has a dark trunk with narrow fissures, quite large pale leaves (12 x 5 cm), and a large yellow fruit about the size of an apple. It grows in both Marantaceae and Mature Forests, but is rare. During a ten year study in the Reserve two individuals grew an average of 1 mm diameter a year, suggesting that the trees of 50 cm cut by foresters are at least 500 years old.

Diospyros melocarpa occurs at high altutude in mature forest. It can be recognised by its distinctive leaf veination. The fruits resemble those of *D. polystemon*, but ripen in the dry season, attracting primates to upland areas.

Diospyros soyauxii is common on some of the higher ridges in the tourist zone in mature forest. It often has multiple trunks and the bark is dark, with well defined vertical fissures. The underside of the large leaf is pale and rough to the touch. The distinctive fruit is yellow when ripe.

Left:

Celastraceae
a) Euonymus congolensis
Dichapetalaceae
b) Dichapetalum barteri
c) Dichapetalum gabonense
Ixonanthaceae
d) Ochthocosmus congolensis
Rhizophoraceae
e) Cassipourea congoensis
Sapindaceae
f) Lecaniodiscus cupanoides

Below:

a) Diospyros abyssinica
b) Diospyros crassiflora
c) Diospyros mannii
d) Diospyros melocarpa
e) Diospyros viridicans
f) Diospyros zenkeri

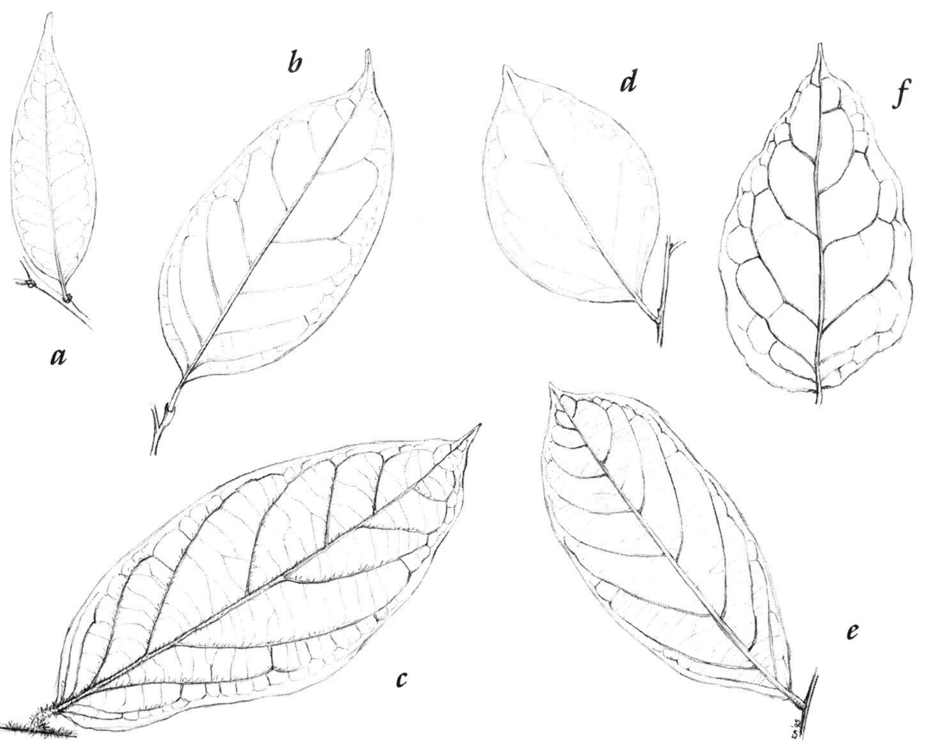

e
f
c
d
a
g
g
c
b
KA95

8/ FOREST RIVERS

The topography of much of the Lopé is characterised by steep valleys with clear, rocky, fast-running streams and rivers. The larger rocks in these water courses are home to a variety of ferns and small flowering plants, some of which trail under water. However, there are very few truly aquatic species in the acidic, nutrient deprived waters, except in low lying areas where marshes are dominated by water-loving sedges and arrow roots (p. 97).

Along the river banks vegetation is often lush, with many ferns, wild gingers and occasionally small, yellow-flowered Begonias. Small trees grow out over the water, their curved branches resembling those of willows. Some species of trees and shrubs are exclusively found close to streams and rivers, so when these are fruiting or flushing with new leaves the galleries become a focus of attention for some forest animals. For others they are home. If you are particularly lucky (and stealthy) you may catch a glimpse of the spot-necked otter as it hunts for fresh-water crabs, whilst the raucous cry of the shining blue or giant kingfishers is often heard as they flash by close to the water. Small forest crocodiles make their nests under logs of long-dead trees embedded into the stream bank and these are occasionally glimpsed by day, although they are most active by night.

Along some of the rivers and streams there are areas where elephants have dug into the bank to feed on soil, creating salt licks. These are used by many of the forest mammals and well worn trails lead into the larger ones from all directions. By burrowing in under their roots, the elephants sometimes bring large forest trees crashing to the ground, creating large openings in which light loving plant species thrive.

Left:

a) Diospyros crassiflora
b) Diospyros dendo
c) Diospyros mannii
d) Diospyros polystemon
e) Diospyros soyauxii
f) Diospyros viridicans
g) Diospyros zenkeri

Heinsia crinita
(Rubiaceae - see p.150)

A spot-necked otter,
Lutra maculicollis

Right:

a) Halopegia azurea
b) Marantochloa cordifolia
c) Marantochloa purpurea
d) Trachyphrynium braunianum

Herbs

AQUATIC MARANTACEAE

Halopegia azurea grows in streams and marshes in all forest types in Lopé. It is similar in form to *Megaphrynium* (see p. 97). A single leaf grows on an erect petiole up to 1 m long. The leaf is somewhat like a long, thin rectangle in shape and is very variable in size, up to 50 x 15 cm. Numerous stems grow off the rhizome, forming a raised tussock. The characteristic purple flower is about 2.5 cm across. The small, cylindrical fruit is rarely seen. It is about 12 mm long, with a single seed partly covered in a small collar of aril. The young leaves and stem pith are eaten by gorillas, particularly during the long dry season. Humans used to burn *Halopegia* to obtain salt from the ashes.

Marantochloa cordifolia is found along rivers and streams and in marshes, particularly in Marantaceae forest. Its erect branching form and succulent stems are similar to those of ***Ataenidia conferta*** (see p. 97) but *M. cordifolia* lacks red bracts. The leaves are green, but one margin on the underside has a slightly darker border, about 2 cm wide. The flowers are white and yellow and can be observed in most seasons, but fruits have never yet been seen in Lopé. The stem pith of *M. cordifolia* is eaten in large quantities by gorillas in the long dry season, when little fruit is available, but is not consumed at other times of the year. It is a 'fall-back' food, which, whilst not preferred at other times of the year, plays a crucial role in periods of fruit scarcity. Chimpanzees do not eat *M. cordifolia* nor any other aquatic plants. It seems, for some unknown reason, that they are extremely reluctant to enter even very shallow water. A second aquatic species, ***Marantochloa purpurea*** is less common than *M. cordifolia*. It is very similar in appearance, but can easily be distinguished because the underside of the leaf is silver, with a highly contrasting green margin, about 2 cm wide, on one side. Its small fruits, which are often present, are bright red berries.

Trachyphrynium braunianum is similar to *Hypselodelphis* spp. (see p. 97), but is always found close to water. It can be distinguished by its small leaves, (12 x 4 cm), its smooth green stem and its small, yellow, fruits. The young leaves are eaten by apes and particularly by mandrills. The stems are used locally to make frames which reinforce the walls of mud houses and elsewhere by pygmy peoples to make their traditional round house frames.

Anubias barteri* (Araceae) grows on rocks in forest streams and has a similar form to *Halopegia azurea

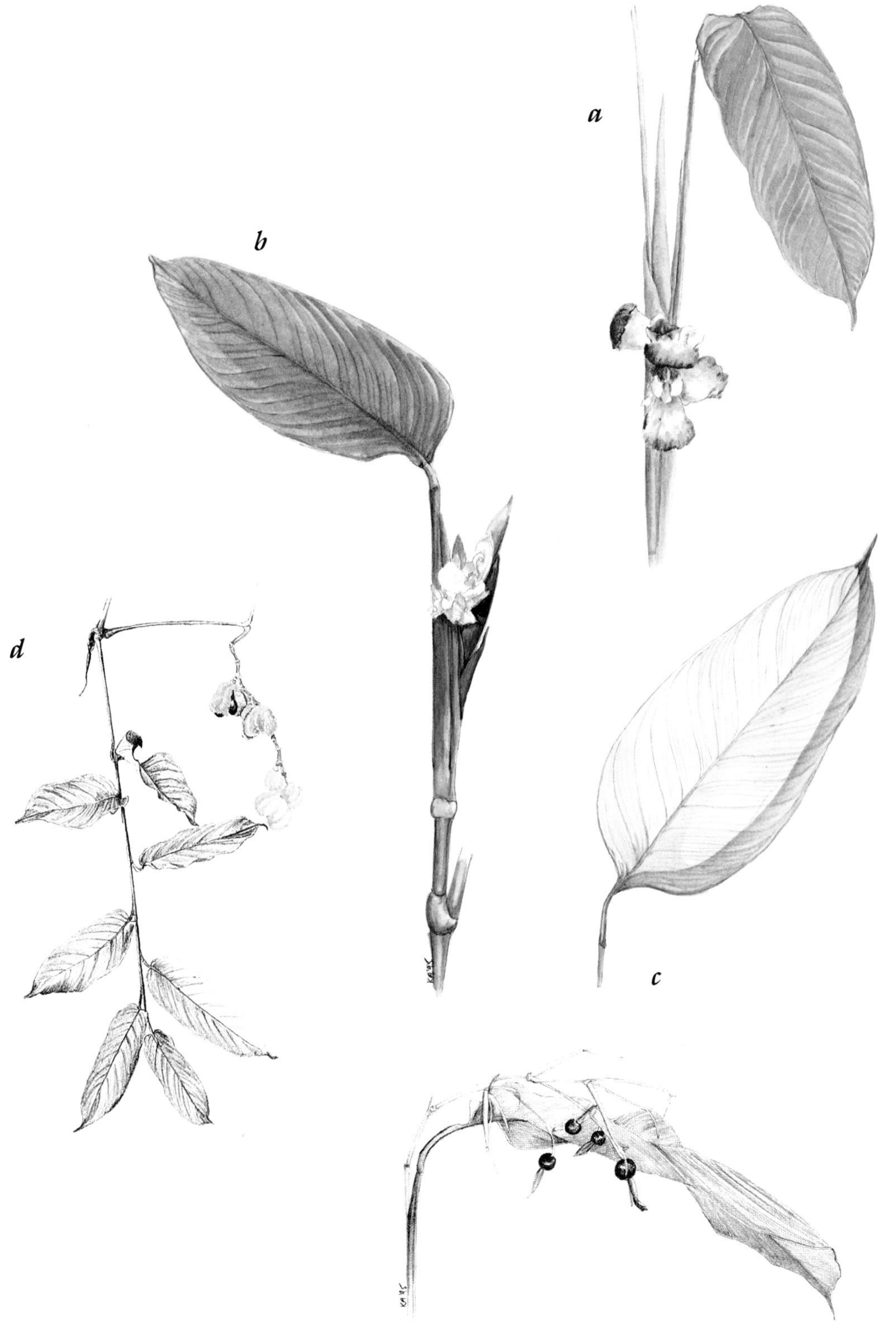
a
b
d
c

Right:

a) Anthonotha macrophylla
b) Berlinia bracteosa
c) Hymenostegia klainei

Trees

LEGUMINOSAE; SUBFAMILY: CAESALPINIOIDEAE

Be they in savanna or in the forest, two general gallery types can be defined in the Lopé. Some are relatively young, resulting from recent colonisation of moist gullies or small streams in the savanna. Other galleries are ancient, consisting of vegetation which survived along water courses during dry periods, when much of the forest was replaced by savannas. The ancient galleries are rich in Caesalpinioideae tree species, which propel their seeds by explosive mechanisms, limiting their dispersal to tens of metres. They therefore spread very slowly and are ideal indicators of forest refuges.

Anthonotha macrophylla is one of the commoner medium sized trees in some galleries. The bark is smooth and greyish. The trunk tends to split low down into several stems. These arch away from the main trunk and send branches up vertically, reaching 15-20 m. There are 2-4 pairs of opposite, symmetrical leaflets (10-20 x 4-8 cm). These have quite bold veination and are silvery on their undersides. They produce white flowers, with four small petals and one larger one, about 6 mm across, in November. The pods are brownish, with velvet hairs, reaching up to 30 x 9 cm. They are covered in roughly diagonal ridges and as they mature they swell around the 2-7 developing seeds, taking on an irregular appearance. They ripen in January / February. The seeds are shaped like small pillows and are eaten by colobus monkeys and mandrills.

Berlinia bracteosa is common along some rivers in the forest and also occurs in the Ogooué gallery. It can become quite a large tree up to 30 m tall and about 1 m diameter. The large compound leaf has 3-5 pairs of leaflets, each 15-20 x 4-7 cm, with well defined lateral nerves. From May to July leaflets yellow and fall, to be replaced with vivid coppery-red new leaves. Each young leaf is enclosed within a protective bract, which falls to the ground as they unfold. *Berlinia bracteosa* is particularly eye catching when in flower. The flower buds are enclosed within bracts about 5 cm long. They have five pure white petals, the largest of which is about 9 cm across, forming large bouquets scattered around the canopy. The fruit is a large, flat pod up to 40 x 10 cm with around 4 seeds each about 5 cm across. Several monkey species, black colobus in particular, spend a lot of time feeding in *Berlinia bracteosa* trees. The young leaves and flowers are eaten by all monkey species and colobus also eat the seeds. In addition, many of the monkeys spend many hours at certain times of the year foraging for insects in amongst the leaves and bark. A second, rare, species, ***Berlinia auriculata,*** is restricted to galleries in mature forest. It is a small tree, rarely reaching 10 m in height. It has 2-3 pairs of opposite leaflets (12-25 x 4-10 cm). Its flowers have a large white petal about 5 x 3 cm, with a subtle, green, lined pattern at its centre. These lines are highlighted by the ultra-violet vision of honey bees, and guide them in to the nectaries. The bee's weight on the petal brings the anthers down and they deposit pollen on its back, which is carried away to pollinate other flowers. The fruits have never been seen in Lopé nor collected elsewhere.

Hymenostegia klainei is a medium-sized tree which grows to about 30 m. Its leaves have 9-11 narrow opposite, asymmetric leaflets (5 x 1.5cm). Characteristic stipules persist at the base of each leaf. It flowers late in the long dry season. The yellow-green petals are enclosed in pink-red bracteoles and when flowering the canopy appears pink from afar. The pods are about 7 x 3.5 cm (see also p. 25).

Distemonanthus benthamianus (Movingui - the sorcerer's tree) is an eye catching tree which is common in galleries, particularly along forest streams and rivers. From a distance its trunk appears vivid brick-red, particularly in younger individuals, and flashes through the greens of the forest like a beacon. Close up, they have several fairly thin orange-yellow buttresses and the trunk is covered in an intricate oyster-shell pattern of persistent scales, which leave smooth, pale indentations when they finally fall. In older individuals the red trunk fades to salmon, becoming yellowish as it rises to the lower branches.

Movinguis are particularly attractive at the beginning of the rainy season in September / October, when they shed their leaves and burst into coppery flush, which gradually changes to a delicate but intense pale green. The young leaves are eaten by many of the primates. The compound leaves have 5-11 alternate, symmetrical leaflets (7 x 3 cm). The flowers appear at the same time as the young leaves. They have reddish-violet sepals and white petals, giving a pink appearance from a distance. The fruits are papery pods about 8 cm long. When young they are red-pink, but dry to pale brown when ripe. They contain about 5 seeds which are dispersed by the wind. As the pods ripen they attract raucous flocks of African grey parrots which can be heard from afar. They eat the nutritious, bean-like seeds, destroying a significant proportion of the crop.

Distemonanthus benthamianus

a
b
c

Julbernardia seretii **(Caesalpiniaceae) - a large tree which occurs in some galleries in Lopé and which is common in some forests elsewhere in Africa.**

Gilbertiodendron grandistipulatum (Abeum) is a large tree restricted to galleries along rivers and streams. It has yellowish, flakey bark similar to that of *Dacryodes buettneri* (p. 116). The large compound leaves have 5-8 pairs of asymmetrical leaflets (up to 40 x 10 cm). Bright pink-red young leaves emerge from a large, protective stipule up to 20 cm long, which persists at the base of the mature leaf. They hang limply, gradually toughening and fading to pale green. The mature leaves are dark green and leathery. The spectacular flowers bloom in November / December. They have bright red sepals which open to reveal the flower. There is one large white petal (10 x 12 cm) and several small pink petals which barely emerge from within the sepals. The fruit is a large pod 30 cm long, covered in golden-brown velvet, with two prominent longitudinal nerves. The large seeds are thrown away from the parent tree when the pod dries out and splits.

Julbernadia brieyi becomes common in the gallery forests of Lopé. It has high buttresses and smooth, pale grey bark. Like *Paraberlinia bifoliolata* (p. 176), the bark is almost always marked by rough patches, where flying squirrels have fed. Pinkish slime often exudes and falls to the ground from areas where squirrels have scraped to the wood, or from other wounds. The compound leaves have five opposite, asymmetrical leaflets which increase in size from 1.5 x 0.7 cm at the base, to 5 x 2 cm for the terminal pair. They flower around Easter. The yellowish sepals and delicate pink petals give an apricot appearance to the canopy at this time. The fruits are pods, about 12 x 6 cm, which are held above the canopy on tough stalks. They dry, splitting with a sharp crack, on hot, sunny days in September / October, projecting seeds (p. 214) up to 35 m.

Gilbertiodendron grandistipulatum

Right:

a) Distemonanthus benthamianus
b) Julbernadia brieyi

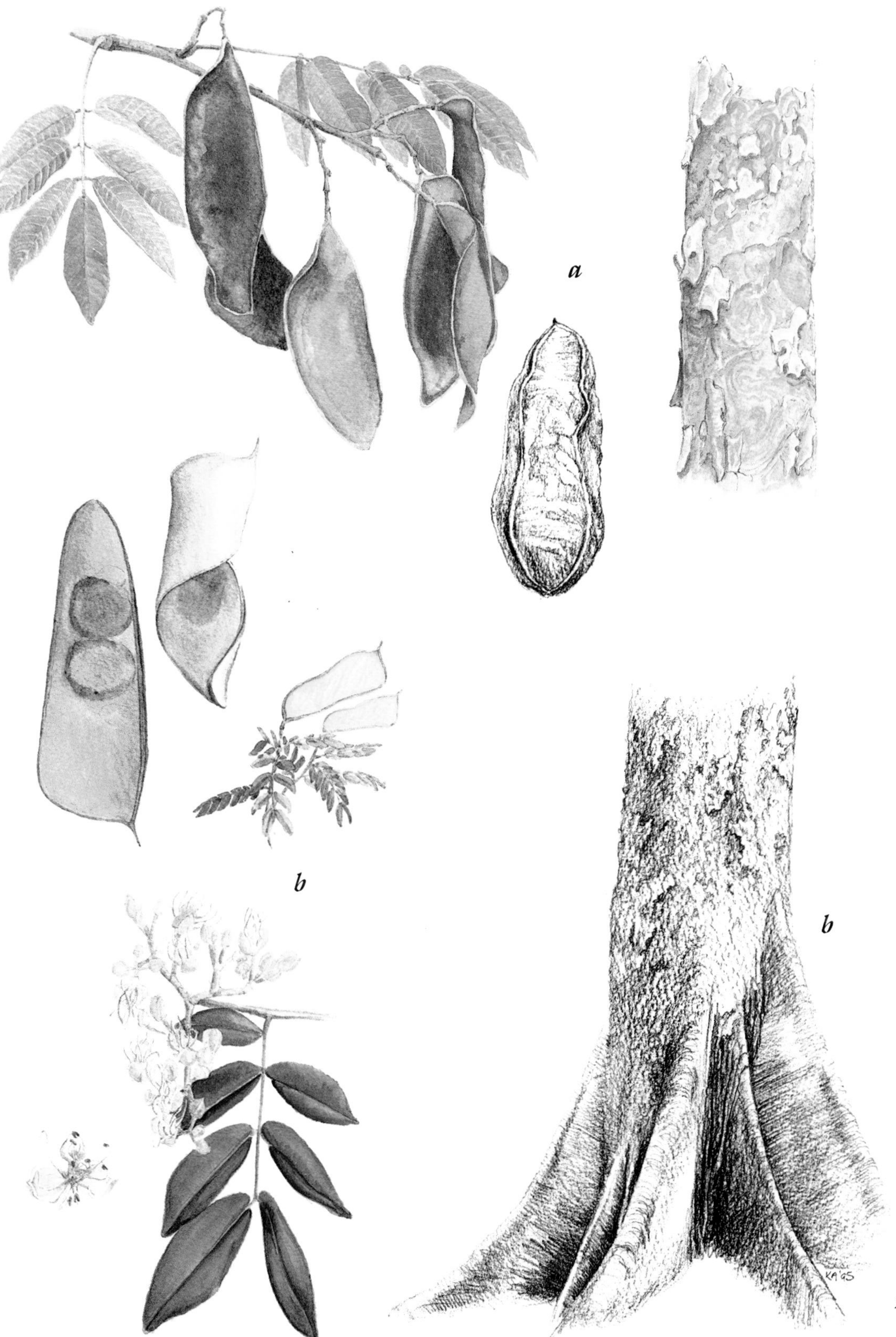
a
b
b
KA'95

Right:

a) Mitragyna ciliata
b) Nauclea vanderguchtii

RUBIACEAE

Mitragyna (Hallea) ciliata (Bahia) is the largest tree found in marshes, growing to 40m tall and 1 m diameter. It has pale grey bark with vertical fissures. The trunk is straight and cylindrical and in large trees the base is often somewhat swollen by thick, rounded buttresses, tapering into roots, which grow on the surface for some distance from the tree. Because of its size and rounded crown it is easily picked out amongst swamp vegetation, where it can form quite large stands. The rounded, opposite leaves (30 x 20 cm) have 7-10 pairs of well-defined lateral nerves, which are often pink, and large stipules (up to 10 x 6 cm). The white flowers are arranged in densely crowded balls about 1.5 cm diameter. These develop into clumps of club-like fruits, each about 5 mm long, which split to release small, winged, seeds dispersed by the wind. It has a light, insect resistant wood which is exploited by foresters, sometimes causing serious damage to fragile aquatic ecosystems.

Nauclea vanderguchtii is a medium sized tree found along rivers and streams and around marshes within the forest. It grows to about 20 m tall and 60 cm diameter, occasionally larger. The trunk is often crooked and partly rotten, without buttresses. The grey-brown bark is fissured like *Mitragyna*. It has straggling branches and a small canopy composed of large leaves (30 x 15 cm or larger) which are easily confused with those of *Mitragyna* at a distance, but which have distinct veination. The stipules are quite large, up to 4 x 2 cm. It is a deciduous species which loses all its leaves in December / February and then, a month or so later, flushes with a crown of reddish new leaves. The white flowers, arranged in heads about, 4-6 cm diameter, at the end of the branchlets, are strongly scented and bloom in May. They develop into large pink-brown fruits with irregularly pitted skins. They contain thousands of tiny black seeds embedded in soft, red-pink, sugary pulp, eaten by many animals and birds. Like *Barteria fistulosa, Nauclea vanderguchtii* has hollow branches which shelter aggressive ants, in this case *Crematogaster africana*. These small ants do not have such a powerful sting as *Barteria*'s *Tetraponera* (p. 92), but they still protect their host from predators.

Another closely related species, ***Nauclea pobeguinii***, is similar in appearance to *Nauclea vanderguchtii* and also grows in flooded areas. It forms stands in parts of the galleries of the large rivers which constitute the boundaries of the Lopé Reserve, sometimes growing in deep flood-water in the wet season. It is most easily distinguished by its small triangular stipules, only about 5 mm long.

***Eulophia seleensis*, an orchid found growing in open, water-logged ground or in amongst islands of vegetation floating on lakes in the Lopé Reserve.**

a
a

9/ DISTURBED AREAS

Two forms of human disturbance occur in the Lopé; cultivation and logging. Cultivation currently has a minimal effect on the Reserve as a whole, since the only human settlements are a few villages dispersed along the dirt road from Libreville to Franceville, which runs through the north of the Reserve, and a logging camp located in the eastern savannas. Small areas are cleared and planted with crops. Once these have been harvested the land is left fallow and is gradually colonised by forest species, resulting in a succession not unlike that which follows savanna colonisation. Along the Libreville-Franceville road stands of mango trees indicate the location of abandoned villages. Other such sites, dating back to resettlements in the colonial period, are just visible in some places within the Reserve.

Logging began in the Reserve in the early 1960's. At this time it was restricted to one tree species, Okoumé, which was exploited in forest close to the savannas in the north of the Reserve and floated down the Ogooué River to Port Gentil. Today almost half of the Reserve has been logged. By building roads and felling trees, foresters cause structural changes in the forest which resemble those resulting from natural treefall to some extent.

When you walk in the forest with your guides some of the trails you will follow are logging roads dating back to the 1970's. At this time the bulldozers and lorries used were much smaller than those seen on forestry concessions today. Nevertheless, the roads are still easily visible since there has been little regeneration along their compacted surfaces. They are lined by light loving trees and shrubs, which are generally only found in large light gaps within the forest. These tracks are used by many of the animals. Buffalo in particular use logging roads as access routes into the forest, whilst elephants and gorillas often feed on succulent herbs growing in the verges. When logging roads are put in they almost invariably follow elephant paths, as the elephants seem always to know the easiest route from one place to another. It is only right that the elephants should reclaim their paths once the foresters have gone. It is refreshing to note that, other than the roads, there is little to attest to the logger's passage in the forests of the tourist zone.

Scleria boivinii **or «razor grass» (Cyperaceae) forms dense thickets along old logging roads** **(see p. 30).**

Logging today is more destructive. Bulldozers and lorries have become much larger and more powerful, and cut wide roads through the forest with ease. A large forest tree can be toppled in seconds, with just one or two shoves from the blade of a bulldozer. Its shallow roots put up little resistance. The logging industry has also diversified in recent years. In addition to Okoumé about sixty other species are exploited.

It is difficult to predict the long-term effects logging will have on the forest as a whole. Obviously construction of roads and camps will result in deforestation and the felling and extraction of large trees will cause further physical damage. There will be a shift in vegetation composition in favour of fast growing species which thrive in open conditions. In Gabon the typical logging operation destroys about 10% of the forest, so once one gets away from major roads, logging seems not to have that great an impact on the forest. This level of damage is low. In most places where tropical forests are being selectively exploited damage levels are typically about 50%.

However, the forest is more than just trees. In order to understand the true effects of logging one must also know its effect on animal populations. Research on the effects of logging in the Lopé has been undertaken at the «Station d'Etudes des Gorilles et Chimpanzés». This field research station, funded in part by the Gabonese government, has existed since 1983, and is a base for research work on many aspects of tropical ecology. Researchers have found that most forest animals are little affected by logging, but that chimpanzees are a notable exception. Chimpanzee densities fall drastically after logging, for reasons which are, as yet, unclear. Partly in response to this problem, the Gabonese government recently changed the status of part of the Lopé, creating an inviolate area which includes much of the northern half of the Reserve.

Elsewhere in Gabon there is generally a sharp rise in hunting when loggers build access roads into a forest for the first time. In some places commercial hunters wipe out most of the large mammals in order to supply the high demand for 'bush meat' in cities such as Libreville. This may have a very serious long term effect on the forest, since large mammals like elephants and primates are vital seed dispersers. If these seed dispersers are eliminated, fruits of animal dispersed plants will fall to the ground and rot and these species will decline.

Right:
Hypericaceae
a) Harungana madagascariensis
b) Psorospermum tenuifolium
c) Vismia rubescens
Ulmaceae
d) Trema guineensis

d
c
b
a

Right:

a) Croton mubango
b) Discoglypremna caloneura
c) Macaranga monandra
d) Maprounea membranacea

Research on the effects of logging in tropical forests is still in its infancy. In Uganda a study was undertaken on the effects of timber extraction on rodent densities. The researcher found that rodents both increased in numbers and in diversity after logging, and that there was little regeneration thereafter, because rats and mice consumed almost all of the seeds falling to the forest floor. Could this be the case in Gabon? The answer is that we do not know. Nor do we know if logging has an effect on insects, which not only represent an important food source for many monkeys and birds, but which also pollinate the majority of tropical plants. Nor can we say what effect erosion of soil from logging roads into rivers or streams has on fish populations downstream, which are an important protein source for humans, as well as many aquatic animals. Until we do posess such knowledge, it is vital that parts of the forest be set aside for protection, to serve as insurance for the future.

When logging roads are abandoned they are gradually recolonised. However, environmental conditions are greatly changed and some species which are otherwise rare or absent in the forest occur. Fast growing species adapted to life in light gaps thrive. Savanna species often colonise the road itself, where the topsoil was removed and the ground compacted. Many species common in young forest and on the forest edge become common: *Barteria* (see p.90), *Lophira* (see p.88) and especially several species of *Xylopia* (see p.74). Species from several families are characteristic of this habitat.

Termite mound on an Okoumé tree.

Shrubs

HYPERICACEAE

This family is very close to the Clusiaceae. They have opposite leaves which are covered in blackish or translucent dots, and exude orange-yellow sap when broken. Those found in Lopé have small fruits dispersed by birds.

Harungana madagascariensis is a shrub or small tree found in disturbed areas in the forest, as well as along the savanna edge, around villages, in old village sites and in savannas which are rarely burnt. It is easily recognised by its large leaves (to 20 x 10 cm), with numerous, parallel lateral nerves. If broken, the petiole exudes orange-red sap. The branchlets are tipped by two young silvery green leaves, tinged with red or orange, which stand erect and are stuck face to face. The small, fragrant white flowers are grouped in broad inflorescences. The small, spherical orange fruits, about 5 mm across, contain 5 seeds. A tea made from the bark is used locally to treat coughs.

Psorospermum tenuifolium is a shrub or small tree up to about 10 m tall and 15 cm diameter, common along old logging roads, but also found in young vegetation types and in Marantaceae Forest. The leaves (8 x 3.5 cm) are covered in tiny black dots. It has small, cream coloured flowers and small, red-pink fruits about 6 mm long, containing 5-10 seeds.

Vismia guineensis is a shrub or small tree, found along old logging roads, which is very similar to *P. tenuifolium*, but which has more than 10 seeds in the fruit. A second species, ***Vismia rubescens***, is a lianescent shrub up to about 6 m tall. It has smooth, pale green leaves (8 x 5 cm) with characteristic nervation and numerous opaque, not black, glands.

ULMACEAE

Trema guineensis is a small or medium sized tree found in disturbed areas. It is quite localised in Lopé, but is common in disturbed habitats all across tropical Africa and Madagascar. Its characteristic, furry, asymmetrical, serrated leaf (10 x 4 cm) is immediately recognisable. Its small fruits (1 cm diameter) are black when ripe and are much appreciated by birds, its main seed dispersers. A tea made from the leaves is used to relieve tooth-ache.

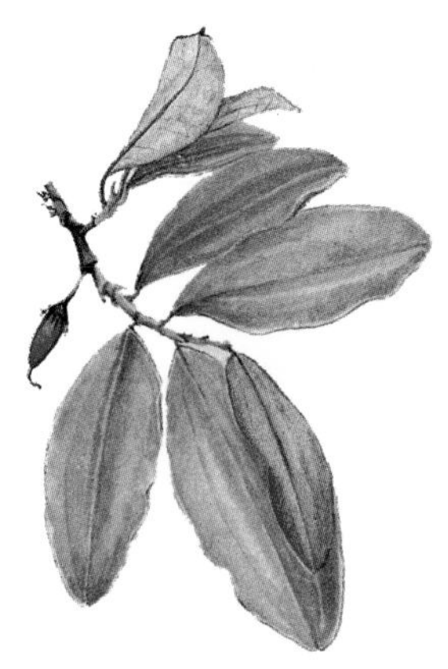

Erythroxylum manni

Trees

ERYTHROXYLACEAE

This family is best known from the shrub, *Erythroxylum coca*, native of Peru, the source of the drug cocaine and half of the origin of the name of the drink *Coca cola* (see p. 156). ***Erythroxylum mannii*** is found on the savanna edge, in young forest types and to some extent in Marantaceae forest, as well as along old roads. It is a medium sized tree, which can grow to almost 30 m tall and about 80 cm diameter. The fissured, reddish-grey bark and upcurving branches are similar to those of *Xylopia aethiopica* (p. 74), which is found in the same habitats as *E. mannii*. The leaves (5 x 2.5 cm) are red when yound and mature to a soft green. They have a pale band along the length of their undersides, either side of the midrib. There are numerous faint, lateral nerves which give the leaf a smooth appearance. The small white flowers are 6 mm long. The fruits are bright red, just over 1 cm long and are eaten by birds.

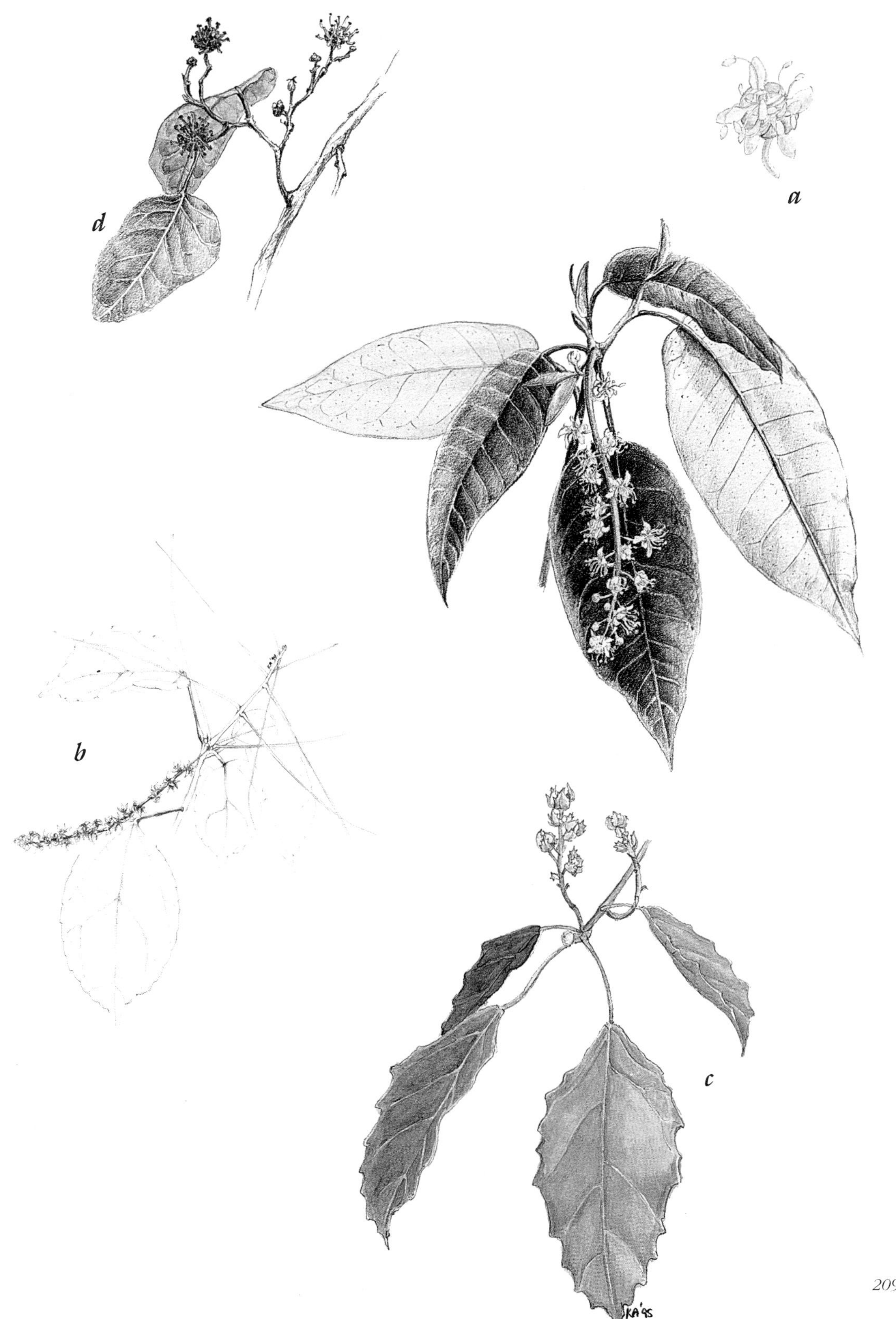
d
a
b
c
SKA'95

Right:

Loganiceae
a) Anthocleista schweinfurthii
Rubiaceae
b) Nauclea didderichii
c) Porterandia cladantha

EUPHORBIACEAE

Croton mubango is a distinctive species found in disturbed habitats and along the savanna edge. The generic name comes from the Greek for 'tick': some species have tick-like seeds. It grows to 25 m tall and about 40 cm diameter, with pale bark, slender branches and light foliage. The leaves (7 x 3 cm) are dark green above and silvery below, with many tiny brown spots, producing an overall effect of shimmering gold. The flowers are on long, pendulous spikes. The petals are white but the calyx is the same golden colour as the leaves, creating a spectacular display when the crown sways in the afternoon breeze. The strongly scented flowers attract swarms of excited bees in September. The fruit is a dehiscent capsule (1 cm long) with 3 valves which split when ripe, throwing small seeds several metres.

Discoglypremna caloneura grows to about 25 m tall and 80 cm diameter in the same habitats as *E. mannii*. The bark is grey-green and large trees develop buttresses. Its rounded leaves (8 x 6 cm) have stalks about 6 cm long and toothed margins. Three nerves start at the base with 2-3 looped lateral nerves above. The leaf can be confused with that of *Macvaranga barteri*. Like all Euphorbiaceae, *D. caloneura* has unisexual flowers. These are small and white, in long branched panicles which are highly visible in December. The green fruits are about 8 mm across, with 3 distinct lobes. When ripe they open to reveal 3 seeds covered in a bright red skin. They have a thin yellow flesh and are eaten by many species of birds and monkeys. Chimpanzees wadge the fruits as they do those of *Psychotria vogeliana* (p. 68). The cleaned seeds are black, with a pitted surface (p. 214).

Macaranga barteri grows up to 20 m high and 40 cm diameter, but is generally smaller. It is only common along old roads. The bark is smooth and greyish and there are thin buttresses or stilt roots. The leaves (14 x 6.5 cm with a stalk of about 5 cm) are a little like those of *D. caloneura*. There are about 7 pairs of lateral nerves and three starting at the base. The flowers are green-brown. The small, spherical green fruit, about 4 mm across, opens to reveal a single seed covered in thin, succulent flesh. The fruits are eaten and dispersed by birds and monkeys. ***Macaranga monandra*** is similar to *M. barteri*, but can be distinguished by its coarsely toothed leaves (13 x 6 cm). It is rarely found away from old roads, where it sometimes forms extensive stands.

Maprounea membranacea occurs in natural gaps in the forest, but is most common in disturbed areas. It is a small, graceful tree growing up to about 15 m tall. The smooth bark is ocre in colour and the branches are long and slender. The twigs and young foliage are reddish. The delicate leaves (5 x 3 cm) have a network of fine veins. It has small red-orange flowers and red fruits, about 6 mm across, containing 3 seeds, which are dispersed by birds.

LOGANIACEAE

Anthocleista schweinfurthii is very similar to *A. vogelii* (p. 92), which is found mostly in marshes. Its cream coloured flowers open rather than remaining closed, and its larger fruits, about 4 cm diameter, are on a thick stalk which hangs down instead of standing erect. *A schweinfurthii* is particularly striking when young and unbranched, because its leaves can reach over 2 m in length. These young plants often form dense stands along logging roads.

RUBIACEAE

Nauclea didderichii (Bilinga) is sometimes over 40m tall and exceptionally exceeds 2 m diameter. Scattered individuals occur throughout the forest, but it is most common in the forest-savanna mosaic and along old roads, where it forms dense stands. Larger individuals tend to have straight, cylindrical trunks without buttresses and yellow-brown, fissured bark. The branches are arranged in whorls, within a dense, rounded crown. The leaves (12 x 8 cm) have rounded stipules (2 x 1 cm). Young trees have pale flakey bark and whorled branches which jut out perpendicular to the trunk. Their leaves are larger (up to 45 x 21cm) and can be mistaken for *N. vanderguchtii* or *M. ciliata* (p. 204). The white flowers are in spherical heads about 2 cm across, which bloom from April to July. The perfumed fruits are orange-brown when ripe from September to November. The fruit surface is covered in small, rough-edged pits and the flesh within is sweet containing numerous tiny seeds. The fruits are eaten by many mammals and birds, and the timber is much sought after by foresters.

Porterandia cladantha grows to about 20 m tall and 40 cm diameter. It is most common in disturbed areas but also occurs within the forest. It has grey bark with characteristic fissures like the pieces of a jigsaw. The branches are roughly perpendicular to the trunk and curve down towards the ground. It has large, rounded, leaves (25 x 13 cm) with stipules about 2 cm long, which can be mistaken for those of *Mitragyna ciliata* (p. 204). They flower between December and February. The perfumed flowers are creamy-white or pale pink outside and yellow within, about 2 cm long. The fruits ripen gradually to orange, between August and October. Hence, *P. cladantha* can be distinguished from the other large leaved Rubiaceae species because they always have either flowers or fruits. Many mammals and birds eat the fruits and disperse the tiny seeds.

Nauclea didderichii

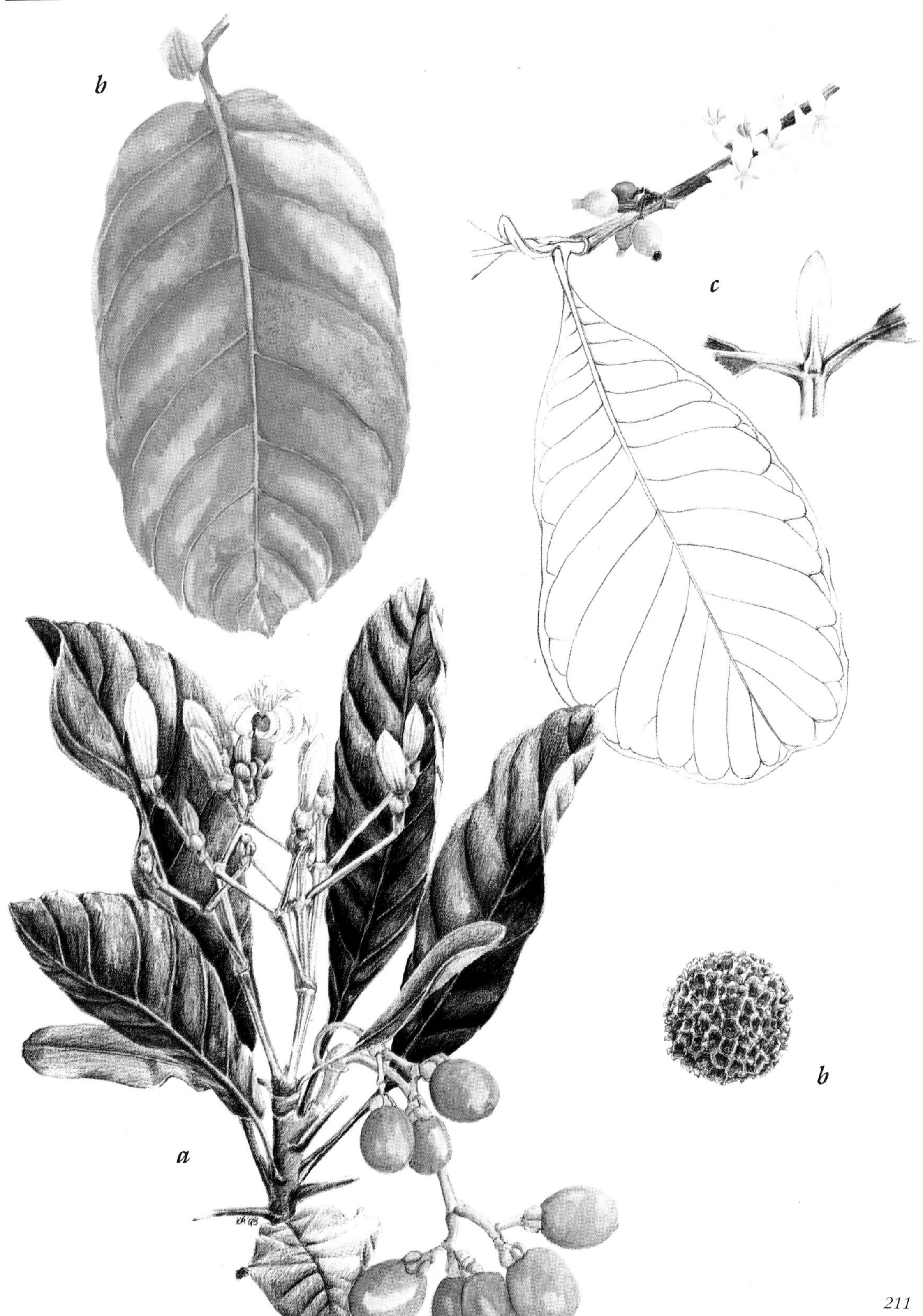
b
c
b
a
KA'93

Syzygium cf. staudtii
(Myrtaceae see p.162)

10/ MOUNTAINS

Lopé is on the edge of the Massif du Chaillu and much of the Reserve is quite mountainous. The highest peak, located in the centre of the Reserve, is 924 m in altitude; about 700m higher than the low savanna plain in the north and just over twice as tall as Mont Brazza, which dominates the view from the Lopé Hotel. On cool, damp mornings, particularly in the long dry season, the taller hills and mountains are shrouded in mist. When one climbs these hills the temperature falls by about 1°C for every 100m, so it can feel quite cool at the top. In the cool, damp conditions many trees are covered in a dense layer of mosses and epiphytic ferns, and in some places Begonias carpet the ground.

In the distant past, in periods when tropical Africa became cooler and drier, forest patches survived on many mountains. These were dominated by species which today are generally only found in truly montane vegetation, above about 1500m altitude. Perhaps because of the cool, cloudy dry season in Lopé, some of these montane species survive today on the highest mountains. Together with some other species, found only at altitudes of about 500m or higher, these plants form a distinct community on the summits of Lopé's higher mountains.

Right:

Ocotea gabonensis
(Lauraceae see p.134) - a small tree found in cloud forest at high altitude known only from the summit of Mount Yindo and upland areas elsewhere, such as Mount Bilinga in the northeast of Gabon.

11/ INTRODUCED SPECIES

Several plant species have been introduced into the Lopé region at different times in the past, including the majority of cultivated species. For example, bananas in the genus *Musa* (Musaceae), originally from southeast Asia or India, were probably introduced into tropical Africa from the north some time in the first millenium AD. Manioc, *Manihot esculenta* (Euphorbiaceae) was introduced to the west African coast from Brazil by Portuguese sailors and gradually spread eastwards. The mango, ***Mangifera indica*** (Anacardiaceae), of Indian origin, is often seen in small stands in the forest-savanna mosaic. They flower at the end of the long dry season and the fruits ripen in November / December to the delight of the gorillas, chimpanzees, monkeys, elephants and humans alike. After feeding on the juicy flesh primates drop the seeds to the ground, where they are all eaten by rodents and red river hogs. Hence there is no natural regeneration of mango trees in Lopé and they all testify to past (or current) human habitation. The lime, ***Citrus limonum*** (Rutaceae) which was introduced from southeast Asia is better adapted to its adopted homeland: its seeds are dispersed by elephants and young trees are found colonising unburnt savannas. ***Bixa orellana*** (Bixaceae) was introduced from tropical America. It is common in villages and is often noticed because of its large pink flowers, which resemble those of *Ipomoea blepharophylla* (p. 39) and its bright red fruits. The seeds yield a red dye.

Below:

a) Mangifera indica
b) Citrus limonum
c) Bixa orellana

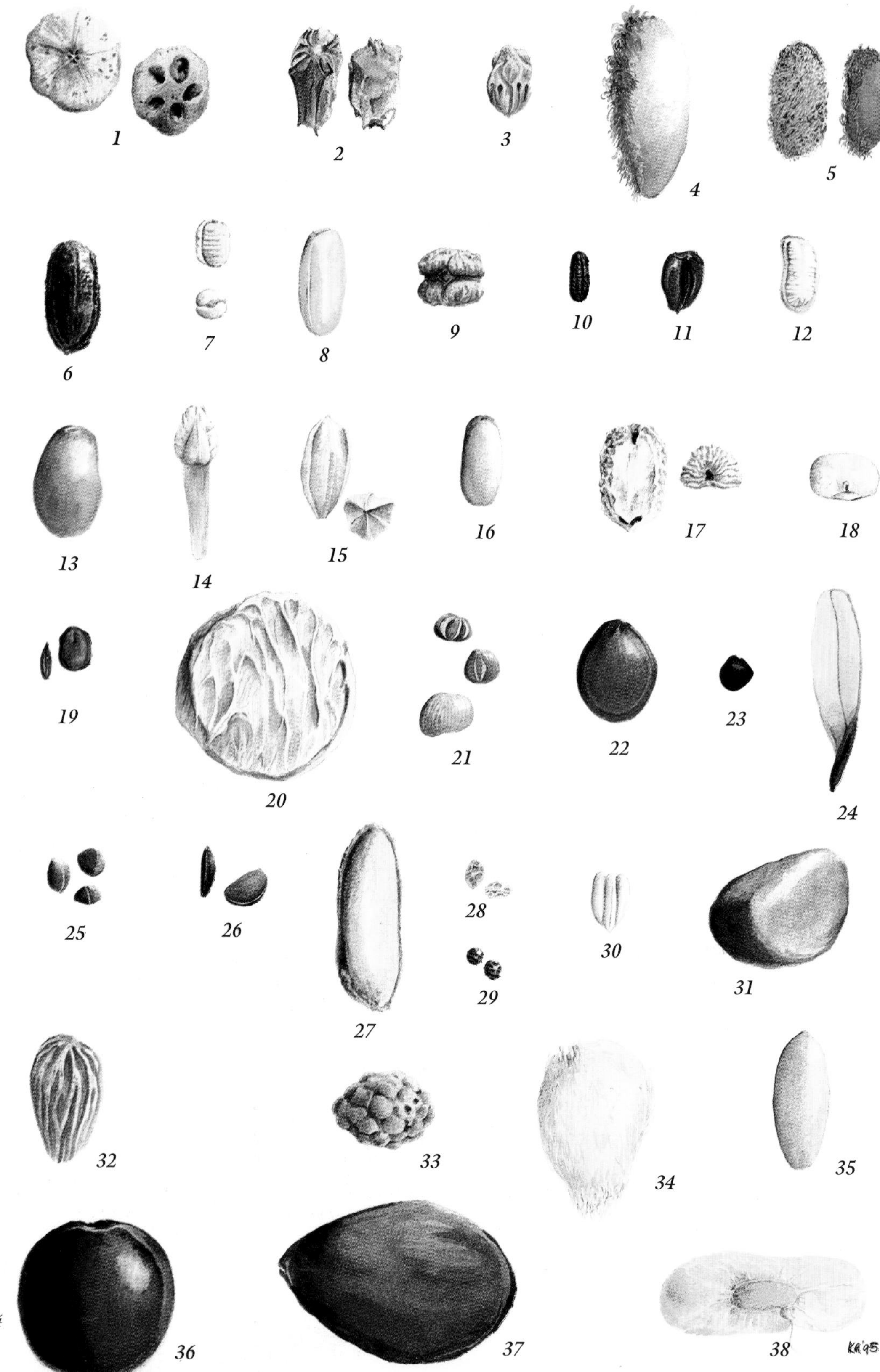
1
2
3
4
5
6
7
8
9
10
11
12
13
14
15
16
17
18
19
20
21
22
23
24
25
26
27
28
29
30
31
32
33
34
35
36
37
38
KA'95

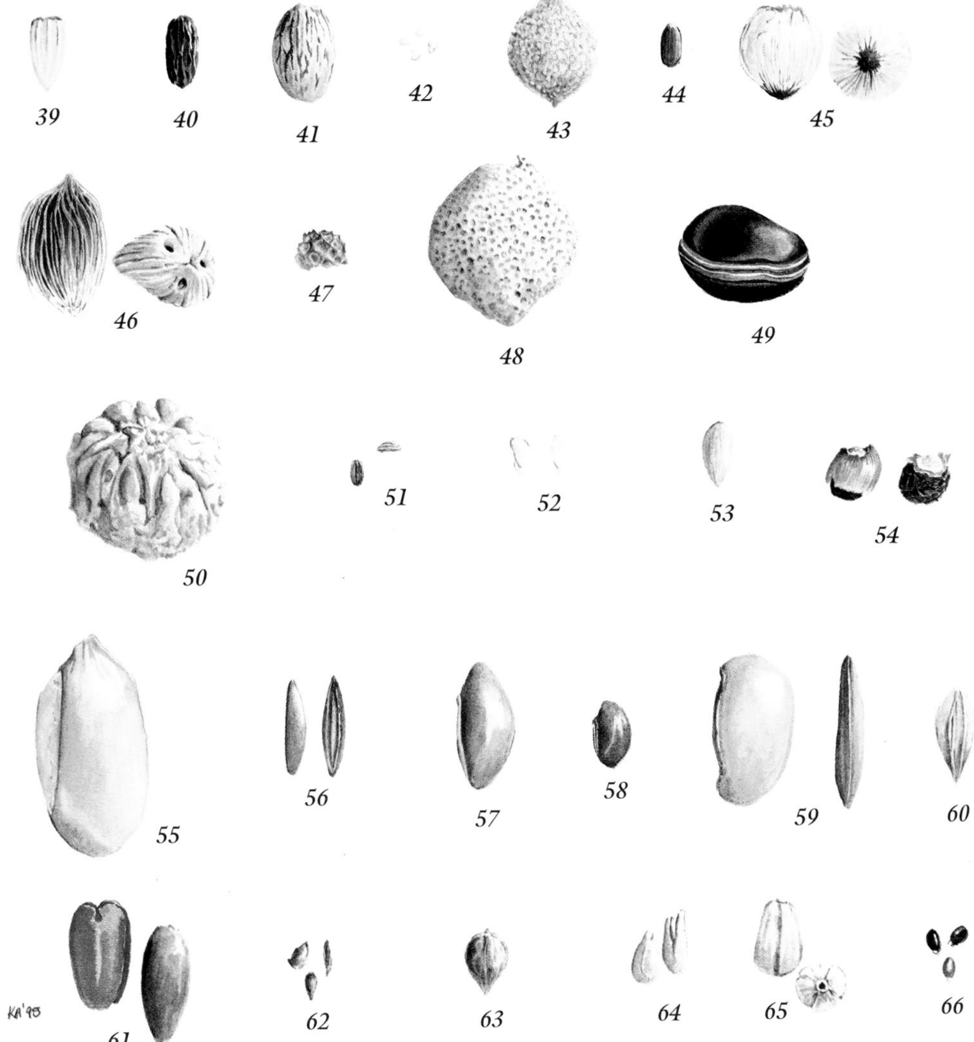

Left and above, the seeds of:

1) *Antrocaryon klaineanum* **(see p.112); 2)** *Pseudospondias longifolia* **(p.112); 3)** *Pseudospondias microcarpa* **(p.112); 4)** *Trichoscypha abut* **(p.114); 5)** *Trichoscypha acuminata (p.114);* **6)** *Enantia chlorantha* **(p. 114); 7)** *Monanthotaxis congolensis* **(p. 105); 8)** *Hexalobus crispiflorus* **(Annonaceae) 9)** *Polyalthia suaveolens* **(p.116); 10)** *Monanthotaxis diclina* **(p. 105); 11)** *Uvaria cf. scabrida* **(p.105); 12)** *Uvariastrum pierreanum* **(p.116); 13)** *Landolphia mannii* **(p.48); 14)** *Aucoumea klaineana* **(p.80); 15)** *Canarium schweinfurthii* **(p.118); 16)** *Dacryodes buettneri* **(p.116); 17)** *Dacryodes normandii* **(p.118); 18)** *Santiria trimera* **(p.120); 19)** *Cryptosepalum staudtii* **(p.25); 20)** *Detarium macrocarpum* **(p.135); 21)** *Dialium lopense* **(p.135); 22)** *Julbernardia brieyi* **(p. 202); 23)** *Swartzia fistuloides* **(p. 143); 24)** *Hippocratea myrioneura* **(p.164); 25)** *Diospyros dendo* **(p.193); 26)** *Diospyros polystemon* **(p.195); 27)** *Diospyros mannii* **(p. 193); 28)** *Antidesma vogelianum* **(p.66); 29)** *Discoglypremna caloneura* **(p.210); 30)** *Uapaca guineensis* **(p.23); 31)** *Mammea africana* **(p.170); 32)** *Pentadesma butyracea* **(p.122); 33)** *Sacoglottis gabonensi* **(p.82); 34)** *Irvingia gabonensis* **(p.132); 35)** *Beilschmiedia sp.* **(p.134); 36)** *Entada gigas* **(p.58); 37)** *Pentaclethra macrophylla* **(p.137); 38)** *Piptadeniastrum africanum* **(p.139); 39)** *Myrianthus arboreus* **(p.86); 40)** *Pycnanthus angolensis* **(p.180); 41)** *Staudtia gabonensis* **(p.180); 42)** *Psidium guineensis* **(p.68); 43)** *Coula edulis* **(p.182); 44)** *Heisteria parvifolia* **(p.182); 45)** *Ongokea gore* **(p.182); 46)** *Elaeis guineensis* **(p.66); 47)** *Laccosperma laeve* **(p.64); 48)** *Panda oleosa* **(p.148); 49)** *Dioclea reflexa* **(p.58); 50)** *Poga oleosa* **(p.148); 51)** *Psychotria vogeliana* **(p.68); 52)** *Citrus limonum* **(p.213); 53)** *Ganophyllum giganteum* **(p.152); 54)** *Lecaniodiscus cupanoides* **(p.193); 55)** *Baillonella toxisperma* **(p.184); 56)** *Donella ogowensis* **(p.19); 57)** *Gambeya africana* **(p.186); 58)** *Gambeya subnuda* **(p.186); 59)** *Omphalocarpum procerum* **(p.154); 60)** *Scytopetalum sp.* **(p.160); 66)** *Cola lizae* **(p.156); 62)** *Duboscia macrocarpa* **(p.160); 63)** *Celtis tessmannii* **(p.162); 64)** *Cissus dinklagei* **(p.52); 65)** *Vitex doniana* **(p.72); 66)** *Aframomum sericeum* **(p.99).**

GLOSSARY

Alternate (leaves) : arranged one after the other along the stem.
Anther : upper part of the stamen containing the pollen.
Aril : a fleshy and often brightly coloured 'envelope' covering certain seeds.
Biomass: total mass of organisms per unit area.
Bipinnate (compound leaf) : see illustration.
Bract : small, usually much reduced or modified, leaf below the flower or inflorescence.
Flute (trunk): semicylindrical vertical groove in the trunk.
Canopy : the leafy section of forest trees (see illustration).
Cauliflores : plants whose flowers grow directly on the branches or trunk.
Compound (leaf) : a leaf with several parts (leaflets - see illustrations).
Buttresses : lateral extensions at the base of the trunk.
Catkin : Inflorescence consisting of tiny flowers whose form resembles a kitten (or its tail).
Deciduous : a plant whose leaves fall before being replaced.
Dehiscence : natural opening (splitting) at maturity.
Dioecious : plants with male and female flowers on different individuals.
Endemic : a species restricted to the area in question.
Epiphyte : a non-parasitic plant growing on another plant.
Stamen : male part of flowering plants consisting of the pollen bearing anther and a thin stalk or 'filament'.
Leaflet : each division of the blade of a compound leaf (see illustrations).
Rain forest (tropical) : forest in humid tropics (more than 1500 mm of rain per year), characterised by several levels or strata of vegetation and great species diversity.
Caudate (leaf) : apex in the form of a tail.
Frond : a large compound leaf - applied to ferns and palms.
Pod : fruit with two valves containing a row of seeds.
Indehiscent (fruit) : which does not open.
Inflorescence : a structure that consists of more than one flower.
Latex : an opaque, milky or creamy liquid which is often sticky secreted by certain plants (especially when wounded).
Lenticel : a pore in the stem of a woody plant,showing as a raised spot, which allows air to penetrate to underlying tissue.
Litter : decomposing leaves and branches on the surface of the soil.
Nervation : pattern of nerves on the leaf.
Opposite (leaves) : leaves attached in pairs at the same point on the stem.
Panicle : a complex branched inflorescence.
Pedicel : stalk of one flower in an inflorescence.
Pinna : one of the leaflets in a compound leaf (see illustrations).
Petiole : stalk by which a leaf is attached (see illustrations).
Petiolule : stalk of a leaflet in a compound leaf (see illustrations).
Stellate hairs : a star shaped hair with radiating branches.
Vegetative reproduction : multiplication from a vegetative part of a plant (roots, stem or leaves).
Sepal : the outer floral leaves borne in a tight spiral or whorled (see illustration).
Spadix : a spike of flowers on a swollen axis.
Spathe : a large bract enclosing the inflorescence.
Sporangium : sac-like structure containing the spores in a fern, moss, mould or alga.
Spore : a microscopic structure for reproduction and dispersal.
Stigma : part of female reproductive organs on which pollen grains germinate.
Stipule : a membranous or leafy appendage, usually in pairs, at or near the base of the petiole.
Style : extension of the carpel (female reproductive organ containing the ovary and ovules) which supports the stigma.
Tegument : seed coat.
Thalweg : line joining the lowest points along a valley bottom.
Secondary vegetation : vegetation changed by human actions.

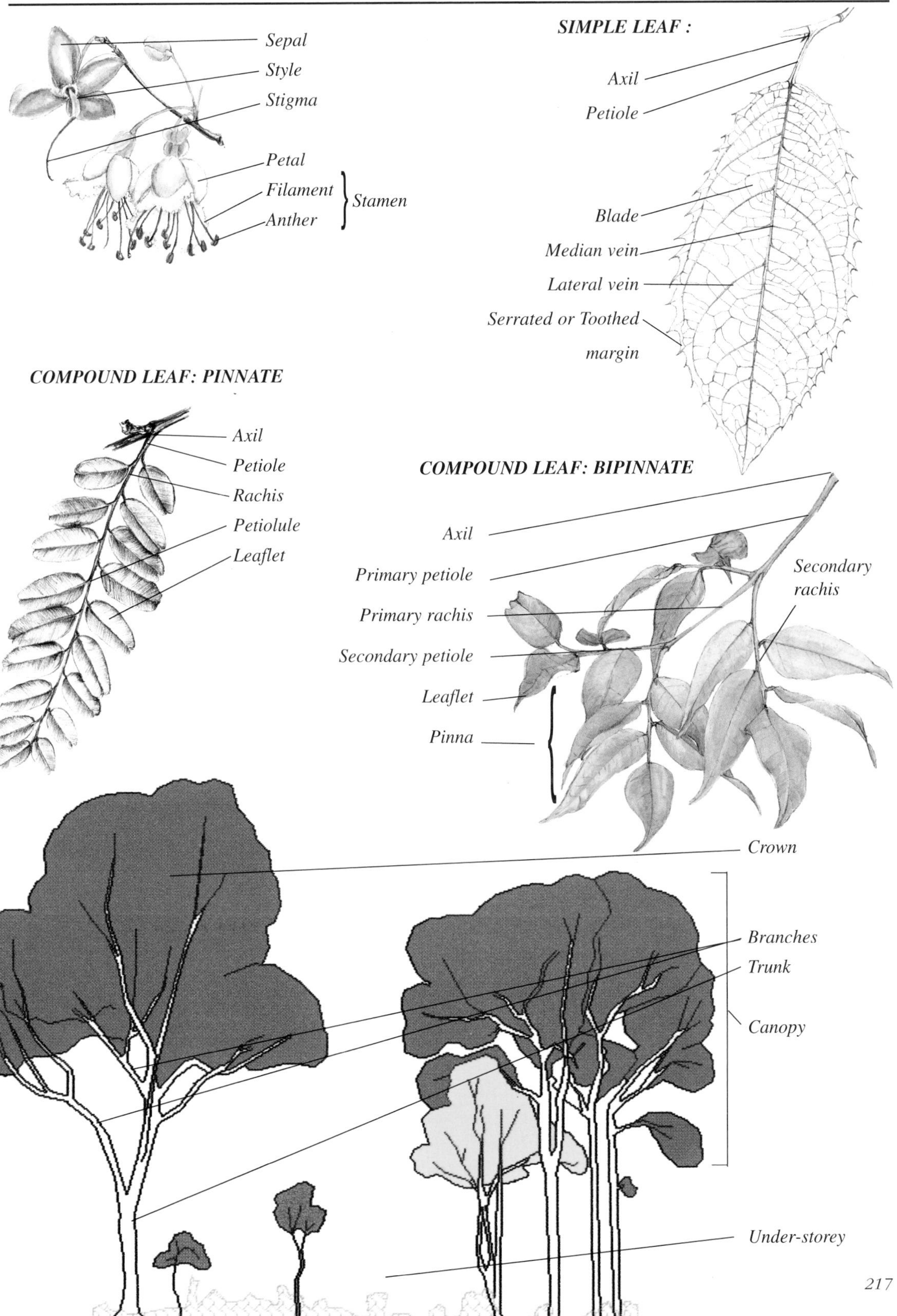
Sepal
Style
Stigma
Petal
Filament
Anther
Stamen
SIMPLE LEAF :
Axil
Petiole
Blade
Median vein
Lateral vein
Serrated or Toothed margin
COMPOUND LEAF: PINNATE
Axil
Petiole
Rachis
Petiolule
Leaflet
COMPOUND LEAF: BIPINNATE
Axil
Primary petiole
Primary rachis
Secondary petiole
Leaflet
Pinna
Secondary rachis
Crown
Branches
Trunk
Canopy
Under-storey
Buttresses

IF YOU WOULD LIKE TO KNOW MORE :

* H. M. Burkhill (1985, 1994 & 1995). *The Useful Plants of West Africa.* Royal Botanic Gardens, Kew.
* P. Christy & W. Clarke (1994). *Guide des Oiseaux de la Réserve de la Lopé.* ECOFAC Gabon.
* R. Letouzey (1982 & 1983). *Manual of Forest Botany: Tropical Africa.* CTFT, 45 bis, Av. de la Belle-Gabrielle, 94130-Nogent s/Marne, France.
* J. Kingdon (1990). *Island Africa.* Collins, London.
* R. Oslisly & B. Peyrot. (1993) *Les gravures rupestres de la vallée de l'Ogooué* (Gabon). Editions Sépia, France.
* A. Raponda-Walker & R. Sillans (1961) *Les Plantes Utiles du Gabon.* Editions Lechevalier, France. (Re-edited by Sépia, 1995)
* G. de Saint-Aubin (1963). *La Forêt du Gabon.* CTFT, 45 bis, Av. de la Belle-Gabrielle, 94130-Nogent s/Marne, France.

This *Urginea sp.* (Liliaceae) grows in the savanna. It has a bulb like an onion, *Allium cepa,* which is in the same family.

INDEX

notes

notes